Black Police, White Society

BLACK POLICE, WHITE SOCIETY

STEPHEN LEINEN

New York · NEW YORK UNIVERSITY PRESS · *1984*

Library of Congress Cataloging in Publication Data
Leinen, Stephen H.
Black police, white society.

Includes bibliographical references and index.
1. Afro-American police—New York (N.Y.)   2. Race
discrimination—New York (N.Y.)   3. Discrimination in
employment—New York (N.Y.)   4. Public relations—
New York (N.Y.)—Police.   I. Title.
HV8148.N5L37   1984   363.2′2′0899607307471   83-23622
ISBN 0-8147-5008-7 (alk. paper)
Book designed by Laiying Chong

*Clothbound editions of New York University Press Book are Smyth-sewn
and printed on permanent and acid-free paper.*

To my father, in memoriam

CONTENTS

ACKNOWLEDGMENTS

I wish to express my appreciation and deep sense of gratitude to those friends and colleagues at Queens College who patiently read and provided assistance and input into this book: Professors Paul Blumberg, Dean Savage, Steve Cohen, Lauren Seiler and Mike Brown. I owe a special debt of gratitude to Professor Bernard Cohen, a long-time friend and colleague at Queens College, who constantly offered constructive criticism and encouragement to complete the book; to Jenny Hunt, who took time away from her doctoral dissertation to carefully read and comment on each page of the manuscript; to Pat Jenkins, who, while not a formal student of the social sciences, nevertheless provided insight into many of the comments quoted in the book; to Joe Ford, who answered many of the theoretical questions I had concerning the working world of the black professional.

Special thanks are due to Rae Simmons, secretary in the sociology department at Queens College, who enthusiastically volunteered her expert typing skills and who never once complained when sections of the manuscript, thought to have been completed, had to be retyped.

Finally, I owe a special debt of gratitude to all the black police officers who participated in the study and especially to Al De-Costa, Clyde Isley and Evrod Williams who spent many hours of their own time answering the many questions I had and helping me gain a better understanding of what it means to be a black policeman in a changing society.

INTRODUCTION

Black Police, White Society is a book about the working world of
the black police officer. The idea for the book, as well as the research for it, came from my own experience as a member of the
New York City police department (NYPD). In the mid-1960s I
worked in the NYPD as a uniformed police officer, then as a detective in plainclothes for approximately nine years, and currently
as a patrol supervisor in predominantly black areas of New York
City. During this time I have met and worked with a large number of black patrolmen and black detectives, and as a result of the
many friendships that developed with these officers I found myself
becoming increasingly sensitized to and interested in the occupational world of the black officer.

An academic background in sociology provided me with the
added curiosity and tools to pursue the various lines of inquiry which
finally ended up as this book. There was something else too, however, and that was the conspicuous absence of anything written on
black police. Aside from a few articles in professional journals,
government reports (which dated back to the 1960s), and scattered newspaper accounts, black police as an occupational group
simply had not received much attention. The one substantial exception was Nicholas Alex's *Black in Blue*,[1] a book which described
the problems facing black New York City police officers in the early
1960s. Yet even this penetrating analysis of the black officers'
working world has proved to be incomplete; since then important
developments have taken place in the struggle of black Americans
to secure a more equitable place in society and especially in the
efforts of black police in New York City and elsewhere to achieve
greater acceptance and equality within their departments. In short,
the rapid pace of social change in this country since the mid-1960s
has required both an update and clarification of much of the data
contained in earlier studies and reports. It was for these reasons

that I undertook the task of gathering data and reporting on black police. I can only hope that the material in this book serves the purpose in which it was collected—to present both an objective and inside view of the impact of changing political, legal, and organizational structures on the position, role, and identity of black police officers in New York City, and by extrapolation in all of urban America.

My approach to this study involved rounds of intensive interviewing over considerable periods of time of 46 black New York City cops, although material was also collected from a variety of other sources including newspapers, magazines, journals, books, and periodicals. The bulk of the statistical data relating actual changes in the racial composition of the police department in New York City and its various divisions, subunits, and ranks was provided by the department's Office of Equal Employment Opportunity and by Roger Abel, an officer in the Guardians Association, a black police (fraternal/political) group.

My efforts to penetrate the working world of the black officer, while I was simultaneously serving as a member of the department, have presented special difficulties beyond the ones normally experienced by the "native" as researcher. From the onset of the project, for example, I found myself occupying a "deviant" status in the eyes of many friends and colleagues on the job. Why, most of them wanted to know, would a white cop want to study and write about such a potentially controversial subject as black police? From white colleagues (and immediate superiors) the subject matter evoked varying degrees of reactions: surprise, bewilderment, annoyance, and occasionally outright hostility. I can recall, for instance, a comment made by a white detective in my team while a number of us were having lunch together. He had just returned from a lengthy vacation and apparently heard that I was speaking to black cops about such matters as discrimination and working relationships and questioned my motives for conducting such an inquiry. Before I could respond to what appeared at the moment to be an innocuous question he added, "What are you, a nigger lover or something?" At the time this comment caught me completely off guard. As I would soon come to learn, however, the subject matter I had chosen to delve into sparked the resentment of more than just this one white policeman.

From my black colleagues, who occasionally found themselves

transformed into informants, questions concerning my motives for conducting such a study took quite a different form. While none expressed hostility, most were curious, if not suspicious, about how I planned to use the material I was collecting. A few, despite my protests to the contrary, passed the matter off very simply—I must be using the material for a college term project. This came across to me most clearly, not by the comments that were expressed, but by the virtual absence of any interest in the project whatsoever during the next two years. It was only when the manuscript was near completion and being reviewed by some of my black col leagues, that interest in the study was evinced by most of my informants. Even today I occasionally receive phone calls from both active and retired officers who participated in the study expressing an interest in getting a copy of the book when it is finished.

A second problem I confronted concerns the study population itself. From the start I had intended to interview a random sample of black policemen from precincts situated throughout the city. After a series of preliminary interviews (with a few of the men I was working with) I began to test the feasibility of this approach by contacting black officers through their assigned commands.[2] I informed each potential respondent of my rank and position in the department and of my purpose for conducting the study. What resulted from these initial contacts was disappointing, yet understandable. Most of the men flatly refused to be interviewed, stating that they were either too busy or just not interested. A few expressed an initial willingness to talk with me and three actually did. Most of these officers, however, seemed reluctant to commit themselves to a specific date or time. After repeated attempts to get together with these men it became increasingly clear that they were not interested in cooperating in the study.

Having been a member of the police department for considerably more than a decade at the time, I could readily appreciate the reluctance of some black officers to participate in a study which might be construed as potentially threatening. (All police officers, by virtue of their occupational role in society, are generally suspicious, and regard any form of inquiry as an investigation of their shortcomings, and any investigation as collecting data for *other* purposes. My being white apparently did not lessen their apprehensions.)

Given that a random sample of respondents was not a realistic goal I decided simply to use a convenience sample consisting of those men who were willing to talk with me. I created an initial base of seven black officers, men with whom I was presently working or had worked with in the past. All were aware of my interest in and motivation for conducting such a study. Not surprisingly I found them extremely cooperative and eager to talk about their occupational world as they saw it. More important, these seven men helped me to gain the cooperation of an additional 36 black policemen over a period of more than a year. In all, 46 men from various commands in the city participated in the study. A formal introduction was made with each potential respondent either by a (black) police friend of mine or by someone I had been previously introduced to and subsequently interviewed.

Each interview seemed to proceed in virtually the same manner—an initial period of reservation on the part of the respondent, followed by a gradual "loosening-up," to a desire in many instances to speak at great length even to the point of returning to earlier questions the respondent felt may not have been thoroughly answered. To insure against the possibility of respondents "clamming up" when sensitive topics were raised and to maintain rapport, background information was elicited at the beginning of each interview. Thus, by the time we moved into what might be perceived by some as "threatening" or "sensitive" areas, most of the men had already begun to feel relaxed and comfortable. I also was aware of the possible aura of antagonism that can affect an interview in which the interviewer and respondent are of different backgrounds.[3] Naturally, I decided that I had better try to eliminate this potential source of trouble. I therefore asked each respondent who was to introduce me to other officers to explain my purpose in interviewing them. Each was informed that my objective was *not* to present an "exposé" of the department but rather to get an insider's view of the black officers' working world, that I would not in any deliberate way distort the contents of the interviews (data), and that I would not reveal names or commands if they so choose. All I asked was that each informant be candid with me and "tell it like it was."

The format of the interviews was focused and open-ended. Most were conducted at one time, lasting anywhere from one to three hours. The open-ended approach was chosen over alternatives for two reasons. First, as mentioned earlier, there is a noticeable absence of literature on black police and this approach is recognized as the most appropriate to explore subjects in which little or no information is available.[4] Second, it was not my intention in this study to draw probability statements about what might be true but rather to describe how black policemen working in black areas of the city themselves perceive their situation in the department and to get some idea of why they felt the way they did. More rigorous approaches may summarize attitudes or may reveal information about a particular direction in which black policemen tend to gravitate, but they do not, as a general rule, describe beliefs held about some issue or problem nor do they attempt to uncover the diversity of reasons behind them.

The questions themselves were quite general in nature, allowing the respondent to consider the issues as he perceived them. However, the opening questions to each topic area (discrimination, working relations, the black community) were highly structured; that is, each respondent was asked precisely the same question. Depending, then, on the response, subsequent (probe) questions were individualized and aimed at uncovering the respondents' particular point of view or feelings about the particular subject. In order not to impose a static view of the material, many of the questions and probes were designed to identify possible sources of change. Initially, there was concern on my part about the possible ambiguities that might arise from the use of "general-type" questions. However, as the interviews progressed it became increasingly clear that multiple-meaning terms contained in some of the questions served a specific need of the study. One question, for example, asked whether black policemen are more effective than white officers in black communities. On the face of it, the question seemed simple and clear enough. Yet, to my surprise, various conceptual distinctions were drawn by some of the officers during the preliminary interviews concerning the term "effective." To quote one,

> Effectiveness? How do you measure this? Effectiveness by the department means collars [arrests] and summonses. The people are not impressed by the "collar game." . . . Effectiveness toward whose standards? Those of the department or those of the community? Bureaucratically oriented officers will naturally believe they are ren-

dering a service to the community by making arrests and giving out summonses, while the community-minded officer sees his function less in terms of making arrests and more by serving the community in other ways. Unfortunately, in Harlem, there is not too much difference in your approach. You wear a uniform and that is enough to make you ineffective.

Aware of the possible ambiguity of terms used in the interviews, it seemed a simple task to change some of the questions by substituting a more precise terminology. Yet, by rephrasing the questions, for example, by adding "crime fighter" to the term "effective," I felt that I would be closing the door to potentially broader areas of concern to the black policeman. Purposeful ambiguities can provide the investigator with a legitimate tool for probing the respondent's interpretation of a particular issue or problem and to elicit contextual meanings that might otherwise be lost. Furthermore, as the interviews progressed, new ideas were constantly being expressed concerning the role of the black policeman in a changing society. In a few instances, these ideas were used to generate additional questions. These questions not only provided useful information, but made the interviewing task itself more rewarding as a whole.[5]

Almost all of the policemen participating in this study declined to have their comments recorded on tape. It was necessary therefore to take notes as the respondents were talking. Most of the interviews were recorded verbatim; a few, however, were carefully written in outline form and later reconstructed to resemble what originally had been said. The officers themselves represented a broad range of backgrounds and experiences, although as I have already implied my research was restricted to police*men*. No police women were included in the sample, substantially because I believed that interviews with women officers would have uncovered a unique and particular set of additional "gender-related" problems that would have greatly complicated the organization, analysis and presentation of the book. It seemed to me the topic was already complex enough.

Virtually everyone who spoke with me had been born and raised in one or the other of New York City's black ghettoes. Approximately a third had moved to nearby suburban communities after joining the department; the others had remained in or near their birthplace. About half the men were enrolled in nearby colleges or had taken college courses in the past. Three have masters degrees and another two are completing their course requirements for the M.A. Most of these men had chosen to major in business administration, although a few are majoring in psychology or criminal justice. Nine of the 46 officers are members of the Guardians Association and participate actively in the organization's affairs; none, however, have attained "officer" or "trustee" status.

As for assignment, slightly more than half of the men interviewed were on uniformed patrol in Harlem precincts where the population is almost entirely black. The remaining men are assigned to various nonuniformed specialty units in the same area, ranging from precinct "anticrime" squads to more prestigious detective commands. In all but a few cases, the men indicated that they had worked previously in other black areas of the city thereby lending some degree of "representation" in terms of geographical assignment. The distribution of these earlier assignments covers most of the city's police precincts, although in Brooklyn, Manhattan, and the Bronx they are overrepresented. As for time in service, the men were members of the police department for at least three years prior to being interviewed and in some cases for more than 20; the median length of time was 11 years. Thus, even though the study population depended on an "availability" sample, it consisted of officers whose views might well represent those of black New York City policemen in general.

It would seem that the findings contained in this study can be extended beyond the New York City police department. My review of the literature on the subject and especially of newspaper articles and journal reports tend to show that black police throughout the country have faced many of the same problems and organizational changes experienced by black cops in New York. Demonstrably, New York was not the only city affected by civil rights laws, that underwent drastic political and social reorganization in the late 1960s and that experienced a genuine need for racial reform in its police department. Nor was the New York City police department the only police agency to respond to "political" pressures for racial change by actively recruiting minorities into the service and, once hired, by expanding opportunities for members of these groups. Further, this department was not alone in experiencing many other structural changes that influence patterns of intergroup relations. However, because the question of generalizability is especially important to the development and refinement of theories of race and ethnic relations, it will be considered more fully in the concluding section of this book, where an effort will be made to focus on those aspects of social change that are relevant not only to the situation black police officers faced in New York City, but also as they relate to the larger population of minority police in the country.

NOTES

1. Nicholas Alex, *Black in Blue: A Study of the Negro Policeman* (New York: Appleton-Century-Crofts, 1969). See also, William M. Kephart, *Racial Factors and Urban Law Enforcement* (Philadelphia, Pa.: Univ. of Pennsylvania Press, 1957), for an earlier review of the racial situation in the Philadelphia police department, and James I. Alexander, *Blue Coats-Black Skin: The Black Experience in the New York City Police Department since 1891* (New York: Exposition Press, 1978), for a particularly interesting *historical* account of the black policeman in New York City.

2. Some of the men were contacted by phone; others I met in person at their commands.

3. For an excellent review of the literature on bias involving the race of the interviewer, see Thomas F. Pettigrew, *A Profile of the Negro American* (Princeton, N.J.: D. Van Nostrand), 1964.

4. This position has been accepted by a number of researchers. See, for example, Billy J. Franklin and Harold W. Osborne (eds.), *Research Methods: Issues and Insights* (Belmont, Cal: Wadsworth, 1971), pp. 382–384.

5. For a similar point of view see William M. Kephart, op. cit., p. 24.

DISCRIMINATION
AND
THE BLACK OFFICER

I'm out there covering some white cop's butt, and I hear over the [police] radio, "Nigger this, Nigger that." Remarks like this you would hear all the time and nobody would say anything. If you happened to be with a white guy riding, you would pretend you didn't hear the remark. . . . I mean, what could a black cop say, where was he going to go?

FROM the time blacks first joined the New York City police force until fairly recently, whites have maintained a position of dominance, relegating blacks to subordinate roles and denying them access to job opportunities and advancement. Thus the first blacks to enter the New York City police department at the turn of the century were assigned exclusively as "doormen." It was not until some years later that they began to receive assignments more in keeping with what police actually do. But, by then, other forms of discrimination had emerged within the department which effectively excluded blacks from all but routine foot patrol assignments in black precincts and districts. The first promotion of a black to the permanent rank of sergeant, for example, was not made until 1926, even though, some six years earlier, this same patrolman had scored high on the civil service promotional exam. The police commissioner at the time, it was reported, simply refused to promote him. The officer had to wait six years until a new commissioner took office. Although his eventual promotion set a "legal" precedent regarding the rights of black policemen in New York City, another quarter of a century would pass before a black in the department would succeed to the civil service rank of captain.[1] Of course, New York City did not stand alone in its application of different standards for black and white police officers; blacks throughout the country faced systematic discrimination and separation along racial lines. However, only within the past decade has any sustained effort been made in our nation's major urban police departments to remove racial barriers to full job equality.

Park I of this book presents a brief historical overview of the accomplishments (and failures) of black police officers in light of these recent efforts. We begin with a general discussion of police race relations, focusing on those problems that have been, and in some instances still are, of concern to black officers everywhere. Next, we consider those social, political, and legal events of the 1960s and early 1970s that have shaped the present character of American race relations in general and police race relations in particular. Data are then presented documenting the attempts made by organized black police groups and the courts to redress the racial problems confronting black officers. Particular attention is paid to the persistent efforts of the Guardians Association in New York City to establish through the Federal courts a racial quota system in hiring and promotion. Finally, we examine the views and opinions of the 46 black police officers participating in this study; how these men feel, the gains they have made over the past few years, and the problems that remain unresolved or ignored. The intention here and throughout this book is to present an inside view of police race relations and to show that the attitudes, beliefs, and behavior of black policemen in New York City are integrally related to changing conditions both within the police department and within the larger society.

Chapter One

Patterns of Discrimination

I was in Brooklyn in TPF [Tactical Patrol Force] and an old black man walked up to me and showed me a retired police officer's shield. And in my conversation with him it was brought out that he was either the second or third black officer hired by the department. And he stated during those times, when he was an active police officer, that black officers could only be assigned to black areas. . . . It was actually stated to him that the only place blacks were good enough to work was in a black neighborhood.

DISCRIMINATION against black police in this country, legitimated by traditional police norms and supported to a large extent by a pervasive racial ideology, was perhaps nowhere more evidently demonstrated than in the common practice in the past of denying black cops any opportunity to work in white communities. Several studies have noted that in most cities across the country black officers, prior to the mid-1960s, were not only concentrated in precincts populated heavily by members of their own race, but quite often excluded altogether from duties in white areas. The practice of confining black police to black precincts or districts was not restricted, as one might have expected, to Southern or border cities. Evidence obtained from a number of related surveys shows that until the mid-1960s it was an accepted practice in Northern cities.[2] In both parts of the country, the rationale behind segregated assignment practices was that black police knew their own people better, that they could command greater respect from them and, that, in many instances, they were stricter with blacks than were white police.

Not only restricted to black districts, black police were, it seems, constrained further to routine foot patrol assignments either alone or with black partners. Again, this type of forced segregation was evident not only in Southern cities where one might, given the existence of segregation laws, expect to find discrimination in assignment and resistance to integrated patrol but also in Northern cities as well. A seminal study of the Philadelphia police department, for example, has shown that the practice of assigning black cops to foot patrol rather than to radio motor patrol or desk jobs was common in most of the city's districts at least until 1956.[3] In Chicago, until 1960, blacks rarely were assigned to patrol cars, and in at least one precinct if no white officers were available for assignment, some radio cars were not dispatched.[4] Similarly, in another study, Martin Alan Greenberg found that prior to the 1943 Harlem riots in New York City, black police had been systematically denied radio motor-patrol duty.[5] Even as late as 1965 black cops in New York City were protesting departmental practices which they claimed restricted them to low-status foot-patrol assignments in black precincts.[6]

Discrimination against black police in assigning special duties also has been reported to be widespread in the past. A study of racial practices in the South, for example, showed that there were only "56 Negro detectives in 1954 . . . , 87 in 1959, among the 146 agencies responding . . . , and 101 among 98 agencies in 1961."[7] Outside the South, patterns of occupational mobility among black police were little better. Until 1961, Newark had only one black detective assigned to the police department, as did Boston.[8] In New York City, black cops complained of the difficulties they encountered when attempting to enter the detective bureau in the early 1960s and in attaining positions in other plainclothes commands. These officers alleged that blacks were automatically excluded from such *choice* assignments as the Homicide Squad, Safe and Loft, and so forth.[9]

Police agencies across the country also have been charged with practicing discrimination against black officers concerning policies other than task and area assignment. For example, in 1967 the President's Crime Commission discovered that in some cities the legal authority of an officer to arrest a white suspect depended heavily on whether the cop was white or black. Drawing upon findings contained in other studies, the commission noted that in 18 of the 28 police departments surveyed, black officers could do no more than hold a white felony suspect until a white policeman showed up on the scene, unless, of course, there were no white officers available. In ten others, the black officer could not arrest the white suspect at all; in most cases he could only keep him under surveillance. The report went on to state that in cases of misdemeanor offenses, the power of the black officer was even more limited. Not surprising, perhaps, was the additional discovery that these practices extended into several Northern cities where black deputies were allowed to arrest white felony suspects *only* if white deputies were not immediately available.[10]

Racial discrimination also was believed to prevail in the area of performance evaluations. In a number of recent studies black police were found to be victims of a biased rating system.[11] Eugene Beard, for example, reporting on a variety of issues directly involving black police officers in Washington, D.C., discovered that the great majority of black officers in that city felt victimized with regard to how they were evaluated by white police superiors and attributed differences in job performance ratings given black and white officers to racial discrimination. In addition, Beard noted a widespread belief among members of his study population that the rules and regulations of the police department were applied inequitably. Eighty-four percent (of his 947 black police respondents) reported that white officers were less likely to receive disciplinary charges than black officers.[12]

Finally, it appears that until fairly recently blacks have been virtually excluded from leadership and supervisory positions in most of the nation's police agencies, especially in Southern and border states.[13] But even in the Northern cities for which data were available, black police were only somewhat more successful in gaining entry into higher ranking positions than their Southern counterparts. For example, a 1962 survey reviewed by the President's Commission on law enforcement disclosed that among the 106 Northern cities responding, six had black captains, 17 had black lieutenants and only 48 had black sergeants.[14] Suprisingly, by the mid-1960s this situation had deteriorated even further. Only 22 law enforcement agencies in the entire country had black officers above the rank of patrolman.[15] In sum, it can be argued that the problems confronting black police in the 1950s and early 1960s were substantial in themselves but were not substantially different from those experienced by blacks in other institutional areas of American life.

As the decade of the sixties began to unfold, public attention became increasingly concentrated on the problems of urban blacks. Major changes in the country's social, political, and legal institutions had begun to make themselves felt and efforts were being made nationaly and locally to resolve the nation's racial problems. In the section that follows we discuss a number of these changes from an historical perspective. Particular emphasis is given to those social forces believed to have shaped the present orientation of the New York City police department toward racial minority groups. Finally, we consider the emergence and growth of black sociopolitical organizations whose efforts throughout the country to secure a more favorable position for black policemen have recently been documented.

The Challenge to White Domination

A sustained, organized, and ultimately successful challenge to exclusive white domination in the United States had its origins in the early 1950s. It was triggered then by a combination of factors, including an apprehension about adverse world opinion concerning America's racial practices, a growing competitiveness between the United States and the Soviet Union for the allegiances of the newly emerging African nations, and by a growing black political activism within this country. It was given a great boost by the landmark decisions of the United States Supreme Court rulings in 1954 and 1956 outlawing racial segregation in public schools and on public transportation. Congress, in turn, through legislation, demonstrated (hesitatingly, perhaps) that the Federal government viewed discrimination and separation along racial lines not only as wrong but as illegal. Although Court decisions and legislative reform succeeded in bringing about change in some areas (and also in raising the expectations of American blacks) they failed significantly to alter the actual conditions under which the vast majority of blacks in this country lived.

Then, in the early 1960s, the challenge to white domination was beginning to shift from the courts to the streets and public accommodations. Largely under the leadership of its then chief spokesman Martin Luther King, Jr., black protest began to take the form of marches, sit-ins, boycotts, rent strikes, and other face-to-face confrontations with established authority. But continued resistance to demands for change throughout the country as well as the growing disparity between black expectations and the rate of "real" economic, social, and political progress eventually was to force many black groups to reconsider their ideological positions. Increasingly, militant tactics were adopted, with some black leaders beginning openly to espouse revolutionary solutions to America's racial problems. Although clear differences existed among the leaders, militant groups were united at least in the belief that racial inequality was widespread in this country and that its institutions were in need of rapid, not gradual, transformation. During this period established civil rights groups which had emphasized legal and nonviolent direct action were openly challenged by the more militant black leaders for their failure to respond adequately to the deeply rooted problems of the masses of blacks in the country. An earlier emphasis on full integration into mainstream American society was supplemented by an emphasis on black pride, nationalism, independence, and the acquisition of power and freedom by radical means. With this, the nonviolent phase of the civil rights struggle had for all practical purposes come to an end. Violent reaction directed against a seemingly unresponsive system appeared to many ghetto blacks the only solution to a long history of exploitation, discrimination, and subjugation.

In the summer of 1964 the nation's first major civil disorder of the decade erupted in New York City's Harlem ghetto. Each summer thereafter for four successive years, urban ghetto riots took their toll in deaths, injuries, and destruction of property. In 1967, for example, racial uprisings in some 56 cities across the country accounted for at least 84 deaths, over 3800 injuries, and hundreds of millions of dollars in property damage.[16] While it is true that the more destructive forms of urban violence were essentially a "black" response to severe social problems that had been mounting over the years, these disorders were triggered in almost every instance by the actions or alleged actions of the police in dealing with ghetto residents, such as the shooting of an unarmed black or the rumor of such a shooting. Whether these disorders turned into random demostrations of violence or into full-scale collective actions against established authority often depended upon the degree to which police officials on the scene were able to exert effective control over their own men. When order broke down within the police ranks, as it so often did, police became subject to the same principles of crowd behavior that motivated their adversaries. Deep-seated racial prejudices surfaced and the desire to vent hostility and to reestablish dominance in the streets frequently became compelling motives for retaliation.[17] In many instances local police became totally ineffective and city administrators had to rely upon outside forces to restore order.

Government Response and the Move Toward Police Reform

Toward the latter part of the 1960s it was becoming increasingly evident that more effective strategies were needed to deal with the problems and general unrest in America's urban slums. In a sense, the riots and disorders which swept through this nation served to "wake up" white America to the conditions and feelings of blacks in this country and to focus attention on the behavior of police who dealt with large disaffected and powerless groups within the society. Early in 1968, after the most extensive outbreaks of rioting had ceased, the National Advisory Commission on Civil Disorders, headed by former Illinois Governor Otto Kerner, "announced the completion of one of the most comprehensive and significant reports ever to be issued by a government-sponsored commission. The Kerner Report placed the major portion of the blame for the socioeconomic conditions of black people on the total society, specifically on white racism. It warned of potential catastrophe if the nation did not commit more resources to solving the problems of the urban ghettoes."[18] Largely as an outgrowth of this report and other studies carried out on behalf of the President's Commission, agencies in the public sector found themselves under increasing pressure to reduce the likelihood of further violence and to address themselves more directly to the changing needs of America's urban populations. Police departments in particular were encouraged to reexamine their internal operations, community-relations programs, and selection and training procedures for minority police personnel. In addition, law-enforcement officers were expected to acquire new social skills, to become familiar with current legal issues and developments, and, above all, to learn to exercise impartial discretion in their dealings with minority citizens.

But it has long been recognized that, like most of the "establishment," the police do not on their own either welcome or institute internal change. For a variety of reasons, including the potential loss of status, prestige, or job security, police officers, as a general rule, cling to familiar methods and norms of conduct. Internal reform comes about only through deliberate, calculated efforts on the part of outside agencies and a progressive government leadership. For some time the International Association of Chiefs of Police (I.A.C.P.) had provided direction and assistance in the area of police reform. However, until fairly recently the dominant thrust of these efforts was in the direction of improving police efficiency and effectiveness through the introduction of new technological developments.[19] Meanwhile, various national commissions contributed to the internal reform of police departments by providing funds to experiment in operational procedures and design programs aimed at upgrading both the quality of personnel and their services. The consensus was that to improve the quality of law enforcement, the quality of individual officers would have to be upgraded through higher education. Findings showed that even as late as 1966, the median educational level of police officers in this country was only 12.4 years.[20] Not only commissions, but individual authorities and police reformers were advocating higher educational standards for police. For example, Rodney Stark (who had studied police riots in the 1960s) argued that police training should be conducted largely within colleges and universities. Similarly, Jerome Skolnick concluded in the *Politics of Protest* that education would help solve police problems. Like Stark, Skolnick felt that higher education could help eliminate the sentiment of racism among police officers by providing students with a background in the role of political activity, demonstration, and protest in a constitutional democracy.[21] What emerged from the Commission's findings and reports was the Law Enforcement Education Program (LEEP). Enacted by Congress in 1968 as part of the Omnibus Crime Control and Safe Streets Act, this program provided police officers and those planning careers in law enforcement with grants and loans to attend institutions of higher learning. Largely as a result of LEEP, police across the country began attending colleges in significantly greater numbers than in the past. In New York City alone, by 1973, some 6500 members of the department were attending institutions of higher learning on their own time and of these nearly 2000 had already obtained degrees.[22]

In some instances, basic changes in police practices were effected by reform-minded city administrators. In New York City, for example, former Mayor John V. Lindsay and Police Commissioners Howard Leary and Patrick V. Murphy provided the necessary progressive, innovative leadership. Under the aegis of Mayor Lindsay, the police department began to promote a philosophy of constructive reform geared to the changing needs of urban law enforcement. One of his first actions after taking office was to institute a Civilian Complaint Review Board (CCRB) that would receive and investigate allegations by private citizens of police misconduct. Members who served on this board were appointed jointly by the mayor and the police commissioner and had investigative and advisory powers. Strongly opposed by the police rank and file the CCRB was defeated at the polls in a citywide referendum not long after its inception and replaced by a board completely staffed by police personnel.[23]

Despite this setback, police practices in New York City continued to undergo serious examination and change. Toward the end of the sixties, the department, then under the leadership of Commissioner Murphy, acknowledged for the first time that the major portion of police work was totally unrelated to law enforcement, consisting instead of a variety of extralegal services provided to the community. As a result of this understanding, attempts were made to "humanize" the police image. Greater flexibility was introduced into the organization and efforts were undertaken to narrow the distance between the police and the civilian population. Altering the traditional perception of the police as a repressive, military-type organization was attempted through fundamental changes in police nomenclature, equipment, and dress. The department, for example, was no longer to be referred to as the police "force" but as the police "service."[24] To promote increased cooperation and rapport between the department and the various minority communities, the traditional "conflict" model of policing was replaced by one that viewed the police and public as partners.[25] Community-relations functions were expanded, police-citizen dialogue encouraged, citizen liaison and advisory boards enlarged, and human relations training for members of the service emphasized. To make the police more responsive to the "unique" needs of certain minority communities, the concepts of "team policing" and "family crisis intervention" were introduced during the early seventies. These programs, once activated in the neighborhood, offered minority citizens an opportunity to see the police providing helpful public services, not simply giving out summonses. Of special importance to black and Hispanic populations was the attempt on the part of the department to promote police restraint in the use of force. Along these lines, personnel training began to stress alternatives to the use of police weapons, encouraging "verbal" rather than "physical" modes of settling disputes between the police and citizens.[26]

Other key changes which were indicative of a break with long-standing police practices included the introduction of women into a wider range of police roles and functions in the early seventies, the civilianization of many traditional police duties including clerical work, communications, and traffic enforcement, the reduction in importance of seniority credit in police promotion exams, and the recruiting and hiring of minority group members in significantly greater numbers than had been done in the past.

We have thus far considered a number of factors instrumental in shaping the picture of relations between white society, police, and the black community in the past two decades. We have discussed some of the reasons for the resurgence of black militancy as an alternate strategy to the earlier nonviolent attempts to bring about real change in the status of American blacks. We then attempted to connect this later movement, if only indirectly, to the spread of civil disorders across the country in the mid-1960s and to show how these extreme forms of intergroup conflict can lead to the restructuring of one of society's key institutions—law enforcement.

Finally, we showed that it was not only local level rebellion by insurgent blacks that accounted for change in traditional police methods but also Federal intervention in local systems. In the pages that immediately follow we consider the combined efforts of Federal courts, progressive city administrators and police chiefs, and newly emerging black fraternal police organizations in bringing about racial reform in their respective departments.

The Emergence of Black Police as an Organized Political Force

Not long after the National Advisory Commission on Civil Disorders published its report depicting severe underrepresentation of blacks in every major police department studied, law enforcement agencies across the country found themselves under increasing political pressure to achieve a more balanced representation of minority group personnel. As a first step, in a number of cities, recruitment drives were launched by the agencies themselves in the hope of attracting qualified minority candidates. Los Angeles, for example, erected "brotherhood" billboards along its freeways. Denver employed an advertising agency. In Washington, D.C., the police department organized community groups to assist in recruiting.[27] And in Kansas City the police department enlisted the services of a black and white recruiting team with the same last names (Brown) to show that, under the skin, all men were brothers. A cash incentive was also offered to any police officer who recruited a new officer.[28] On the whole, however, newspapers, schools, and community center visits were by far the most popular sources of recruitment utilized by large cities to attract minority police candidates.[29] In New York City Mayor Lindsay, spurred on by a favorable economy, earlier campaign promises, and probably by a genuine desire for reform, embarked upon a series of programs aimed at expanding job opportunites for blacks and other minorities. One of Lindsay's first direct actions in furtherance of this goal was to promote a drive to recruit 1000 black and Hispanic officers. This effort, assisted by a $2.9 million grant from the Federal government, was carried out in a variety of ways in the mid-1960s including visits by minority police personnel to college campuses and black community centers, advertising in minority news media, and actually training potential candidates for upcoming police tests.[30]

In conjunction with this recruitment drive, the NYPD also instituted an applicant review process. Informally established under Police Commissioner Howard Leary in 1966, this board (Candidate Review Board) studied every case in which an applicant was rejected for employment. Prior to this a candidate who had been disapproved because of "poor character" or because of cultural factors that were foreign to the investigator stood little chance of being accepted for employment (or for that matter even knowing why he had been rejected). With the establishment of the CRB approximately 80 percent of those candidates—many of whom were from minorities—who initially found themselves rejected by the Personnel Investigation Section were later approved for employment. Even those who were disapproved at this stage had yet another opportunity to appeal the decision before the Principal Hearing Board, which ultimately accepted about half the applicants who came before it.[31]

Still other steps were taken by police departments around the country to eliminate employment barriers to minorities. Slated for elimination in New York and other cities in 1973 was, for example, the standard height requirement for police candidates. The elimination of height requirements opened for the first time the possibility of a law enforcement career for many young Hispanics whose average height would have been slightly below the former standard.[32] In another radical departure from traditional department standards that same year, police candidates from the city's Housing and Transit Authority lists were considered for positions as police officers. Since more blacks and Hispanics had traditionally applied for positions with these agencies than with the regular police force, the department hoped to divert many of these minority applicants into the regular force.[33]

In most of the nation's large cities progress in altering the racial composition of police agencies was achieved through the legal process. The body of emerging law which was used to open doors of police agencies to minorities began with the Federal Civil Rights Act of 1964. Originally designed to assure blacks and other minorities greater access to jobs in the private sector, this legislation also provided those hired with legal precedents to combat certain

forms of discrimination in the work setting. The Federal Equal
Employment Opportunities Act, passed in 1972, extended the
provisions of the Civil Rights Act to cover employment practices
of state and local governments and empowered the EEOC to sue
public employers it deemed guilty of discrimination. This marked
the first time that an independent agency in the Federal government had been created specifically to fight discrimination in the area
of employment. The power of the EEOC was further strength-
ened with the signing of the Affirmative Action Amendment in
1973 and later with the establishment of racial quotas in hiring.[34]
Shortly after passage of the EEOA, the police department in New
York City set up its own independent unit (OEEO) to ensure
that police practices were in compliance with the new Federal, state,
and local laws, regulations and guidelines relating to discrimination in employment. This unit, expanded in 1978 and placed under the direction and control of the Assistant Commissioner for
Equal Opportunity, not only monitored hiring patterns and identified problem areas but also investigated and acted upon individual complaints of discrimination involving such areas as assignment, promotion, advancement, transfer, and conditions of
employment. Any member of the department who felt that he had
been discriminated against in any of these areas had the choice of
bringing the matter to the attention of his immediate supervisor
for informal adjudication or, if that failed, to file a formal complaint with the assistant commissioner.

In order to ensure that department heads, supervisors, employees, and the public were aware of the department's policy on equal
employment opportunity, special meetings were held with upper-
level managers, policy statements signed by the police commissioner himself were posted on all employee bulletin boards, and
periodic checks were made to ensure that they were prominently
displayed. Handouts describing the function of the OEEO were
also distributed to all uniformed and civilian employees; seminars
concerning court decisions were conducted, and recruits were provided with special training describing the creation, purpose and
function of the OEEO. To assure compliance with these new regulations, the assistant commissioner worked with other assigned
OEEO personnel in assisting supervisors to solve EEO problems,
in developing reporting systems that would measure the effective-

ness of the program, in conducting audits of hiring and promotion patterns, in holding regular discussions with supervisors and employees to be certain EEO policies were being implemented, and in ensuring that complaints of discrimination were being written up to the satisfaction of the aggrieved employee. In short, the police department took the position that equal employment opportunity was a fundamental condition that should be judged on the basis of job-related qualifications and not on extraneous factors such as race or sex. In a memo distributed to all commands it enlisted the total committment of every police and civilian employee to this goal and stated that the Office of Equal Employment Opportunity would see to it that this policy was carried out.[35]

The Federal courts meanwhile, were looking into traditional police practices which appeared to circumvent the hiring of minorities. In many instances they ruled against such practices, establishing racial quotas in order to ensure greater participation of minorities in the police departments concerned. In Cleveland, for example, in 1972, a U.S. district court judge ruled that at least 18 percent of all newly hired cops had to be black.[36] A Federal court in Alabama similarly ordered the Department of Public Safety in 1972 to begin hiring black state troopers in numbers equal to whites, until 25 percent of the force was black. (The Alabama highway patrol, it was reported, had not hired a single black trooper in 37 years.[37]) In Philadelphia, a year later, a Federal court ruled that the police department had to begin hiring at least one black officer for every two whites.[38] In Connecticut (in the same year) a Federal judge directed the Bridgeport police department, where blacks and Hispanics made up only 3.5 percent of the force, to "speed up" its hiring of minorities until they constituted 15 percent of the force.[39] More recently, the Chicago police department was placed under court order to impose a racial hiring quota system that would increase the proportion of blacks to 27 percent; in Los Angeles, as a result of a suit brought by minority police, the department agreed to hire about 40 percent nonwhites until the force would be brought up to a level reflective of the racial mixture of the community. San Francisco also reached a similar consent decree in 1979 under which it agreed that 50 percent of its new recruits would consist of racial minorities.[40] Perhaps as a result of the increasing number of police departments that were compelled to hire minorities under court-imposed quota systems, a number of local governments worked out voluntary affirmative action plans for their police agencies. Those departments which reached settlements rather than fight suits in Federal court include Detroit, Tampa, Seattle, Sacramento, Syracuse, Cincinnati, Fort Lauderdale and the Ohio state police.[41] New York City, although it was not under a quota system of any kind, nevertheless increased the number of black and Hispanic cops in the department by 1973 to over 3000, nearly double the number employed seven years earlier.[42]

As their numbers and influence grew in the 1970s, black police across the country began to organize themselves to promote and protect their own special interests in much the same way as black congressmen, lawyers, and journalists had done in the past.[43] In some cities these organizations evolved from social and or fraternal groups seeking redress to racially based grievances, while in others they were formed as an explicit response to racial practices in their own departments. In both cases, interest in matters of internal reform eventually spread to include more general social and political issues involving the police and the larger black community. Soon after their emergence as a "politicized" group, black policemen began speaking out against racial injustices and taking positions on issues that challenged the very foundation of the police system itself.[44] Departments in many cities that had black police organizations were put on notice that racial discrimination, especially in the areas of hiring, promotion, and assignment, would no longer be tolerated. Passive resistance which had for so long characterized black police protest in this country was slowly giving way to a new militancy and assertiveness grounded in the concept of black political power and the law. In a few cities black police organizations engaged in lobbying activities and in publicizing issues of concern.[45] In most, however, direct legal challenges were mounted against discriminatory police practices and were won in the courts, forcing the departments concerned to modify existing racial policies. So strong was this movement that by the mid-1970s black police in New York and other major cities had demonstrated that pressure could be applied effectively from within the organization to discourage long-standing racial practices.

Entrance requirements in the form of written exams, oral interviews, physical tests, and background investigations were some targets selected by black police groups for litigation. In some police departments, it appeared, minority candidates were being systematically rejected for employment by predominantly white police background investigators because of factors related more to aspects of "ghetto culture" than to potential qualifications for the job.[46] In a number of suits brought before Federal courts, police entrance tests and "screening procedures" were found to violate constitutional and Federal law and were invalidated. In Chicago, for example, a Federal district judge in 1976 enjoined the police department when making employment decisions from considering an applicant's socioeconomic status, family history, military service, or even his previous arrest record. A year earlier a similar ruling was handed down in Ohio which prevented the Akron police department from using such arbitrary criteria as the applicant's credit rating, residency, high school record, and neighborhood references for hiring purposes. In Bridgeport, Connecticut, the same Federal judge who ordered the police department to speed up its hiring of minorities substantially also directed the civil service commission to cease giving exams that discriminated against blacks and Hispanics and to submit future examinations to the court for approval. The plaintiffs here included the Bridgeport Guardians, a black police organization, and applicants from minority racial groups who had failed police entrance exams. In a later suit brought by the Afro American Patrolman's League (AAPL) in Chicago, charging discrimination in hiring, selection, and promotion, a Federal district court enjoined the police department from using a 1971 patrolman's exam as well as its background investigation. As in earlier cases of a similar nature, the court accepted as prima facie evidence of discrimination the difference in the acceptance rate between white and black candidates.[47] As a result, Chicago now has a written examination, but there is no passing score for its police candidates. The city's department of personnel merely uses the exam only to make up an eligibility list. Likewise, in New Orleans, black police charged in Federal court that the police department discriminated against hiring blacks back in 1973. This suit included specific allegations that black candidates were subjected to "badgering" and "intimidation" during routine polygraph examinations and were asked questions not asked of their white counterparts.[48]

As pressure and court actions brought by black organizations (and civil rights groups) mounted across the country, significant patterns of change in the hiring of minority police began to emerge. In a few cities only limited gains were noticed while in others the percentage of black (and Hispanic) officers grew substantially. By the late 1970s, for example, the proportion of blacks in the Detroit and Washington, D.C., police departments had reached 35 percent and 42 percent respectively. In San Francisco, Chicago, Philadelphia, Memphis, and Baltimore, blacks now account for roughly one of every five members of the force.[49]

It appears that the New York City police department was determined to avoid the imposition from outside of any quota system and evidently made efforts on its own to increase the proportion of minority police. However, in 1969, the department of personnel released a two-year study of earlier civil service exams for entry-level positions which showed that when test takers of similar employment, education and family background were compared, only the "ethnic factor"—race—affected exam scores. This finding prompted the personnel department to undertake further study of its most recent entry-level exams. The results of this and other related studies supported the personnel department's earlier contention that "greater numbers of blacks and Hispanics could have made perfectly fine cops but never got past the front door because of below passing test grades which may have been unrelated to actual job performance".[50] The crux of the issue, it seems, was that minority applicants were doing poorly on these exams because the tests themselves were culturally biased. This was, in fact, precisely the position the Guardians Association took when it filed suit in 1972 charging that past exams discriminated against blacks and therefore the department should be enjoined from using them in making appointments to the force. The Guardians felt that a test should attempt to find out if a person is capable of training as a police officer and not merely to find out what his knowledge of nonpolice matters might be.[51]

Since hiring, under state civil service laws, for police jobs has traditionally been based on a strict numerical ranking according to test scores, the city enlisted an outside consultant firm to design a new exam that would not be biased against racial minorities, lower job standards, and would be job related and meet all equal-opportunity guidelines. In conjunction with this, the personnel department planned a major publicity campaign aimed at attracting qualified minority candidates. The director's intent was to set up police booths in areas where minorities live, work or attend schools, to set up hot lines where potential candidates could have job-related questions answered, and to tutor minorities for future police tests.[52]

The police department in the meantime continued to hire from the challenged exam lists even while the Guardians suit was in court. Then, the city's fiscal crisis in the early 1970s forced both the department and the Guardians to halt all court actions. However, in 1976 the Guardians renewed their case in court and the police department once again took the position that its prior entry-level exams were in fact valid and job related even though it was unable to produce at the time a written job description.[53]

The final decision on the question of discrimination and job relatedness of police entrance exams in New York City was handed down in 1980 by Federal Judge Robert Carter who, after examining all the relevant issues, ruled that the city not only discriminated against minority candidates but did so deliberately.[54] Carter based his conclusions on "court records stretching back over nearly a decade of litigation, in an uphill and continuous struggle by the city's black and Hispanic cops to reconcile the letter and the spirit of anti-discrimination law."[55] After appeals by the city the court decided that future police hirings should be made on the basis that one of every three be a minority. In order to fill this quota requirement, the police department was forced to lower the qualifying grade for minorities to 84 percent, ten points lower than for whites.[56] Judge Carter's decision prevailed for several months before Federal Appelate Judge Jon Newman stepped in and reduced the quota to one-in-four. Newman gave the city the benefit of the doubt that it had not discriminated intentionally but ruled nevertheless that prior exams were invalid and ordered the quota.[57] The legal basis upon which these court decisions were reached can be traced back to the 1971 Griggs v. Duke Power Company decision. "In that case a group of black employees at a privately owned power plant in North Carolina won a suit against their employer under a section of Title

VII of the 1964 Civil Rights Act, having maintained that the employer was using personnel 'aptitude' tests to discriminate against blacks in hiring and promotion decisions."[58] The Griggs decision established the principle that, regardless of the employer's good intentions, any practice, including tests that have a disparate racial impact, is illegal if it cannot be shown to be related to job performance.

The city administration was not overjoyed with the court's decision but, realizing it had a critical need for more police officers, it agreed to hire minorities under a racial quota system. Beginning in September 1980, the police department added an additional 120 black and 173 Hispanic officers to the ranks. These numbers, although appearing quite small, represented the largest proportion (49 percent) of minority recruits ever appointed to the department at any one time. In 1981, the proportion of minority appointments, while declining somewhat, continued to average better than 30 percent of all police hired. In actual numbers, 303 black and 366 Hispanic cops joined the ranks that year. The most recent class to enter the Police Academy under Judge Carter's racial quota system clearly signals a continuation of this trend. Of the 2779 officers sworn in on January 1982, 332 were black and 315 were Hispanic. This combined total of 647 minority officers raised the proportion of non-whites in the New York City police department to nearly 17 percent.[59]

Black police in New York City and elsewhere did not limit their activities to court actions involving unequal hiring practices. Departmental policies which had for so long restricted the assignments of blacks to predominantly black districts were also challenged. For example, in Hartford, Connecticut, in 1969, black officers resorted to a series of mass sick calls to protest their concentration in high-crime, ghetto areas of the city. This particular issue was resolved when the police department finally agreed to assign its personnel throughout the city irrespective of color.[60] In a related case in Mobile, Alabama, a Federal district judge rejected a "general" policy of assignments based on race, declaring that police officials who attempted to justify such a policy had failed to show adequately that black officers were less effective than whites in white neighborhoods. The court not only ordered the police department to make future assignments without regard to color but also struck down a long-standing practice of refusing to assign black policemen to ride in patrol cars with white partners.[61] In other cities changes in traditional racial policies regarding minority police have been even more dramatic. In Washington, D.C. for example, a white officer who now refuses to ride with a black faces immediate dismissal from the force.[62]

For New York City the question of assignments based on race has been largely resolved outside the courts. While it unquestionably was the practice of the department in the past to place most of its black (and Hispanic) officers in commands situated in ghetto communities, today, evidence indicates that assignments are made on a more or less random basis. Except for a few exclusively black areas such as the 28th Precinct in Central Harlem and the 79th Precinct in Brooklyn's Bedford-Stuyvesant section (where black police comprise slightly more than 30 percent of the patrol force) most precincts located in predominantly black or mixed areas of the city are patrolled by black police in varied proportions. The 25th Precinct in East Harlem, for example, consists of only 10 percent black police, while the 48th Precinct in the Bronx and the 73rd Precinct in Brooklyn consist of 16 percent and 24 percent blacks respectively.[63] Even in white areas of the city, the current trend seems to be to assign officers irrespective of color. For instance, in the exclusively white, silk-stocking 19th Precinct in Manhattan, 15 percent of all patrol officers are of minority extraction. This policy seems to extend, moreover, to civilian employees in the department. Of the 16 nonpolice personnel assigned to clerical duties in the 19th Precinct, 11 are either black or Hispanic.

Black police organizations have also fought to establish equal access to promotions, charging that both written exams and promotional systems which allot additional credit for seniority present competitive disadvantatages to minority personnel.[64] With regard to both the content of promotional exams and eligibility requirements, legal agencies have tended to rule in favor of black litigants. The New York State Division of Human Rights, for example, recently held that grammar questions on an exam for advancement to captain in the New York City police department discriminated against black lieutenants;[65] while in Chicago, a Federal court ruled that a written exam for promotion to sergeant had a discriminating impact upon blacks and other minorities. The

Chicago police department was unable to prove the exam's job-relatedness and was ordered to make up a new one. Similar rulings have been made in other major cities as well. In Bridgeport, Connecticut, the court, after examining promotional requirements, reduced the time-in-grade criterion for advancement in rank from three years to one.[66] In Baltimore, Maryland, police officers with only three years in service are now eligible to take exams for promotion to sergeant, lieutenant, and captain.[67] In New Orleans, the NAACP Legal Defense Fund recently succeeded in freezing all promotions in the police department, charging that current promotional exams gave no indication of who would make better supervisors. The attorney for the black police group also noted that the "seniority factor" which was weighted at 40 percent especially discriminated against blacks because blacks did not have seniority on the force.[68]

In New York City, blacks have made some progress advancing to lower-level supervisory positions. (Between 1974 and 1982, for example, the number of black sergeants increased by 30 percent while the number of white sergeants decreased by 13 percent)[69]. It remains true, however, that the overall picture of ranking black officers in the department has not changed all that much since the early 1970s. Including those holding positions above the rank of sergeant, black bosses in 1974 accounted for only 3 percent of the entire command structure. Today, some nine years later, that figure remains practically the same. Excluding sergeants, there are only 24 blacks holding supervisory positions in the department; of these 18 are either lieutenants or captains.[70] However, the city has recently set up a quota system in promotions which has placed more blacks in lower-level supervisory positions. In addition, seniority systems (which have always been weighted heavily in favor of whites in New York City) and promotional tests (which have traditionally limited the number of blacks holding ranking positions) are currently undergoing revision as a result of successful lawsuits brought by minority police groups.

Also at issue here is the question of black representation in detective and other nonuniformed, specialty units in the department. It is, in fact, in the area of advancement to the plain clothes detective bureau—an appointment based upon achievement, not exam taking—that black police have made the greatest proportional gains in New York City. While there are no available data for the 1960s, we do know that in 1971 blacks accounted for roughly 10 percent of the 2700 member detective bureau, while they made up less than 7 percent of the larger police force.[71] Today, black representation in the bureau is about 12 percent, while the comparative figure for the department as a whole is 10 percent.[72] Recent data from the department's Office of Equal Employment Opportunity also show that blacks have made significant advances once they entered the detective bureau. In 1974, when only 7 percent of the entire police force was black, 10 percent of all first-grade and 11 percent of all second- and third-grade positions were held by black detectives. Today, the proportion remains the same for first- and second-grade positions, but at the third-grade level blacks comprise roughly 13 percent of the detective force.[73]

With regard to other specialty assignments and duties in the NYPD, findings similar to the ones above are evident. An analysis of data provided by the department's OEEO discloses, for example, that of the approximately 8000 officers assigned to specialty units throughout the city today, nearly 800, or 10 percent, are black. More significant, perhaps, is the additional finding that in 25 of these 74 specialty units, black representation exceeds 13 percent.[74]

In concluding this section it can be said that during the 1960s and 1970s efforts by government and aggrieved black groups brought about change in the structure and practices of America's police agencies. Departments across the country were not only pressured into instituting reform in operational procedures aimed at improving relations with the minority public, but were forced to reevaluate their policies and practices regarding minority group employees. Although these efforts to alter customary practices met with initial resistance in some cities, by the mid-1970s changes in the "actual" level of discrimination experienced by black police were becoming increasingly evident. In the section that follows we consider the perceptions of racial reform in the New York City police department as reported by the men in this study. As we shall see, despite evidence of positive change in the overall position of black police today, not all respondents share the view that prejudice, discrimination, and especially inequality are things of the past.

NOTES

1. James I. Alexander, *Blue Coats-Black Skin: The Black Experience in the New York City Police Department since 1891* (New York: Exposition Press, 1978), pp. 11–37.

2. For evidence of police segregation policies in area assignments, see The President's Commission on Law Enforcement and Administration of Justice, *Task Force Report: The Police,* Washington, D.C., 1967, p. 174; Also see, "Many Cities Limit Negro Police Use," *The New York Times,* July 27, 1959; James B. Jacobs and Jay Cohen, "The Impact of Racial Integration on the Police," *Journal of Police Science and Administration,* Volume 6, Number 2, (June 1978), p. 179; Trevor Armbrister, "The Lonely Struggle of the Black Cop," *The Reader's Digest,* March 1971; Nicholas Alex, *Black in Blue: A Study of the Negro Policeman* (New York: Appleton-Century-Crofts, 1969), p. 107; James I. Alexander, op. cit.

3. See William M. Kephart, *Racial Factors and Urban Law Enforcement* (Philadelphia, Pa.: Univ. of Pennsylvania Press, 1957).

4. The President's Commission on Law Enforcement and Administration of Justice, op. cit., p. 173.

5. Martin Alan Greenberg, "Auxiliary Civilian Police—The New York City Experience," *Journal of Police Science and Administration,* Volume 6, Number 1 (March 1978), p. 93.

6. See Nicholas Alex, op. cit., pp. 108, 109.

7. See The President's Commission on Law Enforcement and Administration of Justice, op. cit., p. 173.

8. Ibid.

9. Nicholas Alex, op. cit., pp. 109, 110.

10. See The President's Commission on Law Enforcement and Administration of Justice, op. cit., p. 170; also see, John Grimes, "The Black Policeman in Law Enforcement," John Jay College of Criminal Justice, unpublished M.A. thesis, 1969, p. 55.

11. See, for example, Rita M. Kelly and Gorman West, Jr., "The Racial Transition of a Police Force: A Profile on White and Black Policemen in Washington, D.C.," in John R. Snibbe and Homa M. Snibbe (eds), *The Urban Policeman in Transition: A Psychological and Sociological View* (Springfield, Ill.: Charles C Thomas, 1973), pp. 354–381.

12. See Eugene Beard, "The Black Police in Washington, D.C.," *Journal of Police Science and Administration,* Volume 5, Number 1 (March 1977), pp. 48, 51.

13. The President's Commission on Law Enforcement and Administration of Justice, op. cit., p. 171.

14. Ibid. Interestingly, the first time a black was promoted to the rank of captain in the New York City police department was in 1947, nearly a half century after the first black officer was hired. See John Grimes, op. cit., p. 76.

15. See John Grimes, op. cit., p. 110.

16. Alphonso Pinkney, *Black Americans* (Englewood Cliffs, N.J.: Prentice-Hall, 1969), p. 206.

17. These ideas were drawn directly from Louis C. Goldberg, "Ghetto Riots

and Others: The Faces of Civil Disorder in 1967," in Gary T. Marx (ed.), *Racial Conflict: Tension and Change in American Society* (Boston, Mass.: Little, Brown , 1971), p. 275.

18. See William B. Helmreich, *The Black Crusaders: A Case Study of a Black Militant Organization* (New York: Harper & Row, 1973), pp. 19, 20.

19. See Herman Goldstein, *Policing a Free Society* (Cambridge, Mass.: Ballinger, 1977), p. 326.

20. James B. Jacobs and Samuel B. Magdovitz, "At Leep's End?: A Review of the Law Enforcement Education Program," *Journal of Police Science and Administration,* Volume 5, Number 1 (March 1977), p. 2.

21. Ibid.

22. Press Release, Police Department, City of New York, February 20, 1973.

23. Nicholas Alex, *New York Cops Talk Back: A Study of a Beleaguered Minority* (New York: Wiley, 1976), pp. 76, 77.

24. See Georgette Bennett Sandler and Ellen Mintz, "Police Organizations: Their Changing Internal and External Relationships," in Jim Munro (ed.), *Classes, Conflict, and Control* (Cincinnati, Ohio: Anderson, 1976), pp. 420, 421.

25. Ibid. p. 421.

26. Ibid.

27. James B. Jacobs and Jay Cohen, op. cit., p. 175.

28. Jack Perry, "A New Concept in Police Recruiting," *The Police Chief,* Volume XXXVI (June 1969), p. 42.

29. See Jack Noel Rose, "An Analysis of the Methods used by Urban Police Departments to Attract Minority Group Members," John Jay College of Criminal Justice, unpublished M.A. thesis, 1973, p. 137.

30. For evidence of minority recruitment efforts in New York City and elsewhere see Nicholas Alex, *Black in Blue: A Study of the Negro Policemen* (New York: Appleton Century Crofts, 1969), p. 28; Edward Kirkman, "Police Hope to Triple Minority-Group Cops," *The New York Daily News,* July 2, 1972; Guardians Association, Police Department, City of New York, "We Have a Responsibility," 1971; Herman Goldstein, op. cit., p. 270; Isaac C. Hunt, Jr. and Bernard Cohen, *Minority Recruiting in the New York City Police Department* (The New York City-Rand Institute, May 1971).

31. See Anthony V. Bouza, "The Policeman's Character Investigation: Lowered Standards or Changing Times," *The Journal of Criminal Law, Criminology and Police Science,* Volume 63, Number 1 (March 1972), pp. 120–124.

32. Edward Kirkman, op. cit. See also, The National Center on Police and Community Relations, *A National Survey of Police and Community Relations* (Washington, D.C.: Government Printing Office, 1967), p. 278.

33. See Edward Kirkman, op. cit.

34. See Gerald D. Robin, *Introduction to the Criminal Justice System* (New York: Harper & Row, 1980), p. 120.

35. Official memo issued to all police commands by the New York City police department, September 27, 1978.

36. See "Cleveland Rules on Black Police—18% Quota of 188 New Men Ordered by U.S. Judge," *The New York Times,* July 22, 1962, p. 20.

37. See Gerald D. Robin, op. cit., p. 121.

38. See Deirdre Carmody, "Record Minority Percentage Foreseen for Police Recruits," *The New York Times,* July 2, 1973.

39. See Lawrence Fellows, "Judge Sets a Minority Quota for Bridgeport Police," *The New York Times,* January 31, 1973, p. 10.

40. See Ron Claiborne, "How Other Cities Put Minority Cops on the Job," *The Daily News,* August 31, 1980.

41. See Janice Prindle, "New York's Whitest—Keeping the Melting Pot on the Back Burner," *The Village Voice,* October 15–21, 1980, p. 21.

42. This data was provided by the New York City police department's Office of Equal Employment Opportunity (OEEO).

43. See Thomas A. Johnson, "Many Black Police Feel They're Between Two Guns . . . and a Black Police Chief May be 'in the Middle' Most of All," *The New York Times,* July 18, 1978, p. B1. Also see, Gerald Fraiser, "Black Policemen Denounce Racism," *The New York Times,* June 11, 1971.

44. See Trevor Armbrister, op. cit., pp. 125, 126. Also see, "The Black Cop," *Newsweek,* August 4, 1969, p. 54; Richard Hall, "Dilemma of the Black Cop," *Life,* September 18, 1970.

45. See Hervey A. Juris and Peter Feuille, *Police Unionism* (Lexington, Mass.: Lexington Books, 1973), p. 168.

46. See Anthony V. Bouza, op. cit. For an excellent study of the recruitment process in New York City, see Bernard Cohen, *Minority Recruiting in the New York City Police Department—Part 11, The Retention of Candidates* (The New York City-Rand Institute, May 1971).

47. See James B. Jacobs and Jay Cohen, op. cit., pp. 177, 178.

48. See "Trial Set for Police Bias Case in New Orleans," *The New York Times,* October 11, 1981, p. 36.

49. See John Herbers, "Minority Groups' Distrust of Police Found to be on the Rise Around the Country," *The New York Times,* May 25, 1980, p. 16. See also Ron Claiborne, op. cit.

50. See Janice Prindle, op. cit., p. 20.

51. See Edward Kirkman, op. cit.

52. Ibid.

53. See Janice Prindle, op. cit., p. 21.

54. Ibid., p. 20.

55. Ibid.

56. See Jerry Schmetterer, "The Uniforms are all Blue: Why are all the Faces White?," *The Daily News,* June 21, 1981, p. 35.

57. See Janice Prindle, op. cit., p. 20.

58. See "293 From Minorities Among 600 Police Recruits to be Sworn in Tuesday," *The New York Times,* August 31, 1980, p. 31.

59. This data was provided by the New York City police department's OEEO and by Police Officer Roger Abel, who presently holds a position in the Guardians Association of the NYPD.

60. See Hervey A. Juris and Peter Feuille, op. cit., p. 166.

61. See James B. Jacobs and Jay Cohen, op. cit., pp. 179, 180.

62. See Trevor Armbrister, op. cit., p. 126.
63. This data was provided by Police Officer Roger Abel.
64. See James B. Jacobs and Jay Cohen, op. cit., pp. 179, 180.
65. See Trevor Armbrister, op. cit., p. 126.
66. This data was provided by Police Officer Roger Abel.
67. See James B. Jacobs and Jay Cohen, op. cit., p. 180.
68. See John Grimes, op. cit., pp. 52, 53.
October 11, 1981, p. 36.
69. Data provided by the New York City police department's OEEO.
70. Ibid.
71. See James Sordi, "Do the New York City Police Department's Efforts to Recruit Black and Hispanic Officers Clash With its New Appointment and Promotion Proposals?," John Jay College of Criminal Justice, unpublished M.A. thesis, 1973, p. 47.
72. Data provided by the New York City police department's OEEO.
73. Ibid.
74. Ibid.

Chapter Two

—•◦•—

On the Job:
Perceptions within the NYPD

There's this one [white] sergeant here that loves to refer to [black] people as "those people." If you're black and you refer to black people as "those people" you're treated okay by him. Otherwise you may not be. You get a few black cops who do that sort of thing, guys who have no backbone. *They're* treated by this one sergeant as one of the guys.

ARLIER we presented racial data for the NYPD from a number of sources including government reports, newspapers, and the department's Office of Equal Employment Opportunity. These data, while revealing the statistical accomplishments (and failures) of black police officers over the past decade or so, do not tell us how black officers themselves perceive their situation in the department today as compared with that of the past. Our intent is to try to uncover and present these feelings since they, and not the statistics, create the individual officer's particular sense of identity and of belonging, and influence his reactions to his working environment, colleagues, and to society at large. And it is the individual officer's reactions to his perceived environment that, in turn, help shape the public's view of the department. Stated another way, if the black policeman feels that he is getting ahead in his career with the department, he is apt to communicate these sentiments in various ways to his police colleagues and to the many different people and groups he comes in contact with daily.

Conversely, if he senses that he is being left behind or unfairly treated because he is black, or if his accomplishments are seen as trivial or unimportant by others, those feelings too are likely to be communicated and may eventually become the basis for group dissatisfaction.

Virtually all of the 46 black policemen interviewed for this study were aware of the many and varied efforts in the past two decades to improve the overall position of black people in America. Most were also aware of some of the more direct attempts that have been made to restructure the New York City police department in keeping with the changing interests and needs of the city's black population, including its police. Yet there are clear differences of opinion among the officers as to the effect these efforts have had on the overall situation of blacks in the department and especially on the extent to which individual police commanders and supervisors have lived up to their "official" position of equal treatment for all police personnel regardless of color or ethnic background. What follows in this chapter is a breakdown of these differences into essentially three response categories: (1) those who believe that black officers are now treated in about the same fashion as are white officers, (2) those who perceive a basic discrepancy between "official" department policy which outwardly supports standards of full equality and the "actual" practices of individual white superiors toward black policemen, and, (3) those who are dissatisfied with the overall progress that has been made in removing racial barriers to full job equality and opportunity. We are especially concerned with the perceptions of these men concerning patterns of racial discrimination and inequality in the police department and with the explanations they offer to account for their persistence or absence today.

Where Policy and Practice Coincide

The feeling that black officers are now treated on an equal status basis with white officers is reflected in the views and comments of 24 of the 46 respondents who were asked, "In your opinion are black policemen treated the same as white policemen by the department?" This majority reports that conditions under which black officers work have vastly improved in recent years, and most attribute this change to forces operating outside the police bureaucracy. That is, they do not acknowledge department leaders as having taken the initiative in bringing about racial reform; rather, they view recent gains in their collective position as stemming primarily from formal government intervention, pressures exerted by various civil rights groups and black organizations, and changing police needs in the city.

Changing Political and Social Climate

It is claimed by a number of men in the study that the overall political and social climate in New York City has become increasingly receptive to reform in the area of race relations over the past decade or so. Increased sensitivity on the part of political office holders toward racial problems coupled with more responsive police leadership are thought to have contributed to the gradual erosion of traditional police policies which supported discrimination and racial division within the department in the past. The following statement from a veteran detective is typical:

> You have a liberal city now. You have blacks and Puerto Ricans in power, some of them in key positions. Lindsay started putting things together, the super agencies. He appointed a liberal-thinking police commissioner [Patrick V. Murphy], someone he could tell "This is the way I want it done." People who didn't feel the way he did were simply discarded. And he began to put blacks in office. You had a black fire commissioner. The courts were also stacked with liberal-thinking people. Basically, the whole climate in the city underwent change, and naturally people's values and attitudes started changing.

Prior to Mayor Lindsay's administration of the late 1960s and early 1970s, however, racism was seen as firmly embedded in the city's political, legal, and social institutions. To the extent that the New York City police department attempted to remain within the dominant value system, it reflected in its policies and practices institutional discrimination. According to the testimony of several veteran patrol officers, the police department has always accepted and acceded to prevailing racial policies.

> I would lean toward the fact that blacks are treated pretty much the same as whites now, at least as far as bosses who represent the department are concerned. I don't really think they go out of their way to discriminate against black cops. At one time they definitely did. . . . The department just followed suit, what everyone else did in the city. . . . You have to examine the natural climate in the sixties. There was a major push by blacks for recognition. The department simply followed suit. They were more or less forced into listening to what black policemen had been complaining about for years. They suddenly realized that there was something to it all. Then there were changes, starting in the late sixties . . . The department played the "catch-up" game. . . . Look at it this way, nobody wants to be the "odd ball."

> Now, yes. Ten or 15 years ago I would say no. Why should this department have been any different than any other city agency? There was discrimination everywhere against blacks. Only in the last few years has the department moved in a positive direction, and that's only because the climate in the city changed drastically. It became much more liberal. People began to look at things differently and that's when changes took place. Yeah, they took a real good look at the city's racial problems and I guess they decided that something had to be done finally.

These men do not automatically assume, however, that the same political forces which supported racial equality in the department in the late sixties and early seventies will continue to operate in the future with the same intensity. The last officer quoted speculates on what might happen, for example, if the current "liberal" trend in the city suddenly reversed itself:

> Let me say this too. This is an ultra-liberal city now. If the trend ever swings to the conservative side you'll see the same shit that happened in the past happen all over again. If the pendulum swings back you'll see discrimination of black policemen and black everything else. Basically, New York City goes the way the country goes, and the department goes the way the city and mayor go. Everything that goes on here revolves around the total climate. Things just seem to happen that way.

The comments also reveal a general awareness of the importance and impact of the civil rights movement. As we have already mentioned a major thrust of early black protest was aimed at achieving political, social, and economic equality with whites. And a primary technique used by leaders of the early movement to bring about reform in these areas was to discredit the dominant ideological system publicly in this country by focusing attention on and exposing some of its basic inconsistencies. Commenting on this "tactic" as a partial solution to America's racial problems, and by implication to those of the black police officer, one respondent said,

> I think 75 percent of the improvement in the way the department treats black cops has to be attributed to the civil rights movement. Now it is commonly known that it [civil rights movement] made white people aware of black problems; it made them responsive. It did this by embarrassing a lot of white people with the sit-ins and freedom marches and things. This created a very poor image of whites in this country to people in other countries. You see, the way black people were treated, that was a contradiction of what we, in this country, profess. . . . For example, Martin Luther King pointed out all the basic inadequacies of the system, all the basic frustrations of black people. He served as a test case for what was to come later. King challenged the system and he got a lot of laws changed.

Several respondents felt that the greatest long-term gains in the area of civil rights were indeed attained through court action and litigation. They pointed to a number of court cases that were won during the 1950s and 1960s which achieved "legal" equality for blacks in the areas of education and voting and which later served as important precedents for combating discrimination in employment. For example, legislation enacted in 1964 under the Civil Rights Act and again in 1972 under the Federal Equal Employment Opportunity Act empowered blacks to initiate civil action in the event employers refused to act upon complaints of racial inequality in the work setting. Thus, for the first time agencies in the public sector (such as the police) were faced with the very real possibility of incurring punitive damages should charges of discrimination based upon racial differences be substantiated in court. A number of officers, while not aware of any specific legislation designed to improve working conditions for black police, expressed nevertheless the general feeling conveyed by these new laws. For example,

> That's right, if the climate continued the way it was the city would have lost. It loses every time there is an incident where racial bias can be shown. The city stands a good chance of losing money in a civil action brought by black cops. . . .

One policeman, who agreed that blacks are now treated on a par with white officers, reports on one aspect of the racial situation in the department as he perceived it in the mid-sixties. He claims that departmental reward systems at that time operated to the disadvantage of the black undercover cop by conferring promotions mostly upon white officers who engaged in similar duties.

> Conditions ten years ago were poor for most black cops. I'll give you an example of what I mean. When I was picked up for a special detail . . . and the detail involved infiltrating subversive groups, which at the time was extremely dangerous, I effectively did my job for approximately two years and was transferred from the detail without any reward whatsoever. There were very few white officers in these types of details, but those who were there seemed to get the [gold] shield much faster. I can say, and I think I speak for most black cops, that this was very disappointing.

This same officer—at the time assigned to a prestigious detective unit—then presented a more up-to-date picture of department practices, one which seems to indicate that more rational criteria are now used in designating assignments and promoting members of the service. It is clear from his account, though, that changes in police practices are not seen as having been motivated altruistically. Rather they appear to have been established by the department to ward off the possibility of bad newspaper publicity and costly legal entanglements that would, no doubt, involve the city and its minority police personnel.

> Well, as I said before, the whole climate of the job has changed since those days. People are now promoted mostly on the basis of how well they do a job, not whether they are a certain color. A lot of this change has come about through the activities of civil rights

groups. Blacks became united, especially in this job. They became, so to speak, a force to be reckoned with. Things like I just described, passing up a guy for the shield just because he was black, that sort of thing simply would not be tolerated anymore. There would be hell to pay. . . . You know conditions today were forced on the department. It wasn't a humanitarian gesture on their part, this equality pitch. It was so the lid didn't blow off. The department and the mayor were afraid of repercussions. Complaints of discrimination might leak to the newspapers. Civil suits might be brought against the city and this would hit the city where it hurt the most, in their pocketbook. Basically, the department didn't want any waves so a lot of concessions were made. This is pure fact. It's like in the Jewish community, if it means sending in more cops to prevent complaints, they'll do it. They just don't want any more waves.

Although many of the black policemen in this study pointed to an increasing sensitivity on the part of local government leaders in the late 1960s as an important source of change in the department's racial policies and practices, there is also widespread awareness that this professed liberalism was in large part a direct response to the growing politicization of blacks in the city and to the trend to resolve racial problems in court. No doubt, the relative success of Federal law suits brought by black litigants in other cities across the country contributed to the feeling expressed here that any shift in the city's position toward its minority police was designed largely to preclude the possibility of law suits and unfavorable news media publicity.

But there were other forces operating in the late 1960s, early 1970s that would serve to insure that any changes in the department's policies met the needs and interests of its black minorities. One was the increasing politicization and militancy of black police themselves.

The Rise of Militancy Among Black Police and Their Associations

The shifting emphasis of civil rights protest in the mid-1960s toward black nationalism was accompanied in many instances by a resurgence of racial pride and solidarity among black Americans. As part of that larger movement black police officers across the country began, as we mentioned earlier, forming separate organizations for the purpose of promoting changes in the policies and racial practices of their departments. As these organizations grew in size, strength, and external support, it became increasingly apparent to police leaders that their demands for improved conditions for blacks both on and off the job could no longer simply be "shrugged off." Our respondents felt that the expression of racial solidarity communicated by black policemen in recent years has in a number of ways forced the police department to meet many of the demands of the more militant black leaders and supporters. For one said

> I don't really see how conditions could not have improved for black cops. You see, you began to have blacks closing ranks, forming militant groups, finally getting their shit together. There was strength there, there was leadership. There was pride. Especially a lot of the younger guys started to become vocal. You know, they started questioning a lot of the shit that was going on. They felt, why should they always do the city's dirty work and not get anything in return. They had a lot of complaints. . . . The department finally made some changes, promotions, things like that, but only after these guys threatened to go to court. Again, I say you can close your eyes in the precinct, pretend you don't see what's going on, things that are basically wrong, but you can't close your eyes in court. There you've got to answer. . . .

This is not an isolated view. The belief that "pressure" can be effectively applied from within the ranks to eliminate long-standing racial practices is expressed by other black policemen as well. For example,

> There's another reason too. A lot of pressure has been put on the department by black officers and black [police] organizations. For example, the old practice of confining black cops to menial jobs in the station house is gone. There's just too much pressure from black organizations like the Guardians for things like that to ever happen again.

In short, the growing sense of racial pride and solidarity among black policemen has unquestionably contributed to a more aggressive, assertive posture on their part. But underneath much of this militancy and assertiveness lies the belief that black policemen now have avenues of redress outside the department in the event that internal grievance mechanisms prove ineffective. One avenue, of course, is the courts. The other two are black politicians and the news media.

Black Politicians

One of the most significant developments in recent years to advance and protect the interests of blacks in this country has been the steady rise in the number of non-whites holding public office. In 1967, for example, there were approximately 650 blacks elected to public positions. By 1971 the figure exceeded 1600, and by 1975 it more than doubled again.[1]

The increased participation of blacks in the political arena is believed to be a consequence of a number of interrelated factors. First and perhaps most important, there was the rapid movement of black populations from Southern rural farms to Northern and Western cities in the 1950s and early 1960s.[2] During this period blacks made significant gains in education, permitting them to enter the middle class and the political life of America's urban centers. Accompanying this was the removal of structural barriers to voting and other means of political expression through the Civil Rights Act and Voting Act of the mid-1960s which assured black citizens the right to elect to public office those persons most likely to represent their interests. Finally, the emergence of a climate of opinion which was both receptive to and supportive of increased participation of blacks in the political arena no doubt contributed to the increase in the number of black leaders in such cities as New York, Newark, Cleveland, and Detroit.

Although it is difficult to estimate the actual extent to which black office-holders are able to exercise influence over racial policies and practices in the NYPD, the fact remains that many of our respondents are inclined to view black political power as a key to further progress to overcome racial inequities. They feel that internal racial problems are amenable to political intervention today and that such problems are consequently more easily translated into affirmative action. As one detective explained,

> Another area I have in mind is that blacks have reached strong political positions in the city now and can give legal advice and even direct help in cases where there is obvious discrimination against black cops. Today, at least now, there are black lawyers around, and as I said black politicians who are willing to help. You have some place to go when you feel things aren't on the up and up . . .

He went on to say

> There's no heavy problems now as far as I can see, but if something comes up that affects me personally, I'll go see someone, maybe Senator ———. I'll make sure he knows about the problem and maybe there won't be a problem after that.

The feeling that black police officers now have access to avenues of redress outside normal department channels is encouraging to a number of men in this study. But even more important from a preventive standpoint, according to a detective with over 20 years of service, is the feeling that police executives who ultimately decide and act upon internal policy are also aware of the existence of these avenues. They now take steps to check discriminatory practices before serious problems develop or come to the attention of black office holders.

> Well, now the black cop has a place to turn to relieve his frustrations. There are black organizations outside the department as well as inside. There are also black politicians in the city, people who don't mind getting involved today. . . . I feel that the department is aware that black cops have something to say and someplace to go with their grievances. They listen now, they sort of have to listen. . . . Now there are legitimate efforts to prevent problems before they go public. The higher-up bosses know they just can't sweep a racial problem under the rug like they did years ago, because there's bound to be political repercussions.

Our respondents also were keenly aware that these outside means of grievance redress did not always exist for the black police officer. A few of the men reflected on the belief that influential black politicians, for example, were too few or too loosely scattered in the past to wage a successful battle against racial discrimination in the department. Moreover, they felt that those few blacks who held public office in New York City prior to the mid-sixties were almost always forced to conform with the existing system if they were to gain favor and status among their political peers. This often meant that black politicians had to "soft-pedal" racial problems coming to their attention regardless of the effect these problems had on their constituents in the black community.[3] One officer summed up the past predicament as he perceived it:

> In the past the black politicians weren't there and the ones that were there, weren't really there anyway.

More recently, however, it is believed that black officeholders have reached a position of numerical strength in the society which allows them to be effective agents of change when needed.

> I would like to think that, let's say, with the upswing of black political power, blacks as authority figures in society are more accepted, more commonplace and this would stimulate an atmosphere of more respect and cooperation for the black officer. . . . Since the advent of black political power there's less fucking with black cops. The line personnel, you see, have got to the point where they accept blacks as police officers. . . . It's an atmosphere of more unity. As years pass by the racial issues become less important, you might say.

Outside civil rights groups, such as the Human Rights Commission, also provide support in obvious discrimination cases. One officer explained

> Personally, there are certain things I will take and certain things I will not take. There would be a militant attitude if conditions ever reverted back to the old days. This is the way most black cops feel today. . . . Black cops have recourse now. There is recourse with the Human Rights Commission. You have these boards and they definitely work, because if you don't come to them with problems they go out of business. So when they get a complaint they enter-

tain it. So the department knows this and they try to keep things level.

The News Media

In contrast to the antipathy held by most police toward the news media a number of respondents in this study have come to regard this institution as an ally of the black officer.[4] As one detective remarked,

> For the most part I feel things are on the level. In some places though shit still goes on that shouldn't go on, not today. Look at ———. He worked for over seven months on the ——— case and didn't get grade out of it. Four or five white detectives got it though. . . . Well, he comes to me with all of this stuff, about not getting grade. He's really pissed off. I tell him if it were me I'd be screaming. I also tell him don't come crying to me, go tell your tale to the papers. Go see the newspapers. They would just love to hear shit like that. I tell him that I would want to know why I was passed over and most of the white guys got grade, and if I didn't buy the story a lot of people would be reading about it the next day. If I didn't get any satisfaction, you can bet people would hear about it, even if I had to go see ———. And if they [the department] fucked with me after that, they would read about that too the next day.

Although it is not a commonly accepted practice among police officers, white or black, to bring complaints about the department to the newspapers, a number of officers felt that this was one way of redressing long-standing racial grievances that have not been acted upon by the department. These men did not view themselves as "snitches" or "traitors" and even if they did, judging from their remarks, they did not seem to care what "others" thought.

The potential power of the press in shaping public opinion is seen by these same men as a force the police department has had to come to grips with in recent years. They apparently feel that the department can be intimidated by negative press coverage concerning the treatment of its minority personnel. For example,

> The news media gets into everbody's ass on everything. I can tell you of an instance when a black guy on this job made out great by

speaking to the press. He was promoted to third grade [detective] because of his involvement in the ——— case. He spoke to the press and they said, "The man did all that and all he gets is third grade." Well he eventually got jumped to second [grade].

Racial complaints are now entertained. They weren't in the early sixties when I came on the job. Why would they be entertained now? Basically, I feel because this same black guy can turn around now and go to the papers. Then you got a monster on your hands if the beef is heavy.

This, of course, was not always the case. In the past the press relied heavily on the cooperation of the police for their stories. Journalists and reporters knew that by antagonizing the police newsworthy material would not be gained easily. It is not surprising, therefore, to find that some of our respondents believe that the newspapers, in the past, would not have risked alienating one of their primary sources of information by printing unfavorable articles concerning racial practices in the department. As a case in point, a veteran detective points to the early futile attempts of a New York City detective to expose police corruption by going to the press. He said,

A black cop who had a problem knew he couldn't go to the papers. Look what happened to Serpico when he first went to the papers. They didn't want to hear his story and they certainly weren't going to consider printing it at the time. Don't forget, the papers needed the department for their stories. If they started printing every piece of dirt some cop dug up they would have been cutting their own throat. Of course, all this corruption business was exposed later but by then things were really hot and the papers couldn't ignore it. And it did a lot of damage to the department's reputation.

In this officer's opinion the press did not entertain Serpico's story at first because it did not want to upset the delicate relationship it had established over the years with the police and it certainly, by implication, would not have wanted to risk upsetting this relationship by printing racial stories that placed the department in an unfavorable light.

What then accounts for this apparent change in media policy toward the department? One possible answer lies, as the officer quoted below states, in the recent creation of a centralized police department bureau (Public Information Division) which gathers and disseminates reports of unusual occurrences to the news media, regardless of how they may feel about a particular paper, radio or T.V. station. News reporters, consequently, are not as dependent upon individual officers or unit heads for their stories as they once were and thus may no longer feel the strong sense of obligation to protect the department's image by passing up stories that tend to discredit either its members or its practices.

> I knew black police officers ten years ago who were beaten up [by white officers] and the papers would not print the story. The reason they didn't print the story was that they wanted to keep a good rapport with the department so that they could get their stories. So everything was squashed. Now, this is not necessary. Public information services in the department give them all the stories anyway. I think they are required by law, I'm not sure. In any event we've done a complete turn-about here. Now they print anything and expose everything that comes to their attention.

Our respondents are not only aware of the enormous power and influence of the press in shaping public opinion, but they are especially sensitive to its often contradictory role in reporting the news. It is common belief, for example, that while newspaper reporters profess to operate under a code of professional ethics which requires that they adhere to standards of impartiality, accuracy, fair play, and responsibility to the public, they nevertheless seem to be drawn to the negative, scandalous aspects of police work and will at times "play up" an incident or situation that tends to discredit the police in order to attract readers. They know too that the department has become increasingly sensitive in recent years to allegations of discrimination or to other wrongdoings, particularly when these charges are born within the ranks themselves. They recognize, and rightly so, that these types of complaints attract readers and can bring unfavorable attention to the department and its internal operations.It is for these reasons, many of the men claim, that police commanders in New York City have found themselves under pressure from high city officials to adopt and maintain a policy of equal treatment for all personnel and to respond affirmatively to racial grievances before they are brought to the attention of outside groups or made public through the news media. The following quotation is typical of the views of those black policemen in this study who regard the press as an ally in the struggle to ensure equal opportunities for members of their group through a willingness to print stories exposing discrimination in the department.

> The papers would eat these types of stories up. *The Village Voice, Post, News.* And we will go to the papers if necessary. . . . I personally look at the press in a friendly way. If I feel there's a problem that can't be handled properly inside the job, or won't be handled properly, and I feel it warrants some attention, I will give it to the press. As long as it has a certain public interest, the press will pick it up. Race is a public interest story now. As far as the job's concerned they don't want these problems now. They've become supersensitive to racial problems leaking to the press. . . . All this talk about professionalism and racial equality, you know we're supposed to be a professional department and all that. Well, the department is concerned about bad publicity more than anything else except maybe law suits which we already talked about. That's basically why we have some semblance of equality today.

While it is not altogether clear what precise impact black politicians and the news media had in bringing about a more equitable distribution of opportunities and rewards for black cops, it would seem from available newspaper reports that the threat of "public" exposure of discriminatory practices along with the loss of Federal revenue-sharing funds that could accompany such disclosures, prompted city government and the police department to take a "preventive" position regarding *even* allegations of discrimination in the work setting.[5]

Changing Police Needs

In the wake of the civil disorders of the mid-sixties, and the growing crisis in police-minority relations, outside pressure was exerted on municipal police agencies to increase the number of minority group personnel. The feeling generated by Federal agencies and commissions at the time was that the ethnic makeup of the police should be representative of the population at large. This was based in large part upon the notion that such representation would serve to enhance communication and understanding between police and the diverse groups they served.

A few policemen, in their comments, connected the gains made by black police in the late 1960s, early 1970s and especially the increase in number of minority officers brought into the department, to the ghetto uprisings of the mid-1960s and to the inability of a white-dominated department to reduce conflict between the police and the public in these areas. Former mayor John Lindsay, our men argue, responded to community cries for more black police by instituting drastic changes in the city's recruitment and hiring practices during his term in office. One observed that

> Basically, I think the black officer is treated pretty fairly now. This is certainly true in the precinct where I work. . . . But then again you had to have some changes. You had a revolution going on in the city. In the department you desperately needed black cops to calm things down in the ghetto, better relate to people. This was Lindsay's idea to recruit more black cops, once and for all get rid of the quota system. [What was that?] Well, you had a black candidate for the police department who got arrested at one time for some bullshit misdemeanor charge, drunk driving, something like that; he got knocked out. That's when, remember, you got all those black guys moving to Transit and Housing [P.D.] because they knocked them from this job. They kept knocking these guys off for petty bullshit. . . . He had black cops and black sergeants investigating police candidates along with white cops.

The department's purpose in increasing the number of minority group policemen in the early seventies was not limited solely to the goal of promoting good will and rapport between black citizens and the police. The department decided that minority officers were also needed to counter the threat of some of the more revolutionary black groups, particularly those factions espousing illegal, military-type attacks against public property and established authority. It also concluded that officers from the minorities could serve as undercover narcotic agents in black areas of the city much more successfully than white policemen could. It was felt that the black officers' "visible" ties to the community together with the special training they received would allow them to serve effectively in these roles while at the same time minimizing the risk of exposure as police informants. Although many of the black policemen who undertook such assignments were eventually elevated to the rank of detective and transferred to prestigious specialty commands in the early seventies, most of the men in this study remained suspicious of the underlying motives for these promotions. One is led to believe from the responses that these rewards were not conferred out of a basic sense of fairness or equality. Rather, one is left with the impression that the department simply had no other choice. Consider the following comment from a detective who received the gold shield in 1970 after having spent nearly three years in an undercover capacity:

> There are a lot of black detectives that are here because of the sixties. For example, who could you get to go to 8th Avenue and 116th Street to buy drugs? . . . When things were all over what could the department do but promote these guys. . . . You see there was a lot of pressure to make these promotions. Politicians like to jump on that shit. . . . Take a guy like Lindsay too. He felt he owed it to the guys. So he forced their [the department's] hand so to speak, and got a lot of black undercover guys moved up.

Others similarly argue that these promotions were simply a way of avoiding a potentially embarrassing confrontation between black police activists and the department. For example:

> I want to think about things directly involved with the police department. I know you are speaking of certain areas. . . . I'll give you an angle that you probably never heard. In the sixties there were a number of black officers that were doing some fantastic jobs for the police department, guys like Wood. . . . It goes back to this. Blacks were never seriously considered for special squads unless they were really needed. Well, they needed them in the sixties to infiltrate the BLA [Black Liberation Army] and some of the other groups. And I think the fact that they did such a fantastic job made officers and bosses more aware that they deserved to be promoted. Maybe they weren't promoted because of fairness or because of the type of

job they did but because they had no other choice. . . . I think the department was more or less embarrassed into it.

What is noteworthy about all the comments quoted is the virtual absence of any direct reference to the role played by the Guardians Association, the black police officers fraternal organization, in bringing about racial change in the department. Clearly this black police group *was* the compelling force behind Judge Robert Carter's imposition of a racial quota in both hiring and promotion. Why, then, were the Guardians not mentioned as being instrumental in forcing the department to alter its hiring policies and practices? One reason might be that only token gains had been made by blacks in the late sixties, and early seventies as a result of the efforts of this group. The greatest gains by far were achieved in Federal court only after the interviews for this study were conducted.

The Guardians, of course, were only one of the major forces behind the accomplishments of black police in the past decade or so. Changes in Federal and local policies, combined with a growing political support for reform in the area of police race relations, accounted in large part for the gains made by black police in New York City and throughout the country. This leads to the conclusion that before a major urban police department will change its policies and practices regarding racial minorities certain conditions must be met. First, legislation must exist which provides a legal basis for the elimination of discrimination in hiring, promotion, and assignment. Second, a political climate that is both receptive to and supportive of racial reform must prevail at the local government level. Third, local government administrators must experience a genuine need for racial reform in the organization. And finally, owing to the likelihood of internal resistance from those perceiving change as a threat to their "established position," there must exist avenues of grievance redress within as well as outside the organization. Interestingly enough, in New York City, as in other major urban areas that undertook racial reform in their police departments, these conditions were fully operative by the early 1970s.

In the section that follows we consider a condition common to all social arenas undergoing change—namely, the disjunction that emerges between newly established policies and traditional courses of action. As we shall see the mere fact that a particular policy proscribing discrimination in the work setting has been put into effect by no means guarantees that all those in positions of ensuring compliance with such policies actually do so.

Where Policy and Practice Diverge

In any organization, police or otherwise, inconsistencies are likely to develop between "official policy" as set down by management and the "actual" practices of individual supervisors. In describing how they are treated by the department, a second group of 11 black policemen called attention to just such inconsistencies. They felt that, although the department itself had responded positively to the question of racial discrimination, the fact remains that some police supervisors still acted independently of and, in some instances, in direct contradiction to, the "official" rules which prohibit discrimination based upon racial considerations. The following quotations provide a general outline of these basic inconsistencies as seen by the men in this group:

> No . . . I don't believe the department discriminates by policy. There are instances of discrimination on an individual basis, however. This cannot be helped. You aren't going to change everyone's attitudes overnight . . . attitudes that have been around for so long. . . . I would say there is not so much overt discrimination as there was say ten, 15 years ago, but in some places, among some bosses, it's still there. Overall, there has been a good deal of change from when I came on the job [in the early sixties].

> Generally, yes, I would say it's not the policy of the job to promote people just because they're white. Of course that doesn't mean some superiors don't discriminate against black cops. You have to be blind not to see that. There are still a minority of individuals who still are racists and discriminate against black cops.

A detective with over 15 years of service, while flatly rejecting any notion of a "hidden plan" to discriminate against black police officers, acknowledges "occasional" instances of racial bias on the part of some white police superiors. Again, it is the emphasis on *individuals* rather than on the department which characterizes this group of respondents.

> Since the late sixties I would say things have improved for the black policeman. But I still feel that there is still room for more improvement. Personally, myself, I have never had any problems, ever. On occasion there are what appears to me to be instances of personal prejudice against black detectives with certain bosses. On the whole I would have to say that blacks are treated pretty fairly now. I don't believe there's any secret plan or policy to discriminate now. You would be able to sense it if there was. You would know. . . .

When this group of men was asked how they had been affected by the discretion of individual supervisors acting against official department policy, they pointed to two specific areas affecting not only themselves but the efficiency of the department as a whole, and those were recognition and reward, and long-term support from superiors.

Recognition and Reward

Research into large scale organizations, as well as common sense, tells us that praise and recognition are important to developing a sense of job satisfaction. Most police officers, regardless of color, appreciate a sincere word for a job well done and work better in an atmosphere of acceptance and approval. To the extent that recognition is perceived as lacking from some white supervisors, it is not difficult to see how black policemen could become bitter toward the job and even toward their white colleagues. An officer agreed:

> Yeah, this is the type of job that a black cop can work and work and never get (a good word) from some white sergeants. With these bosses you rarely hear, "You did a good job."

Speaking on both the personal need and fundamental importance of recognition in the work setting, a detective added that

There are a few things I could point to. For instance, there's plenty of good work by black detectives in my office, and rarely does it go noticed by the boss. He just doesn't seem to feel that it's important to tell a black detective he did a good piece of work or maybe handled a sensitive situation well. There's just no communication here at all. In other places I worked, it didn't seem to matter what color you were, you did the job and you heard about it. It was a good feeling you had. I think all the black guys in the office felt the same way.

He continued,

Look, I'm not a little kid that needs a pat on the head everytime a case is broken or a collar [arrest] is made. But, at the same time it doesn't hurt once in a while to bring a guy in and let him know he did a commendable job. You would be surprised how far this would go in a lot of ways, especially in the area (of) race relations.

Recognition and reward, we are told, can cut across racial lines if the subordinate happens to share the same values as his immediate supervisor. The obvious problem here is that values are quite often attached to membership in a particular racial group. An example of this dilemma is pointed out by a black patrol officer, who observed,

If you're white and disagree . . . you're a "shithead" with [Lieutenant] ———. But if you're black and disagree, then the animosity toward this disagreement may be doubled or tripled because guys like him, bigots, feel that as a black you have no right to disagree about anything.

Some black officers in this group were angry and resentful over what appears to them to be an unequal application of the principle of "fitting the man into the job for which he is best suited." White policemen, they argue, are often given "choice" assignments regardless of whether they are qualified for the job. Black police officers, however, who may possess special qualifications for a particular assignment, are generally relegated to performing routine patrol functions.

My pet gripe. Let's say, for example, that there are two guys, one black and qualified for a certain kind of job, and the other white and not qualified. The way I see it, in some precincts, not all, it's usually the unqualified white guy who gets the job. This I feel has happened to me personally. . . . Why should I always be in the field getting my head busted when I have special qualifications which should allow me to work in the ———— squad. There are white guys down there who had no prior experience in this sort of job, and they had to be especially trained to do the job. This is what I mean. I put in for a transfer and it gets knocked. This is not on an overall basis, because I feel that things have changed for the black cop. They've gotten better. But it's still there in some places and it makes you mad.

The reluctance on the part of some police supervisors to place black officers in positions for which they may be better suited can lead not only to dissatisfaction with the job but to loss of the employee as a productive member of the service. This is particularly evident in the following account of a black policeman who, we are told, had compiled an impressive arrest record in a specialty area but failed to win recognition or compensation for his performance:

I worked with a guy a few years ago, a friend of mine. His thing was car stops, good stops. He knew cars inside and out. He accumulated in a few years well over a hundred collars for stolen cars and forged licenses and registrations. . . . . All he wanted was a shot at the Auto Squad. He got a few interviews he told me, but never got in. He also had a clean record, never had any problems that I know of. . . . There was no reason why this guy wasn't transferred to this outfit. He felt personally that it was because of prejudice on the part of the white lieutenant who interviewed him. His attitude now is "fuck it" with everything. When I see him all he talks about is getting out in 15 [years].

Of course in some instances failure to receive serious consideration for a particular assignment may be due to the reluctance of the officer himself to "follow up" on transfer requests submitted through official department channels, rather than to actual discrimination on the part of individual superiors. Thus, blacks in the department seeking transfers are advised, as was the officer mentioned in the following comment, to stay on top of the situation.

> I feel also that some black cops are misplaced so to speak. They're working in places they really don't belong. Some of these guys are funny too. There was this one black cop who really wanted a transfer to some office downtown because of his background in electronics. I forget the name of the office. Well, anyway he put in a 57 [transfer request], had one interview for an opening and never heard anything more. So he let the matter slide. He just kept crying that they didn't take him because he was black. Maybe so, but if it were me I would have followed up on it, if it meant that much. I would have looked into all possibilities. . . .

However, it should be noted that this reluctance is itself a reaction, however premature, to the belief that preferential treatment is invariably weighed in favor of white officers. Though not strictly a result of discrimination per se, such an apparent reluctance may be a result of an environment perceived as discriminatory.

Support from Superiors

Policemen feel that one of the most important qualities of a supervisor is his willingness or courage to represent all of his men equally on issues which appear to threaten their security. They feel that a supervisor worthy of his official designation must continually strive to maintain an interest in the personal well-being of his subordinates regardless of their color, and must, above all, support them when legitimate grievances are brought to his attention or when problems arise in the field. Quite naturally police officers resent supervisors who always seem to turn their back on problems, or who "disappear when the going gets tough." Particularly disturbing to the black policeman, we are told, is the white supervisor who uses race as a basis of differential treatment in times of trouble or personal crisis. This was illustrated by the reply

> Treated equally? That's not an easy question, because basically I feel yes and no. On the job level I think yes. When you drop down to

the individual level, say with some white sergeants, I would be inclined to say absolutely not. What I'm directly thinking of here relates to a couple of experiences I personally observed with white sergeants who turned their back on black cops who I guess you might say found themselves in a ticklish situation. . . . I feel that if you're black and this one sergeant in particular is working, you've got a problem. You're on your own. I get the feeling that if I personally ran into a ticklish situation and he knew it was me involved, he'd be in the wind or if I was dead wrong he'd look to stick one up my ass [prefer formal department charges]. Fortunately, we don't have this problem anymore because he just got transferred.

One black policeman's concern over the lack of support in "ticklish" situations is brought to light in the following quotation. Unlike the other men who voiced this complaint, however, this policeman does not suggest that race itself is a basis for differential treatment, but that such problems are common to most bottom-level policemen regardless of color.

Again, I'm not sure whether it's color that matters here so much. Both groups I think have common problems that are founded in fact. . . . I think it boils down to the fact that some bosses today haven't had the experience some of the younger men have had. They seem to disappear when the going gets tough. They don't back their men at all. How many supervisors do you see today going down to the trial room to testify on behalf of a cop brought up on bullshit charges? I'll tell you, very few. They're afraid to stick their necks out. They're afraid they'll lose their spot [detective superior designation] if things go bad. This is especially true with those bosses who have the money [e.g., a detective sergeant or lieutenant who is receiving special compensation because of his supervisory position within the detective bureau].

It is, as the officer quoted above implies, often difficult to sort out a generalized phenomenon from a particular instance of discrimination. Quite possibly some blacks anticipate rejection and discrimination in the work setting and create by their own behavior a self-fulfilling outcome.

Discrimination in Policy and in Practice

The assumption that the New York City police department and its supervisory staff treat black officers in much the same way as white officers—an assumption seemingly obvious to most of the men in this study—was largely rejected by nine of the policemen interviewed. While there are a number of attitudes that separate this group from the other two, perhaps the most important is the feeling they have that discrimination along racial lines not only exists today but that it extends beyond the "individual" level into the operation of the whole department. Although the men in this group did not always agree as to the form discrimination takes, they remain united in the belief that black cops on the whole are far from enjoying the real meaning of the term "full equality of opportunity." Not surprisingly, this group of respondents consisted of mostly younger members of the service who were assigned for the most part to uniform patrol rather than to detective commands or other plainclothes duties. Young, uniformed officers, it appears, are more likely than their senior counterparts to have experienced what they perceive as discrimination or to have witnessed instances of racial bias in the department.

Our principal interest at this point is to uncover both the form discrimination is thought to take as well as the areas in which it is believed to operate today and to see to what extent these constitute a justified charge of *racial* discrimination. We begin with the most frequent charge: that black cops are subjected to and suffer most from the practice of favoritism.

Favoritism

In police organizations, as in most large-scale bureaucracies, employment practices stem largely from policies developed within the framework of the political, economic, and social environment in which the organization operates. Presumably, these practices are aimed at maximizing productivity and providing effective services to its clientele. Decisions to promote an employee, for example, or to move him or her laterally, or for that matter the conferring of rewards in general are ideally based upon such universally accepted criteria as the value of the individual to the organization. In actual practice, however, the use of purely rational criteria in dispensing rewards is often replaced by other less-objective practices. One such practice which takes its form from earlier political patronage systems is "favoritism." Defined simply, it is a practice which involves the selection of favored individuals in the organization for preferred duties or assignments over others who may possess equal or even superior qualifications.

As a "way of life" on the job today, favoritism is thought to prevail in virtually every area of opportunity and to involve all levels of the organization from the precinct clerical staff to the highest ranking officials. Regardless of background, members of the police service, as an example of those who work in any public or private organization, who happen to know people in the "right places" are often singled out for preferential treatment over others not so well connected. But how does one come to acquire those important personal contacts and what are the implications of not having people in the right places? In some instances simply being affiliated with a particular civic, religious, or social or fraternal group can help. In other cases important contacts are established through the process of informal social exchange. Subordinates, for example, who have served a superior well in the past can reasonably expect the latter to express his gratitude by repaying the service when the occasion calls. In other words, a social bond is created between members of unequal rank by the initial provision of services and by the expectation and obligation that services will be returned in the future. In most cases, as we shall see, just being a member of the "established" group can result in the acquisition of the "right" contacts on the job. What this means in effect is that in some, if not most, police commands an officer's potential or actual performance may become substantially less important in terms of receiving rewards and favors than his personal contacts or membership group within the organization.

For a number of black policemen interviewed for this study, the practice of distributing rewards and privileges based upon informal group ties constitutes an active and sometimes deliberate form of job discrimination. These men argue that, as a group, blacks occupy a "newcomer" status in the department and consequently have not had the same opportunity as most whites to develop important personal contacts, or to move into informal positions of power within the structure of the organization. Put into more systematic form their complaints can be stated as follows: (1) The distribution of rewards, privileges, and favors in the police department has traditionally depended to a large extent upon membership in "exclusive" white groups or cliques. (2) Blacks have been unable, except on a token basis, to penetrate these groups or to develop close and lasting ties with white officers occupying "strategic" positions within the command (e.g., precinct) structure. (3) On a collective basis, blacks have found it difficult to establish independent sources of power and influence within the organization which would allow them to participate more fully in the reward distribution system.

Generally speaking, these men have come to believe that it is their "position" within the organization that results in their being assigned routine patrol duties while whites frequently move on to more desirable duties. They have, consequently, come to regard with distrust, if not outright contempt, any practice which confers rewards and privileges on the basis of informal group ties. A patrol officer assigned to a Harlem precinct outlines a form of favoritism thought to operate in his command.

> I guess it's just a gut feeling I have about how blacks are generally received. Take something like precinct assignments. Sometimes details are not posted on the board; they are passed from mouth to mouth. White guys who become aware of these details somehow tell friends who are also white and blacks get shafted in the end.

Another patrol officer who has adopted a posture highly antagonistic toward favoritism within the department also argues that this practice, as it currently operates, is almost entirely confined to "white" ethnic groups. He concludes that black officers who lack personal ties with key white officers find themselves at a distinct disadvantage when it comes to competing with whites for "choice" precinct assignments and duties.

> Blacks, I don't feel are treated equally. I'm not sure whether this is racial discrimination or not. It may not exactly be racial discrimination as it is defined in a dictionary, but discrimination by personal contact. . . . An example, if there are two cops who put in for a special detail, the white cop will get it, whether he merits it

or not. Why is that? They have people in the right places. . . .
Friends do favors for friends, and white cops have white friends in
the right places to do favors for them. That's what it boils down to.

The first officer quoted above went on to point out that because
it is often so subtle, favoritism has resulted in complacency on the
part of high-ranking police officials and even lower-level precinct
commanders who actually believe that blacks are getting their fair
share of rewards today.

So in effect what you really have is just a different way of discriminating against black cops. And what makes it all the worse is that
you really can't claim discrimination because you really can't prove
it. It's there and you can't prove it. But people downtown and even
some of the C.O.'s think that they're on top of the situation. They
don't hear the complaints so they think things are on the up and
up.

The perceived inability of black police officers to participate more
fully in the "informal" reward distribution system can perhaps be
better understood by examining some of the influential positions
in the department.

The clerical position

In the New York City police department positions of power and
influence often exist apart from the formal command structure. One
such position is the clerical or staff post. Traditionally, police officers holding this position have tended to be veteran members of
white ethnic groups, selected in large part because of their time on
the job and presumed knowledge of precinct politics and operations.[6] Working out of precinct, borough, and headquarters of-
fices, members holding these positions perform important administrative functions. Although much of their work involves routine
matters such as preparing roll calls, duty charts, and sick reports,
there is an element of their job which not only allows, but in many
instances requires, them to have access to important decisions and
developments affecting members of their command. The clerical
officer, for example, is usually one of the first bottom-level members of the department to learn about such matters as personnel

transfers, upcoming details, openings in specialized units, and vacancies or "seats" in patrol cars since he is usually in charge of
maintaining records of such assignments.

There is another aspect of the clerical officer's position that merits consideration. Clerical officers, because they perform a number
of important administrative functions for the commanding officer
and his staff, have developed over the years a special bond or trust
between themselves and the staff supervisors. Consequently, when
a situation arises that requires a decision to be made concerning a
particular officer in the precinct, in many instances the staff supervisor (or even the commander himself) will turn to the clerical officer for input or advice. It is at these times that the clerical officer,
who serves as a "liaison" between management and employees, can
influence the outcome of decisions effecting other members of the
command.

A final, and perhaps most important, aspect of the clerical officer's position concerns the background of both the officer himself
and the recipient of his influence. Since clerical officers have been
chosen for the position largely on the basis of seniority, they tend
for the most part to be white. And it stands to reason that the
principal recipients of influence are also likely to be members of
the established group with whom they shared experiences in the
past or with whom they at least identify personally—in other words,
other white police officers.

Our respondents agreed that these strategic positions have traditionally been held by white officers who often withhold career
advancement information from black officers but circulate it among
their white friends and colleagues. This practice, they argue, constitutes a deliberate form of discrimination which almost always
operates to the disadvantage of the black policeman. As a Harlem
patrol officer put it,

> In most of your clerical positions, or in positions where things are
> apt to come up, there are no black cops in these positions. Say if
> there's a detail or something, it always seems that men are already
> picked. Only certain people know about it. You don't get a chance
> to vie for these details. . . . Recently, when they had the BLA de-
> tail, there was a call for black cops. That's the only time when blacks
> got details. Anytime a detail comes up, certain people (black cops)
> are the last to hear about it.

In reflecting on the position of black policemen in the city, another patrol officer agreed that most "influential" positions are held by white officers who naturally do favors for other whites when they can. However, he also felt that this practice depicts a different type of discrimination than had existed in the past; the black officer today has simply traded one set of "race-related" problems for another. That is,

> It's just more subtle now. It's not quite right out in the open as it was in the past. What has happened is that they just painted it a different color, that's all. It's the same thing, has the same effect on black cops. What do I mean? Years ago a black cop didn't bother to put in for a detail. He knew right up front that he would be turned down, so he didn't even bother. Today, there is a feeling that the department can no longer do that. There are laws now against discrimination. So now they exclude you "unofficially" by letting the roll call man make up assignments. . . . He generally picks men for details, sometimes with the sergeant's approval. Naturally everyone involved is white so they naturally pick friends who are also white.

In sum, it can be argued that the informal power vested in the clerical position serves to establish a reservoir of binding obligations which the incumbent can tap when the occasion calls or the need arises. Those receiving favors or services become obliged to reciprocate in the future should they be promoted or moved to a higher position within the organization. It also creates networks of communication between the provider and receivers of services needed to maintain the position itself. But most importantly, from the point of view of some black policemen, it helps maintain the established groups' position of dominance within the organization by insuring, where possible, that certain choice assignments and duties continue to be filled predominantly by white males.

The white sergeant

The police officer's immediate supervisor occupies another key position within the command structure and much like the clerical officer can use his position to influence the outcome of decisions involving others. But unlike the clerical officer the sergeant uses the formal power vested in this position to distribute rewards and privileges. For example, he can either recommend advancements or transfers through the rating process or prevent them through formal disciplinary procedures. And herein lies much of the resentment of black policemen. According to the men in this group, white police supervisors also play the "favoritism" game, choosing officers for preferred assignments and duties and providing them with other services based upon factors totally unrelated to an individual's capability or performance. A patrol officer described favoritism involving white police supervisors as he thought it operated in his precinct as follows:

> The climate of the job has not really changed that much. I can remember some years ago when there was outright instances of discrimination against black officers in all areas. Now it's done more underhandedly. [How is that?] Well, for instance, competent black officers in my precinct haven't been assigned to anticrime patrol. This I observed personally. White sergeants who are in the majority choose white cops for these assignments when they come up. This is because they are close to these guys. They drink with them after work and they live near them, so naturally who do you think they are going to pick when an opening in anticrime comes up . . . ? And it doesn't really matter much whether the black cop is more suited for the assignment. You see, blacks don't ordinarily get involved with whites off duty. They generally don't fraternize with white sergeants after work and they certainly don't travel home with them.

Much of what this officer said is true. Friendships which develop between police officers and their immediate supervisors outside the work setting do tend to carry over into the job and can result, as some of our respondents intimate, in an unequal distribution of rewards and favors. Moreover, changing economic and social conditions in the city during the past two decades have added a new dimension to the development of relationships between white supervisors and white subordinates. It might be recalled that as a result, in part, of deteriorating city services, increasing crime rates, and expanding ghetto boundaries, white police at all levels in the department began to move from the city in the late 1960s to the surrounding suburbs.[7] Because many of these officers now had rather long distances to travel to work, car pools were organized which, in many instances, white police supervisors joined, thereby increasing opportunities for new and more intimate relationships to develop between them and their subordinates in the precinct. Inasmuch as black police tended to remain within the city or to move to nearby black communities there was little, if any, occasion for them to travel together with whites and hence little opportunity to increase their contacts with white bosses under conditions that could lead to preferential treatment on the job. The result, we are told, is diminished opportunities for favors and advancement for black police and increased opportunities for whites.

> There are sergeants who go home with white cops in car pools. Blacks are not involved in that type of thing. The sergeant will give the detail to the white cop he rides with first. The black cop will be the last to be considered even when he's more qualified.

Such accounts reveal something of the disadvantages facing black police officers as a result of their location within the structure of the organization. Although it would be difficult to document instances of favoritism or discrimination stemming solely from membership in a particular racial group, the fact remains that a number of policemen in this study felt that such practices not only exist in their commands but constitute an integral part of the operation of the department. The question is, how then can disadvantages which result from such practices be effectively neutralized? The most obvious solution, one officer tells us, lies in increasing the number of blacks in supervisory and command positions:

> It's my estimation that there is still discrimination in a lot of areas. It *now* depends upon friends in the precinct and officers of higher rank whether you're going to get a detail or possibly put in for the shield. . . . The situation strictly depends on your relationship with some higher up. The tricky thing here, and I speak for a lot of guys you talked to, is that there are too few black bosses. And a white boss might be more inclined to do a favor for a white guy, just as a black boss might do for a black cop. What it boils down to, the bottom line, we need more black bosses.

This view, however, represents an isolated case. As we shall see, black police officers share, for the most part, a marked skepticism concerning the role of black superiors in promoting and protecting the interests of lower-level black cops.

The black superior

Policemen interviewed for this study have very definite ideas about the role of black leadership in the department. Fourteen were asked whether black bosses had been effective in fighting discrimination on the job; 12 responded in the negative. Generally it seems that black officers in formal positions of power are clearly in the minority and have been unable to develop the network of informal, interlevel and intergroup ties needed to exercise effectively the power vested in their position. Lacking this interrelationship blacks occupying positions of authority often found it necessary, and at times even politically expedient, to play down or to turn their backs on issues of concern to their brother officers on the job.

Not only were the policemen in this study aware of the numerical scarcity of blacks in supervisory and command positions in the department, but many felt that this disparity is particularly acute in the upper reaches of management where important political decisions are made. They argue that because of the absence of blacks in high and intermediate positions, lower-level black bosses (i.e., sergeants and lieutenants) are virtually without internal sources of power and may therefore hesitate to be outspoken with regard to racial issues and problems. Indeed, the black superior who would take up the role of spokesman for his group may feel that he is jeopardizing both his present position as well as his future career chances. A veteran patrol officer expresses his view on the matter:

> They [black superiors] definitely won't speak out against policy. There's no one backing them. If they open their mouths too much, they never go any further.

Another officer was a bit more explicit. He said,

> I don't really see that they have been much help. That's because there hasn't been a united effort, a 100 percent effort. You get partial ef-

fort, that's all. Look at it this way—the white boss generally has some chief he can call if he is unhappy about something and wants to rearrange things or maybe he wants some of his buddies moved up. A black boss, who does he have to call? Those black bosses on top, they're not going to do anything because they aren't united, there aren't enough of them. Besides, they're bureaucrats now, and they don't want to make waves. These guys were handpicked because it was felt that they wouldn't make any waves. So this feeling filters down to the black lieutenants and sergeants in the precinct. Now, they learn not to make waves. Black sergeants, they generally hide and pretend they don't see anything, that everything is cozy. They don't make any waves because they have ideas about moving up.

As some of these same men see it, the higher up the organizational ladder the black superior advances, the more removed he becomes from the problems and affairs of his lower-ranking brother officers, and the more he comes to identify with the "organization" and its traditional values. This may be especially true of those few blacks who, over the years, have gained positions above the rank of captain and who aspire to climb even higher in the police bureaucracy. According to one respondent, black superiors near the top are almost impossible to reach.

> Chief ———, for example, wouldn't do a thing. That's because he was "looking up." In fact, you can go to the highest ranking black in the department if you have a problem or want a favor, and he will say, "I'll see what I can do." You know he's just jerking you around.

As has been said, it is common practice for white supervisors to grant favors and provide services to white subordinates on the basis of friendship and interpersonal ties. Since the black superior is formally vested with the same "official" powers as the white superior, he ought to be able to use his position to the advantage of lower-level blacks. But this does not seem to be the case. Most black superiors, we are told, go out of their way to uphold standards of fairness and equal treatment in order to show that they are not favoring fellow blacks on the job. The following excerpts testify to this belief:

Most black bosses bend over backward to show that they are not
prejudiced toward black cops. They definitely won't go out of their
way like some white bosses to do favors for their own.

I would say not. . . . A white superior may put a man in a slot
[give him a special detail] because he is a friend. A black superior
is in the minority. He is not as willing to do favors as the white
superior. He might feel that everybody is watching him.

The black superior may indeed feel that he is being watched.
Because of his "minority" status, both in terms of color and actual
number of black superiors on the job, he may sense that his actions and decisions are being closely scrutinized by white subordinates as well as by white superiors above him. If his desire is to
move out of routine patrol or be considered for a specialty assignment, he may take special pains to avoid behaving in a way that
spells out or even hints of racial favoritism on his part. What this
translates into is a competitive disadvantage for his black subordinates who, lacking in many cases the appropriate credentials and
informal group ties of their own, generally find that they cannot
count on the black superior for favors or preferential treatment. A
detective summed up the predicament of the black superior and
indirectly that of the black police officer:

He's like a raisin in the white ice cream. Everything he does is put
under a microscope, and if he's looking for a slot himself, he certainly can't have charges of reverse discrimination being made against
him. If this happens, he goes nowhere.

The interpretations of the role of black leadership in the department today tend to support the widely held view that upwardly
mobile blacks are often caught up in the dilemma of competing
loyalties. Should the black superior identify too strongly with those
forces from which he derives his official power and chances for
further mobility within the organization, he risks alienating himself from lower-level blacks on the job. In contrast, should he
publically sympathize with his brother officers by acting, for instance, as their spokesman on racial issues, he risks losing favor with
his white colleagues and support from those above him. Yet, as we
shall see, this dilemma is not faced exclusively by blacks holding

supervisory or command positions, but as well by black officers of lower rank.

Rationalizing preferential treatment

Not all black policemen in this study viewed the practice of favoritism in a negative light. Some see it within the context of an occupational philosophy—a "way of life" on the job that has been shaped by the interests and practices of earlier generations of police officers. For this and other reasons having "connections" in the department is regarded by these men as a legitimate mechanism through which a measure of upward mobility can be attained. Although the two groups of officers clearly differ as to whether favoritism constitutes an active form of discrimination, both see it tied to such organizational factors as seniority, friendship cliques, and the scarcity of blacks in "strategic" positions. For example,

> I really can't say that the department treats me any different than a white cop. I can understand that some black cops may not feel that way. But it's not really based that much on color, but on things like seniority and mostly friendships. . . . People will do favors for others who they are friends with. This is a natural thing in all areas of life. It's something all cops have to learn to live with if they are going to get by on the job. In the department, right now, there are not enough black cops in the type of positions where they can do favors for other black cops. That's it, in a nutshell.

A detective, in making essentially the same point, points up the distinction between racial discrimination and inequality. Implicit in this officer's comment is the notion that one may experience the latter without experiencing the former.

> In all honesty I would have to say there is no outright racial discrimination as far as I've seen. Any inequality that exists has to do with time over junior men, guys you know in the precinct who can do favors for you. Otherwise, it doesn't really exist.

In summary these black officers seem to take a purely pragmatic position regarding favoritism in its various forms. Their view seems to be that since nothing can be done, one simply must go along with it. Besides, they argue, the black officer can also benefit from having people in the "right places."

> What you're asking me, are blacks discriminated against more? There isn't any of that as far as I'm concerned. This is based on my own personal experiences. People who have the ability to move others usually move friends, who also happen mostly to be of the same color. Cops do favors for guys they know, guys they ride with, guys they travel with. The only catch here is that it's not always the best guy who winds up filling a special slot. But this has always been the way in the job and it will probably always be that way. You can't fight it. Cops who like each other stick together and look out for each other. I've seen blacks moved up, favors done for black cops by white bosses who are their friends. So it's not really a racial thing. . . . I remember after a few years on the job, I was really pissed when I saw mostly white guys getting special favors, anticrime, tit jobs [choice assignments] in the precinct. Then I saw that this is the way things are done all over, not just here in my precinct. As I said, you can't fight it so you accept it. You just hope that eventually you make the right friends too.

> Things are pretty much on the up and up now. The department doesn't practice discrimination by choice. I may have thought that it was policy years ago. Maybe it was then, but not really today. You have bosses and even patrolmen in certain positions who can manipulate other officers into good jobs. But I don't look at this as racial discrimination anymore. It's really present in all types of areas . . . favoritism. I think in your language, nepotism. . . . And it goes for black cops as well today, to be honest. Black bosses choose blacks who are friends or belong to the Guardians, you know for special assignments when they can.

It is evident that some black cops not only accept, but even defend arrangements which bestow rewards and favors based upon seniority and informal group ties. Unlike others these men seem to view any disadvantages confronting blacks on the job not as a result of departmental discrimination per se, but as a function of their "newcomer" status and position within the organization. But more than that, their acceptance of favoritism as both an integral and legitimate feature of the job has allowed them to rationalize away any hostility that might result from the belief that differential treatment is tied solely to membership in a particular racial group.

As we have seen earlier, however, this seemingly "apologetic" view is not shared by all black policemen. A substantial number still view favoritism, nepotism, or whatever one cares to label the practice as a powerful organizational mechanism capable of advancing both the individual and collective interests of white police at the expense of equally deserving blacks.

There is yet a third point of view, one which incorporates the key arguments of the other two. Although the claim has been made that membership in a particular racial group can help influence decisions regarding assignments, transfers, advancements, and promotions, affiliation alone cannot guarantee that favorable decisions will be forthcoming. Personal experience and contacts with hundreds of officers over the past 17 years has shown that whites who lack the "appropriate connections" on the job fare only somewhat better than non-whites when competing for choice assignments such as Emergency Service, Harbor, Aviation, Forensic, Bomb Squad, and so on. Like blacks, whites who apply each year for these and other specialty duties also find that they are routinely turned down, not because they lack the requisite qualifications, but because they lack the right contacts. It may, therefore, be misleading to label the practice of favoritism as *racial* discrimination since the practice itself, while currently operating to the disadvantage of blacks as a group, clearly affects whites and may occur in those commands where racial distinctions are not made in designating assignments and promotions.

Some Specific Areas of Concern to Black Policemen

Although a number of respondents indicated the general form discrimination is believed to take, a more complete picture of the concerns of some black policemen emerges when the question is directed to the specific areas in which discrimination is believed to operate today.

Task assignment

Much of the disatisfaction with the department stems from the belief that task assignments are racially designated; that black officers are generally relegated to routine patrol duties while whites receive most of the more desirable assignments. Moreover, there exists a feeling among a few respondents that habit and custom still play a major role in the exclusion of blacks from preferred assignments. As one patrol officer put it,

> There has been for the last two years a high-visibility team working in my precinct. There has never been to my knowledge any black officers assigned to this team. The captain gives these assignments to white cops. This is the way it's always been, and this is the way it still is. A black cop, as I said, doesn't have a chance to move around here.

Another policeman, who appeared bitter about conditions in his command, charges that white superiors generally pay lip service to the principle of equal opportunity especially when it comes to selecting officers for specialized precinct details. His complaint was directed specifically at what he felt was a long-standing practice in his command to exclude deserving blacks from plainclothes anticrime assignments.

> Anticrime here is almost all white. There's only one or two black cops assigned. The bosses who run these details say they pick their men based upon activity and ability. Well that's a crock of shit. They pick white cops over blacks who have more collars (arrests) and are more effective in the street. I know this to be true because I was personally passed over. . . . Some white guy in the precinct with less than three years on the job and much less collars than I had got anticrime. . . . Equal treatment, that's a laugh. It's only for the newpapers.

However, another patrol officer, who works in the same command, offers a contrasting picture of current precinct policies regarding the selection of personnel for anticrime units. He contends that because of their "natural" ability to blend into community surroundings, black police officers are often picked for anticrime details in black precincts. But he concedes that the black officer may find similar opportunities greatly limited in predominantly white precincts. That is, white police superiors often have serious reservations about the effectiveness of black policemen who, for example, when operating an unmarked police car in civilian clothes, can present an identity problem the precinct commander may be looking to avoid.

> In certain black precincts, for example where I work, I would say the black officer has an equal chance of being selected for anticrime details or for some detail that comes up. You see he fits in, so here he can make good collars. In other words, he's needed. But this is only in black precincts. I've also worked in white precincts. There, blacks are hardly ever picked for anticrime. I got the feeling that maybe because it's a white area blacks are not good enough. You see, a lot of people there don't want a black cop riding around in civies for a lot of reasons. So they don't put you in for these details. If you work there you do routine patrol in uniform so there's no question as to who you are.

Civilian-clothed, anticrime assignments present a special case for consideration here. Of the 18 precincts located in the boroughs of Manhattan, Bronx, Queens, and Brooklyn that were sampled in an effort to determine minority representation, it was discovered that there were a total of 186 anticrime officers assigned, of which, interestingly, 12 percent were black. This figure, however, may be totally misleading in terms of proportional representation. Only one precinct (the 28th in Harlem) had more than two black cops assigned to anticrime duty. In four of the predominantly black or mixed precincts there were no black anticrime cops at all, while in five precincts only one black cop was assigned to each. In the two predominantly white precincts sampled, there were no minority officers at all in the anticrime units. Although one might expect this situation to prevail in a white precinct where, as the officer above stated, there is a possibility of an "identity" problem arising should two black cops patrol the street in an unmarked car wearing work clothes, the absence of black anticrime cops in some of the black areas where their natural ability to blend into the surroundings would present a definite asset in fighting street crime, seems strange. Moreover, one finds that in the department's citywide Street-Crime Unit (a centralized counterpart of the precinct anticrime unit), which operates in high-crime areas of the city, black cops accounted for only 6 percent of the unit.[8]

Why aren't blacks represented in greater numbers in all-black and mixed precincts or in citywide units which serve these areas? While favoritism and individual discrimination in assignment might explain these conditions, it is also possible that they are a result, in part, of a process of "self-elimination." It is conceivable—and a number of interviews tend to support this explanation—that black police themselves are often reluctant to volunteer for anticrime duty because these units are predominantly, and in some precincts, *all* white in composition. Also it is this type of assignment that has, over the years, attracted and retained the more aggressive white cops in the department. The point is that anticrime cops have traditionally assumed an aggressive approach to fighting street crime and many qualified black officers may find it uncomfortable working in an environment in which they would be expected to conform to certain occupational values that they did not share and to behave aggressively toward other blacks in their community who are often only suspected of having committed an offense. Rather than subject themselves to these competing pressures and loyalties, it may simply be easier in the long run to avoid such assignments altogether. So, what may appear at first glance as a policy of racial exclusion in some precincts may, upon closer examination, be the result of a selection process controlled in part by the black officer who, although sharing the department's goal of reducing street crime in the ghetto, rejects outright some of the traditional police methods of doing so. As one officer put it,

> Let me tell you something you probably don't know. A lot of us would want anticrime and would relish the chance to get in there. But we feel that we would be put in a sort of a bind. What do I mean by that. Well, for example, I know the anticrime cops here and except for ——— they're all white. These guys are demons in the street. Not that they're bad guys but they fuck with people a lot, stopping people for no *real* reason, tossing them, sticking guns in their faces. . . . And when they find that a dude's not dirty [i.e., he's not carrying a weapon or drugs] they just go on their way. No apologies no nothing—just go on their way. This leaves a bad taste in people's mouths; and I personally can't work under these con-

ditions. Some guys can, maybe. I can't. These guys don't give a fuck about people here anyway. They were the same in uniform.

Area assignment

The systematic assignment of black police officers to black precincts in the city is another area of concern to some of the men in this group. The following comments support what other studies have shown in the past; that some black policemen deeply resent the practice of "enforced segregation": [9]

> There are more blacks in this precinct than any other precinct in the city. Blacks are overrepresented in black precincts and underrepresented in white precincts. Personally, I feel this is not right particularly when it's forced on you and you really don't have a say in the matter.

> I think the department discriminates in a lot of ways, but mainly as far as representation. They put blacks into black areas most of the time. And this is certainly not equal treatment as far as I see it.

A few are resentful of such practices because they result in the disproportionate exposure of black police officers to the potentially violent and dangerous conditions found in some ghetto communities. A detective had this to say:

> Blacks are overrepresented in black areas. Manpower is allocated by race, not by qualification. The department is using the wrong criteria. Now, if you ask me whether this is a form of discrimination, yes it is. Anytime you shift men around by color and some have to work in more dangerous precincts for prolonged periods of time because of their color, it's discrimination. There's just no other way to cut it.

Compounding the resentment of some blacks toward so-called "restrictive" assignments is the belief that it is extremely difficult for them to transfer out of a black precinct once they have been assigned there. One respondent went so far as to assert that an "unwritten" department policy exists which makes it practically impossible for black policemen working in areas such as Harlem to transfer to white precincts.

> Transfers from say Harlem to midtown or Queens precincts, they are difficult to come by. Blacks are placed in Harlem and that's where they stay, most of them anyway. The department has an unwritten policy about this. I think this is discriminatory.

In addition, we are told that white policemen usually are not subjected to the same assignment restrictions as black officers; transfers out of precincts located in Harlem or Brownsville, for example, are not that hard to come by if one happens to be white. A detective sees this as a form of "double discrimination" against blacks:

> And then on top of this there are white cops who put in 57s [transfer requests] to get out of Harlem for one reason or another. This, you see, is possible. There's black officers who put in 57s to get out and they can't. I don't know what you would call it, but I personally feel that the black cop who finds himself locked in a black precinct while white cops move around freely is being discriminated against twice.

The practice of assigning black police officers to precincts located in black areas of the city has indeed provoked protests of discrimination from some of the men in this study. Yet, there is no evidence to indicate that in making these assignments the police department acted solely with the intent of discriminating against its minority personnel. In fact, it might be recalled that during the turbulent 1960s, black civil rights activists, black politicians, black news media representatives, and black citizens alike were calling for greater representation of black cops in their communities. For example, when black cops were hired and assigned to patrol beats in Harlem in the mid-1960s a leading black newspaper, the *Amsterdam News,* rejoiced: "We believe that from our vantage point of being the community newspaper we can feel and report on the pulse of Harlem better than any other media, and it is a pleasure to be able to say at this time that Harlem is in a state of peaceful calm."[10] Similarly, the chairman of the African Nationalist Pioneer Movement reported: "The assignment of more Negro patrolmen to the

Bedford-Stuyvesant area will go a long way to improve community relations with the police."[11] In making these assignments the police department perhaps was simply responding to community demands, expecting that the placement of additional black officers in black communities would lead to an easing of tensions and a better understanding between the police and the community. Moreover, as we shall see later, not all black police have been opposed to such restricted assignment practices. Indeed, some of the men interviewed seemed to prefer assignments in black areas of the city where they felt they could serve the people better. In short, then, the existence of restrictive assignment practices should not necessarily translate into racial discrimination since the practice itself may be a response to political pressures emanating from within the black community.

Promotion and advancement

Some policemen charge that access to the detective bureau is restricted for blacks even if they have met the formal requirements for promotion such as accumulating an impressive arrest record. One officer recalls the difficulty he encountered advancing to the rank of detective:

> I was promised the gold shield first in 1965 then in 1966 and 1968. I finally got it in 1972, well after some white cops who worked with me. This I feel is because there is discrimination against black cops. I can't prove it. It's not something you can prove easily but that's how I feel—case closed.

This officer's comment is important, not for what it suggests about racial practices in the NYPD today, but for what it reveals about the effect of past experiences upon current beliefs and attitudes. When asked whether black police are treated the same as white police, this officer replied by pointing to a situation which he claims existed as far back as 13 years ago when he was assigned to a narcotics undercover detail. As we shall see this *type* of response is not uncommon among the men.

A few policemen interviewed were among a larger group of black officers who were called in the late sixties to infiltrate subversive, extremist organizations, to gather intelligence information on their activities, and to work as undercover narcotics agents in some of the city's most hazardous precincts. Although all of these men re-call actual life-threatening experiences while engaged in under-cover activities, not one complained about the work he had done, nor did any of the men appear to share initial misgivings about the dangerous nature of such assignments. Rather, the major point of contention was that the department had failed to honor earlier promises of advancement for blacks who undertook hazardous un-dercover duties. Consider the following comment from a former narcotics officer:

> While in one command years ago I found that minorities were being used for undercover work a lot. Undercover men rarely ever got the gold shield. I did a survey and found that in not one instance was a minority undercover cop promoted or had ever been promoted.

And, they allege that while passing over blacks, police officials awarded the coveted gold detective shield to white undercover of-ficers who worked in considerably less hazardous areas—a prefer-ential treatment which has caused much resentment. For example as one officer stated,

> Well, for example, in narcotics we were expected to make heavy drug buys in the street in high-crime areas, whereas white officers were able to go to white areas and buy marijuana and pills. The white officers were recognized and got their gold shields way before many blacks who worked under much more dangerous conditions.

Whether such accusations stem from real or imagined denials of equal access to promotions in the department cannot be known from the limited and often contradictory accounts revealed in this study. What is important is that these men *believe* that the distri-bution of rewards in the mid-sixties was strongly influenced by ra-cial factors operating at the time and that these beliefs have col-ored their perceptions of racial conditions in the department today. As one officer very candidly stated,

I have to go back to my experiences in narcotics. In narcotics they expected more out of blacks than whites. Blacks were in the street making heroin buys while whites were working in white communities, in Wall Street, parks and discos. There was always the risk for the black cop of being taken off or getting killed. . . . If blacks didn't want to do this type of work they had a difficult time getting out. There was always the threat that you would be put back in uniform even if you spent a few years in undercover. . . . As I said my attitude was formed at that time.

Complaints were also directed at forms of racial discrimination believed to operate even after a black officer had been upgraded to the rank of detective and assigned to a field command. Some of the men contend that white detectives received systematic advancements in grade while black detectives generally remained at the lowest possible level (ie., third grade) for comparatively longer periods of time. One detective relates the difficulty he experienced advancing in grade.

There is definitely discrimination in promotions in grade too. I was put up for grade five times in about eight years. Each time I was in the top third. Three times a white detective who was under me in evaluations got grade money.

Another detective offers a similar tale:

I had been recommended for second grade [when promotions were common practice] a couple of times and never received it. It seems that I was always being passed over. I was always low man on the totem pole. I can't explain it any other way except through discrimination. White guys always seemed to get grade ahead of me.

Nor do these officers appear to be entirely satisfied with the way in which assignments were meted out once they entered the detective bureau. A specific charge is made that many competent black detectives were not only initially excluded from speciality units during the shift to "specialization" in the early 1970s, but passed over as openings in these units later became available. As one observed,

Well, there was a tremendous amount of discrimination during the move to specialization as to who was going to a speciality unit and who was going to P.I.U.'s [Precinct Investigative Units], which were [initially] believed to carry less prestige. Almost all blacks went to the P.I.U's.

A patrol officer who feels that blacks are victims of differential treatment at the hands of the police bureaucracy points to several speciality units in the department which he claims are still "all white" in composition.

There are no blacks in the Helicopter Squad, the Boat Squad, the Hotel Squad, the Bomb Squad. There are quite a few choice commands that don't seem to include blacks in their plans. What does all this tell me? It tells me there is still racial discrimination in the job. . . . Once in a while they place a black guy in one of these places. All that is is tokenism.

And still another patrol officer sees whites dominating the ranks of such specialized units as Homicide and Robbery. He said,

Also, there is still discrimination in assignments to specialized units. For example, Homicide and Robbery. The percentage of blacks in these outfits is still very low. It's just difficult for black detectives to get assigned to these units.

When asked to estimate the proportion of black detectives in a particular Homicide Squad in Harlem, however, the above officer qualified his position somewhat to exclude specialty units serving black areas of the city.

Well, I would have to say there are probably more black detectives in the 6th Homicide. I would estimate probably around 25 percent are black. But that's just in Harlem. You don't find this kind of proportion working in homicide in other areas.

At issue here essentially is that access to the detective bureau is restricted for black police and that even if they are assigned to a detective command, blacks remain at the lowest grade level (i.e., 3rd grade) while whites are systematically promoted to higher grades and into more prestigious units. Although this seems to be the belief among some black officers, data from the department's Office of Equal Employment Opportunity tell us otherwise. They show, in fact, that black police are slightly overrepresented in the detective bureau at all grade levels and that this proportion has remained fairly constant since the early 1970s despite the loss through attrition of over 900 detectives between 1974 and 1982.[12] And, although this loss obviously affected blacks, it was not due, as some claim, to a policy of racial discrimination but to a general fiscal deterioration in the mid-1970s which forced the police department to substantially reduce the size of the detective bureau by freezing advancements and promotions.

It should be mentioned here that advancement to and within the detective bureau has traditionally depended, among other things, upon seniority and performance. Considering the fact that blacks, as a group, were "newcomers" to the department during the 1970s and even into the 1980s, it can be argued that those black officers who achieved formal recognition did so more on the basis of performance than on seniority. This, in turn, suggests that organizational pressures to reward superior performance, regardless of color, were operative during this period. An alternate argument, of course, is that the department, in its attempt to preclude the possibility of court litigation brought by the black Guardians Association, simply moved blacks into the detective bureau and once there, into higher grade levels in approximate proportion to their numbers on the force. This basis of making advancements is evident in the average breakdown of approximately 12 percent blacks at each grade level in the detective bureau. In either event, the data from the department's Office of Equal Employment Opportunity do not support the claim that black cops were denied access to, and advancement within, the bureau during the 1970s.

Discipline

Complaints of racial discrimination in the area of discipline were, interestingly enough, for all intents and purposes nonexistent in this study. When 16 respondents were asked whether black officers receive more complaints (i.e., departmental disciplinary charges) for alleged rule violations than white officers, only two responded in the affirmative. One of these men, although he himself had never been the subject of formal charges, felt nevertheless that blacks were more likely than whites to be singled out for disciplinary action because blacks are often more outspoken on racial issues. The other policeman offered a different reason for this perceived disparity. He said,

> There is no doubt about it. Black cops get more complaints than white officers. It happened to me and other black guys. This is because the complaint will be entertained downtown.

In contrast, the majority of men were of the opinion that racial discrimination was not the basis for formal punishment. Departmental disciplinary charges, they felt, are largely a function of personality clashes between subordinates and supervisors. However, in a few instances they were thought to result from an individual officer's poor overall performance, general lack of motivation, or both. For example,

> I have no feelings that black officers receive more complaints, although there are plenty of prejudiced white supervisors. Complaints are individual. If a supervisor knows that a guy is a good worker he might speak up for him if he screws up. If a guy is a general fuck-up, no matter what his color, he will get one [a complaint].

It is also believed that black officers now have recourse when charges of misconduct appear to be "racially" motivated. While this has eliminated the "formal" application of different standards of conduct for black and white police officers according to some of our respondents, it has not curtailed the unequal imposition of "informal" sanctions upon black policemen by white superiors. Supporting this, a black officer observed that

> If a boss gives a black officer a complaint, he [the officer] has recourse, and I don't think a supervisor would want to have a weak complaint aired today, especially when it involves a racial issue. He would hesitate to give a complaint that would not seem to be fair, but he would turn around and give the black officer a shit detail.

Police supervisors, like supervisors in any public organization, have at their disposal any number of informal means of securing compliance with departmental rules and regulations. A supervisor need not proceed formally against a subordinate who has broken one of these rules, unless, of course, the rule violation itself is of a serious nature or if the offender has ignored earlier warnings concerning his behavior. Instead, the supervisor may proceed by administering an informal punishment which is often more severe. For example, what the officer above refers to as a "shit detail" is a frequent form of informal sanction administered to subordinates who intentionally violate department rules or who displease their supervisor in other ways. "Shit details" are basically unpleasant duties which may include standing fixed posts for a set of tours, assignment to indoor clerical duty for an extended period of time, assignment to parade details, DOA's, (standing guard over a dead body), or temporary assignment to other precincts or commands.

If informal sanctions are to continue to be used by police supervisors in order to modify unacceptable behavior and if it is to maintain its legitimacy in the eyes of subordinates it cannot very well be meted out arbitrarily and capriciously. In fact, in order to protect subordinates from the capricious actions of superiors and to preserve order in the department, precinct commanders routinely rotate unpleasant assignments among their officers. Should a particular member find that he is receiving a disproportionate number of undesirable details and should he feel in addition that these assignments are related to his race, he has recourse up the precinct chain of command, and if that fails to relieve the perceived disparity, he can file a formal complaint with the department's Office of Equal Employment Opportunity

As for the question of formal discipline, even though it does not seem to be of concern to most of the men in this study, the fact remains that in the early 1970s black cops did receive disproportionately more departmental complaints than white cops.[13] This finding, interestingly, contradicts the predominant views expressed and suggests that black officers were either singled out for disciplinary charges more often than whites or that they simply engaged in misconduct more frequently than whites. However, Bernard Cohen, reporting on police misconduct in New York City, pointed out that neither interpretation need be correct. Complaints issued by superior officers were found to be a function of work assignments and black officers were assigned disproportionately to those units in which *all* police officers, regardless of color, were more likely to receive disciplinary charges.[14]

Overqualification and conformity as preconditions to advancement

Some of the men in this study who claim to have experienced discrimination in assignment feel that if the black officer is to be considered for advancement in the department, he must perform substantially better than his white counterpart. In other words, he must be overqualified for the position.

> The only time the black can get assignments to good details is if he is needed for the job. That goes for street crime units and the bureau. Otherwise there is discrimination when it comes time to be considered for promotion. There is always a question mark as to the black officer's competence. . . . The black officer always seems to be passed over when it comes to promotions. He must be three times as good as the white cop to even be considered.

Underlying such expectations, these men claim, is an attitude toward black capabilities deeply rooted in the stereotype of the black man as inferior to the white man and incapable of succeeding if advanced. The following quotation from a patrol officer suggests that most black policemen are not viewed by white superiors in the department as equals, but as inferior performers lacking both the intellectual credentials and potential ability to perform more challenging duties:

> As I said before black cops are picked up for special details more on the grounds that they are needed in these areas. For example, the BLA [Black Liberation Army] detail, whites obviously could not be used. If he is not especially needed and if he wants to get into a specialized unit he has to prove his worth. He has to convince the brass that he is qualified, while the white officer is just picked regardless of his qualifications. . . . This equality thing is bullshit. The black officer has to be ten times better because the department is concerned about his performance. A lot of bosses feel that blacks

are dumb, stupid and have to be led by the hand. This is a misconception. . . . So you have to go out and prove your worth. You have to work ten times as hard to show that you can handle some mickey-mouse detail.

Besides lacking the capability of performing more specialized duties there is also the feeling among some white bosses, according to a Harlem-based detective, that blacks cannot be trusted in "sensitive" assignments.

> I'm not sure why this is. I think maybe it's the mentality of the white bosses on this job. I don't think half of them trust a black cop, especially when it comes to sensitive jobs. Say, they call some guys up for a detail. You find that they always explain things over two or three times to the black guys. I guess they feel blacks don't catch on easily. I've personally heard about instances in other commands where they didn't even tell the black detective everything he should know and they wouldn't let him do certain things. Not only didn't they feel the black guy was capable of doing a job, worst of all in some cases they didn't even trust him. That's some hell of a comment, that he might sell information.

Not only is pressure believed to be exerted externally on the black officer, but internally as well. One respondent explains that black detectives often feel they have to work harder to gain recognition equivalent to that won by their white counterparts because the black police officer's background, like that of so many other blacks, is marked by severe educational deficiencies. Because of this fundamental disadvantage, we are told, many blacks in the bureau are not able to express themselves as well as most of their white colleagues when they write reports. In order to compensate, the black detective feels he has to become more proficient in other areas of the job. For example, he might put greater effort into his investigations, hoping that this will offset his failure to master the English language and its complexities.

> Let me answer it this way. Some black guys I know recognize their own inability to handle written reports properly. They are quite competent to do an effective job in the field, but because they dropped out of school, they can't express themselves—say as well as some of the other guys on paper. To a lot of bosses in this job,

paperwork is important; it's really the only thing that counts. They couldn't care less about the case, just be able to "cover yourself" on paper. In my office a couple of black guys are always being criticized about nickel-and-dime things like spelling and grammar. This to me is not fair. These guys walk away after their sergeant grabs them about some stupid spelling mistake, feeling like shit. So they feel they have to prove themselves in other ways. They work twice as hard on their cases to make up for things like spelling.

A related criticism offered here centers on the "expected" role of the black policeman who shows an interest in achieving promotions. If the black officer is to be seriously considered for advancement, commented one detective, he must at least outwardly demonstrate support for the convictions of his immediate superiors, regardless of whether these convictions conflict with his own set of values and beliefs. Above all, the black officer must never become outspoken or openly critical of his superior's views unless, of course, he is willing to suffer the consequences. Unlike the views expressed by most policemen in this study, this is seen as pervasive in the department rather than subject to conditions enforced by *individual* superiors. Consequently, these policemen are unwilling to consider conformity even as a strategy for acceptance or advancement. The following comment is typical:

For a black to move in the detective bureau, you couldn't be outspoken. It seems like you have to play some sort of a predesignated role, and if you don't play this role, if you criticize the choices your boss makes for, let us say, promotions or assignments, then they sort of delete you, "X" you out. You're just no longer considered for anything but shit details. When ratings come around you wind up 16 out of 15. . . . My old boss used to be like that. He always used to criticize black politicians, but never white politicians. He'd say, "Look how they're letting their people live." Well, I'd say to him, "What about Nixon and the others?" He didn't want to hear about that., so I was evaluated on the bottom of the list, because I was outspoken. As far as I'm concerned if I have something to say I'll say it. I don't give a fuck if they put me 100 out of 50.

Another officer talked of "outspokenness" in a way connecting it more closely to the racial stereotype believed to be operating in the department today:

One thing is you can't keep a stiff backbone. They try to bend you and break you. The attack is on your manhood. You see, the manhood will be tested at every turn. It's hard to give specifics. If you follow it back to slavery, you'll find that any manhood, any type of aggression was snuffed. What aggression means today is another thing. Aggression today would be, I suppose, independence, asserting yourself and your beliefs.

While it is true that, with most police supervisors, criticism or disagreement from any quarter is unwelcome, some black officers feel that they are more likely to suffer from such differences when the subject is race or race-related. Thus we find, as we did in the discussion of black superiors, that the black policeman may feel that he is being asked to conform, that is to become a little "whiter." This can lead to pressure on the black officer especially if he is seeking advancement in the department. Should he accept the role whites would impose upon him in order to move up or at least out of a routine assignment like patrol, he may discover that the psychological cost to his own identity as a black man outweighs the benefits conformity brings. If, to the contrary, he rejects outright the established group's definitions of what he ought to say and how he ought to think and behave, he may find attempts to gain acceptance and recognition hampered or even blocked by those above and around him.

Several observations might now be in order. Denials of progress in eliminating racial discrimination in the police department have come largely from the younger, less-experienced officers. Young black policemen appear more likely than their senior counterparts to interpret job-related problems within a racial context. Several possible explanations can be offered to account for the negativism of black officers and especially of the younger men. First, the fact that younger black policemen appear more disenchanted with conditions on the job and the apparent absence of racial reform may simply reflect their lack of experience and appreciation of the more overt forms of discrimination characteristic of earlier years. In this sense, the older, more experienced black officers are, in many ways, better equipped to recognize and evaluate changes that have come about in recent years. They have personally experienced the gradual dissolution of traditional racial patterns which, in the past, effectively excluded all but a few from full acceptance in the organization, and their awareness of these changes seems to be reflected in their comments. Second, many young black policemen coming on the job in the early 1970s were initially thrust into low-visibility specialty units such as narcotics, Organized Crime, and the Bureau of Special Services where the department felt it could best utilize their talents and especially their visible ties to the black community. Ironically, however, by assigning large numbers of young blacks to these nonuniformed, "low-contact" units, the department, in effect, lowered their visibility and accessibility to other blacks, creating in the process a false image of institutional discrimination in assignment and reward. Third, the negativism expressed by some of the black policemen in this study may be a reflection of the concept of relative deprivation which can be set in motion when a period of objective improvement in conditions is followed by a period of sharp reversal and when the gains made earlier (as in the late 1960s) create expectations that are increased more rapidly than the actual changes. Conditions under which black police worked had improved substantially by the early 1970s and may have created expectations of even greater improvement in the future. These expectations, as we know, failed to materialize as the city's economy began to deteriorate in the mid-1970s. Perhaps, it was the combination of the earlier gains and the unfulfilled expectations for the late 1970s that led in part to the belief among these disenchanted black officers that whites were progressing at a faster rate than they were or that they were not advancing at all. This leads to the related possibility that some men in this study responded in strict racial terms to job situations and conditions in the mid-1970s (e.g., the freeze on hiring, promotions, and advancements) that most police officers, white and black, were experiencing both prior to and during the period the interviews for this study were being conducted. By attaching subjective meanings to these conditions and being so strongly influenced by their own particular interpretations, they refused to accept or even consider alternative ones. Or, finally, as the officer quoted below states, some of the responses alleging widespread and systematic discrimination in assignments may simply reflect an attitude of "sour grapes" as these men saw others move ahead while they remained behind, assigned to routine patrol duties.

I'll tell you what the problem is with alot of guys (both black and white). You have more cry babies on this job than you have in cribs.

As for the specific claims that blacks are disproportionately underrepresented in non-investigative, specialty units such as Harbor, Bomb Squad, and Aviation Unit, it might be recalled that these types of assignments are virtually closed to members of the service, both white and black, who do not possess the appropriate technical qualifications or "contacts" on the job. In this sense, the young black officer suffers doubly from his marginal position in the department, for he is a "newcomer" both in terms of his ethnic affiliation and length of service. Both serve to delay full acceptance and the opportunity for upward mobility.

In the final analysis, then, the question of *purposeful racial* discrimination with regard to the area of specialty assignment is problematic. What may appear as conscious racial discrimination to some of the younger (and older) blacks on the job today, may more accurately be described, as one officer put it, as "discrimination by personal contact." If we refuse to accept or even to consider this term independently of any racial connotations then we confront yet another problem: how to account for those whites who claim to have been denied access to preferred specialty units and duties because they lacked the right connections on the job. In other words, can we label favoritism a *racially* discriminatory practice *only* when it operates to the disadvantage of blacks or other ethnic minority groups?

In Part II of this book we deal with working relations between white and black policemen. Here, too, a fairly consistent pattern seems to emerge between attitude and time in service. Black patrol officers who came on the job in the early 1970s are more likely than their senior counterparts to feel that relationships with white officers are not that good. In addition, they are more inclined than older blacks to view this condition as a function of negative racial sentiments operating both within the department and the larger society.

NOTES

1. Nicholas L. Danigelis, "Black Political Participation in the United States: Some Recent Evidence," *American Sociological Review.* Volume 43, Number 5

(October 1978), pp. 756–771. See also, comments by Alphonso Pinkney, *Black Americans* (Englewood Cliffs, N.J.: Prentice-Hall, 1969), p. 197. Recent evidence suggests that in the future black citizens are even more apt to get to the polls and to elect blacks to public office.

2. During this period it was reported that the total black population in the North and West increased by almost 4 million. See Thomas F. Pettigrew, *Racially Separate or Together?* (New York: McGraw-Hill, 1971), pp. 2, 3.

3. See especially the quote by Edward Banfield and James Q. Wilson in Harold M. Baron, "Black Powerlessness in Chicago," in Norman R. Yetman and C. Hoy Steele (eds.), *Majority and Minority: The Dynamics of Racial and Ethnic Relations, 2nd ed.* (Boston, Mass.: Allyn and Bacon, 1975), p. 387.

4. See Nicholas Alex, *New York Cops Talk Back: A Study of a Beleaguered Minority* (New York: Wiley, 1976), pp. 124–129.

5. In Chicago, for example, a Federal court withheld $95 million in revenue-sharing funds earmarked to pay police salaries until the police department complied with a racial quota system. See Gerald D. Robin, *Introduction to the Criminal Justice* System (New York: Harper & Row, 1980), p. 121.

6. It seems that there has always existed a feeling throughout the police community in New York City toward senior officers which in many ways resembles the attitudes people in our society hold toward age in general. For example, seniority has and still determines to a large extent which police officers in a particular command will be eligible for "soft" details and assignments. Seniority also determines vacation selections and days off.

7. Between 1960 and 1972, for example, there was an increase from 7.7 percent to 37.2 percent in police personnel residing in suburban communities outside New York City. See Michael Peter Forbell, "The Commuting Policeman— A Comparison of the Effectiveness of City and Non-City Resident New York City Police Department Patrolmen," John Jay College of Criminal Justice, unpublished M.A. thesis, 1973, pp. 3, 4.

8. Data provided by the New York City police department's OEEO.

9. See, for example, Nicholas Alex, *Black in Blue: A Study of the Negro Policeman* (New York: Appleton-Century-Crofts, 1969), pp. 105–108.

10. Ibid., pp. 28, 29.

11. Ibid., p. 29.

12. Data provided by the New York City police department's OEEO.

13. See Bernard Cohen, "The Police Internal System of Justice in New York City," *Journal of Criminal Law, Criminology and Police Science*, Volume 63, Number I (March 1972), p. 57.

14. Ibid.

WORKING RELATIONS BETWEEN BLACK AND WHITE POLICE OFFICERS

Going back to what I said before, this pride thing caught on in the sixties. Blacks started dressing differently, feeling differently, and in some instances whites began copying them.

I N Part I we considered a number of key political, social, and legal developments of the past two decades to uncover their effect on traditional patterns of racial discrimination in American police agencies. We then examined the views of 46 black policemen in New York City concerning the treatment they felt they received from white police occupying both formal and informal positions of power in the department. It was discovered that, despite the important advances that have been made in the direction of removing institutional obstacles to full job equality and opportunity for black policemen, and an optimism toward future improvement, problems linked to the structure and "informal" operation of the department still remain.

In Part II we explore further the occupational world of the black policeman, focusing on working relations between whites and blacks assigned to different units and branches of the service. Although our concern is with how black police feel they get along with their white colleagues in general, we are also interested in identifying those factors that are thought to give rise to individual, and group, sentiments of acceptance, or rejection, in the work setting.

"What are some of your feelings about working relationships between black and white cops? Would you say, for example, that they have improved, remained just about the same or gotten worse in the past ten years or so?" When this question was asked of the black policemen participating in the study the following response categories emerged: (1) Considerable (or moderate) progress has been made in the way black and white police get along on the job. (2) Interracial relations are for the most part as poor today as they were some ten years ago. (3) Factors other than race influence relationships.

Chapter Three

Forces Favoring Improved Relations

For one thing [early] civil rights leaders forced new laws to be passed. I think these laws eventually affected relations between blacks and whites. [How is that?] Well, if you have laws which discriminate as you had prior to the sixties—blacks weren't allowed to go to the same schools as whites, they couldn't eat in the same restaurants, that sort of thing—then you can't have good feelings and intentions about whites. You see the laws worked against you. Once you change the laws, you eventually change people's attitudes about each other.

AS we have indicated, the 1960s and early 1970s were periods marked by broad and far-reaching challenges to traditional racial policies and practices. These challenges were divided along two major lines; one essentially conservative in character, the other more radical. The early civil rights movement was basically conservative in its approach towards integration and equality for blacks in America. It committed itself largely to working through the existing legal and political system and accepted the prevailing values of the country as a whole. The later, more radical, movement, which accepted a militant posture with regard to America's racial problems, concentrated less on notions of equality and integration and attempted rather to promote racial pride, black nationalism, and an increased self-respect and awareness among blacks.

Our respondents were, for the most part, in some agreement concerning the positive impact that black protest has had on race relations in the country and on relations between black and white cops in particular. There were differences, however, as to how black protest actually influenced these changes and more importantly regarding the contribution of each phase of the movement.

The Early Black Movement and the Push for Social, Legal and Political Reform

The comments of one group of respondents suggest that many black policemen in the city not only supported the strategies and goals of the early civil rights movement, but associated this phase of the black struggle with what they saw as a general trend toward improvement in the area of race relations. These policemen seem particularly impressed with the approach of early civil rights leaders, especially their commitment to fight discrimination through institutionally prescribed means even in the face of violence and victimization by government leaders. They felt that this approach eventually achieved for blacks greater acceptance by arousing a sense of moral shame among many white Americans. As one officer put it,

> Well, it's my feeling that the Martin Luther King period was very important. . . . A lot of people had to be moved, impressed by the fact that King and his people stuck to their beliefs no matter what happened. He opened a lot of eyes all over the country.

When asked why he felt relations between black and white cops have improved in recent years, another respondent also spoke in terms of overall improvement in race relations in the country as a result of the efforts of early civil rights activists.

> This is a question that probably has a lot of answers. Behind all this I suspect first and foremost is the fact that certain civil rights groups worked rather conservatively in getting things together. I mean they didn't organize riots and that sort of thing. They pretty much went by the book and got a lot of changes slowly. . . . I feel these changes were not really resented that much by whites. There was even a lot of white support in places. . . . You could even see changes in the attitudes of some of the cops in this job too.

A number of policemen spoke of racial reform specifically in terms of the various civil rights laws that had been enacted in the early sixties. Yet it is not altogether clear from their comments just how these laws succeeded in changing the attitudes and behavior of white policemen toward their black colleagues. One possibility, of course, is that the passage of these laws had a reciprocal effect on the views each group held toward the other. If, for example, members of a traditionally defined subordinate group begin to experience positive changes in their situation as a result of legislation designed to improve conditions for that group, they may then begin to react less negatively to members of the dominant group, who, in turn, may respond in kind. A detective suggested such a line of reasoning:

> In the early sixties, conditions in the department were different (than today). Those were hellified times. Those were sensitive times, the peace movement. . . . There was a clash of traditions which brought out animosities in all aspects of society. It's interesting to know that the difficulties during those times resulted in better relations between the races in general and of course in the P.D. . . . Once the smoke cleared, everybody stopped to look at each other for a moment and it was easier to understand each other's point of view— from a black perspective too. Had it not been for the tough times of the sixties, I don't think we would be enjoying the calmness, more understanding, more tolerant times that we have today.

The passage of antidiscrimination laws is, it seems, a necessary but not a sufficient condition for gains to be made by minority groups. One need only review the history of the early civil rights movement in the South to find evidence that legislation designed to reverse existing racial patterns was successful only to the extent that that legislation enjoyed support and enforcement from local government officials. In those instances in which local government support was lacking the impact of the new laws was effectively neutralized. It might be argued then that the legal efforts of early civil rights activists to eliminate discriminatory practices in employment in New York might not have been nearly as effective had these efforts not been accompanied by a political climate in the city that openly favored and supported reform in this area. A detective presented this argument quite nicely:

I think relations on the job have improved a lot. Actually, there was no way they could have stayed the same. First of all the political atmosphere in the city changed [in the mid-sixties]. It was favorable to better relations between blacks and whites. . . . This was due to the arising of political sophistication among blacks. They (blacks) joined civil rights groups and created new laws. These groups also put pressure on the city for change. . . . Then you had Mayor Lindsay and his liberal appointments. I think Lindsay and other liberals moved on a lot of racial issues. It seemed that what the laws were saying Lindsay supported. It worked something like the domino principle. Lindsay's appointments would more or less express his feelings. People who didn't feel the way he did had to undergo change or quit. If you had a Southern redneck politician in office at that time, relations would still be back in the stone ages, even with all the antidiscrimination laws.

This detective indicates a strong belief in the power of legal change, combined with strong supportive government in bringing about better working relations between whites and blacks through improved working conditions for blacks. Yet it is difficult to know precisely how the liberal climate generated by Lindsay and his political constituents succeeded in penetrating the traditional conservatism and resistance of the New York City police department. Judging from some of the comments, however, penetration *did* occur with the appointment of a progressive-thinking police commissioner in the late 1960s. In fact all of the men who touched on the political aspects of racial reform in the police department mentioned Commissioner Patrick Murphy and agreed that he did more to reconcile the department's internal racial problems during his term in office than any other police commissioner before him. Implicit in the explanations offered by most of these men, including the officer quoted above, is the belief that reform (in this case racial change) is increasingly facilitated as succeeding hierarchical levels of authority are filled (or replaced) by like-thinking individuals.

Recently, they're pretty good, but not excellent. They've improved because of the overall improvement in race relations in the country. I would guess that the civil rights groups were very much responsible for this. Years ago, for example, a black man could only be a passenger on a bus. Today, the laws have changed. Blacks are now bus drivers and cops. . . . You also had people in office like (former commissioner) Murphy. He became commissioner under a very liberal administration. Murphy made a big thing about racism. This was one of his pet peeves. He instituted a number of policy changes on the job, even though he made some enemies—people who maybe didn't want these changes so fast. But he had the final say and from there things went uphill. Let's face it also, there are still some guys on the job today who still don't cater to blacks. Now they generally don't show it. They pretty much keep their feelings to themselves. Before Murphy got in these guys showed their feelings in a lot of ways. That made it pretty tough to feel good about whites on this job.

Other policemen who spoke positively about the impact of the early phase of the civil rights protest, then contrasted this movement with the surge of black militancy that was sweeping the country in the late 1960s and 1970s. According to one officer, the antiestablishment posture of some of the more revolutionary black leaders succeeded in stirring up once again racial antagonisms among white policemen thereby making the prospect of "getting along" that much more difficult. Concerning the latter movement and its effect on police race relations at the time, he explained that

> To my way of thinking people like [H.] Rap Brown and Stokely Carmichael instigated trouble, riots, things like that. They were responsible for groups like the BLA [Black Liberation Army]. Cops were killed, both black and white cops. . . . They also caused people who were not really involved in the movement to riot. This was definitely not a plus for blacks, the rioting I mean. I feel that relationships went downhill in some precincts. In fact, where I worked they were real bad. All in all, as I said, I think they've improved considerably. Once the militancy fad disappeared, relationships definitely took a turn for the better.

A veteran detective seemed equally convinced that the sudden rise in the popularity of the black militant movement and its "separatist" ideology in the late 1960s served to dampen interracial relations in the police department considerably. He felt that both he and other black policemen were being put in the position of having to defend themselves against a philosophy which, in fact, did not reflect their true feelings and beliefs. He went on to say,

It seemed to me that all of a sudden I was being looked at by a lot of white cops as the enemy. No, relations definitely went down then. They weren't good at all. I can remember one (white) guy I was pretty tight with. We always kidded around together, joked around, even went out drinking together a couple of times. One day, I won't forget it, he comes up to me very cooly-like and he asks me how I feel about these guys that preach violence. I knew who he was referring to and I told him first of all that I wasn't sure that they entirely preached violence but that I also didn't necessarily approve of groups who did. I also told him that I understood where these guys were coming from, what they were trying to accomplish. . . . We talked for a while and stayed somewhat friendly, but not like before. Our relationship cooled down quite a bit, even today. I constantly had the feeling after that that I had to somehow prove myself. I guess you might say I had to prove my loyalty to the other guys.

What this officer is saying is not that black cops necessarily supported violence as a means to an end but that there *were* legitimate injustices facing blacks at the time that needed somehow to be resolved. What happened, however, was that the distinction between the legitimate demands for equality and opportunity and the means used by militant groups to achieve them were, in the minds of many white officers, becoming blurred to the point that they were often unable to separate the two. Many white policemen assumed that because blacks favored social change they therefore supported any means used to bring about change. The black cop was therefore considered to be guilty of rejecting traditional values (e.g., bringing about change through institutionally prescribed means) and supporting revolutionary tactics simply by virtue of his membership in the black race. Not all aspects of the militant movement, however, resulted in increased polarization of white and black police. Some, as we shall see, operated to strengthen ties between the two groups.

The Militant Phase and the Growth of Black Consciousness

The arguments of those police officers who expressed some support for the basic philosophy of black militancy differ in several important ways from those of officers who identified more clearly with the early forms of the civil rights movement. First, of course, there is a general rejection of the concept of "working within the system" as an effective means of bringing about long-term changes in intergroup relations. Opposition to this concept was clear too in those officers' belief that the early civil rights movement had been far too conservative to have implemented anything but "cosmetic" changes in the area of race relations. Secondly, there was an overt sympathy with one of the major concerns of the black militant movement; the providing to the masses of blacks in America with a positive cultural awareness and identity. It was felt that by providing their people with a set of cultural values with which they could identify and through which they could develop a sense of pride and respect, blacks would eventually acquire the strength needed to affect change in America's institutions.[1] (In the late 1960s the effect of this new militancy was becoming increasingly evident in the contributions of black artists, writers, and educators, the proliferation of black studies programs in colleges, the wearing of African clothing, and even the growing popularity of Afro hairstyles.)

For some of our men, interest in these new forms of cultural expression was aroused not so much by the fact that they provided blacks with a set of positive symbols but that they altered the way blacks were beginning to see themselves in relation to whites. The following excerpt is typical of the feelings expressed by those policemen who identified with this part of the movement and who visualized its long-term effect on intergroup relations:

> The mere fact that a black person knows where he stands now in relation to whites makes it easier for him to cope with everday dealings in life. Belonging allows him to relate better to white people. . . . Going back to what I said before, this pride thing caught on in the sixties. Blacks started dressing differently, feeling differently, and in some instances whites began copying them.

When pressed about what he meant by "copying them," this officer continued

> For instance, ten or 15 years ago do you think most whites knew what a "fro" was, or even cared? Today, you see many whites who

are wearing Afros. One of the white sergeants I work with is very proud that his son is wearing one. This he personally conveyed to me.

In the 1960s it was not unusual to see black policemen openly expressing their "newly found" identity by sporting Afro hairdos under their uniform caps and by wearing African clothing and jewelry when they were not on duty. While some of these new expressions of racial solidarity and pride may have initially alienated whites in the department, their long-term effect, we are told, was to promote greater respect toward, and acceptance of, black police, at least on the job. As one policeman put it,

> Relations have definitely improved. That's because there is more acceptance and equality now. Actually, since the sixties there's no way in the world that conditions could have gotten worse. The white cop accepts the black cop more as an equal today, than say, ten, 20 years ago. That's because the black cop sees himself in a different light today. He no longer walks around acting like a "Tom." He generally stands up, speaks up. He doesn't let racial remarks slide like he used to.

Similarly, another policeman, drawing upon previously held racial stereotypes of blacks, explains how newly developed pride and self-respect often go hand in hand with more harmonious relations:

> I would say that before you can get the respect of others you have to build your own self-respect. . . . Respect yourself and others will respect you. That's basically it. Would you be able to respect a cop who didn't respect himself? Absolutely not. As I said before, if you respect yourself, other guys will respect you, they got to. You can't have respect, for instance, for someone who goes around saying "yassuh" and laughing all the time.

It is both interesting and significant given the fact that most policemen in this study grew up in the ghetto where violence was often used as a means of settling disputes and resolving problems, that not one of the respondents expressed approval of violence as a means of reconciling America's racial problems and conflicts. A few did feel that the tactics of some of the more revolutionary black groups contributed indirectly to a growing sense of solidarity between black and white police in the city. For example, by openly supporting violence against the "establishment" and especially by targeting black and white police teams for assassination, black extremist leaders furthered the attempts already being made by the department itself to promote a sense of common identity and purpose along occupational, not racial, lines. Thus, a policeman in the study responded,

> How did it improve relations? It's obvious. It was a movement against the establishment. The movement got violent. Cops represented the establishment. The movement, you see, wasted black and white cops alike. . . . Once a white cop saw a black cop lying dead in the street, shot, he couldn't look at another black cop and say you didn't pay your dues. The violence was an education to both black and white cops; the very militant black cops as well as the bigoted white cops were mellowed.

Another officer explains how the sporadic attacks upon, and killings of, uniformed cops in the early 1970s eventually forced policemen of both groups to channel their aggressions and hostilities against their newly found "common enemy," rather than against one another.[2] He said,

> Relations have definitely improved. . . . Mostly, I think, because of the BLA and the cop killings. In those incidents both black and white cops were gunned down. The BLA deliberately choose black and white cops to make a point. They said they wouldn't have chosen two white cops or two black cops. . . . So from there it was a "we versus they" feeling among most cops in the city. It's kind of a tragic way for guys to get their shit together. I don't feel relations will ever revert back to the old days. How could they?

Such comments not only show how police victimization can help minimize racial differences among policemen, but it supports the wider notion that "dramatic events" occurring at a time when blacks and whites are experiencing interracial conflict can trigger sharp changes in the attitudes held by members of each group toward the other.

A number of men in this group also expressed the feeling that New York City government itself had taken some very definite steps in the direction of improving police race relations. Mentioned most frequently were changes in the racial composition of the department, the erosion of barriers to promotion and advancement for blacks, the introduction of human relations training programs, and the emphasis on higher educational achievement for all police personnel. These changes are considered separately in the following pages.

The Influx of Blacks into the NYPD

Earlier we described the changes in the racial composition of the police department as a result of the efforts of reform-oriented city officials and the black Guardians Association. Our respondents felt that this was an important time for the black officer, and that the resultant increase in the number of black cops in the 1970s produced a desirable effect upon relationships between them and their white colleagues. That is, after blacks were admitted to the ranks, it was argued, the department created a working environment in which blacks and whites experienced greater interracial exposure and an understanding of and tolerance toward each other. A policeman explained:

> You learn from each other. Whites who never had any dealings with black police now had more opportunity to work with them. In some precincts a white cop may have had to work mostly with blacks. This was definitely a learning experience for both. You learn something about the other guy each time you work with him. Mostly, you learn to get along. . . . I personally found that the more I worked with a guy the more we found we had in common. There's one catch. Sometimes you didn't get to work with one guy long enough to find out where he's really coming from.

To reiterate, it is quite possible that increased interracial contact over the past years is beginning to dispel the long-standing fears and misunderstandings held by white and black police toward each other. According to one detective it was precisely the absence of this type of "extended contact" in the past that ensured the persistence of racial stereotypes and antagonisms.

> The mere fact that you have to deal with black cops as partners more often will automatically bring about better relationships. . . . It's very simple. If you don't have to deal with and never have dealt with a green Martian, then you would not have the vaguest idea of what he is all about. You won't understand him and you will fear him until you get to know him. The same thing applies here. If you're exposed to blacks more, you get to know them and you will fear them less.

In addition, by altering the racial composition of police precincts and detective squads, it is believed the department reduced the potential for intergroup conflict by providing additional support in the event discussions or problems of a racial nature got out of hand. As one detective remarked,

> The situation has gotten much better lately. I think you can see it in my office. In my team you got four black guys [out of nine men]. We're around each other a lot. To be honest you feel more relaxed, more comfortable when other blacks are around. There's less tension, definitely less problems . . . practically none at all.

This same officer went on to speak about the importance of seeing blacks in his office the first day he was assigned to a Harlem-based detective squad:

> It's funny, before I got there, I was wondering how I was going to fit in. I was under the assumption that most detectives were white. I thought I might be the only black face in the office and if there was a problem who would I have on my side. When I got there I saw the men they had and it was a lot of white guys and a lot of blacks. I said, "Oh, shit, I'll be able to fit in," which I did. I was able to work with no problems at all.

According to a seasoned patrol officer who has spent most of his career assigned to ghetto precincts, the influx of blacks into the department in the early seventies contributed to the image of a black man occupying a position of authority and power in society. Presumably, this "new image" resulted in greater acceptance of black police and greater accord between policemen of both racial groups.

> I never had any real problems myself, but I've heard stories about guys showing their shield [when off-duty] and still being questioned by white cops until they produced their I.D. cards. . . . But you hear these stories less and less now. This, I believe, is because there are considerably more blacks on the job. Years ago there were only a handful. Now there are a lot more. This adds to the credibility of a black man being a cop.

The Breakdown of Racial Barriers to Promotion and Advancement

Among its policy recommendations, the Kerner Commission report of 1968 not only called for increased representation of minorities in police departments across the country, but also recommended that substantial changes be made in department policies and practices regarding the promotion of minority policemen to supervisory and leadership positions. Not long after these recommendations were delivered to the public, the New York City police department began to promote blacks into some of its highest ranking positions.[3]

Virtually all of our respondents acknowledged the advances some blacks made in the late 1960s to top leadership positions within the police bureaucracy. A few considered promotions of blacks as being essential to the growth of cooperative relations between black and white police in the city. As an example of this, a black officer stated that

> If I can see black officers in top positions and other blacks moving up finally, I feel that I can relate much better to the department and to other white cops I work with. I feel that I have a chance to advance if I so choose. The opposite is also true, of course.

Another policeman, emphasizing pride in identification, expressed the feeling that the promotion of blacks into high administrative positions had improved his attitude toward the department and its predominantly white officers. He put it this way:

Like you see a black bum in the street and you feel bad. A guy has a much better image of himself seeing some black chiefs rather than all indians. It's easier to work in a department that includes black bosses in their plans. You can identify with the high-ranking boss which means that you can identify with the department or at least you feel that the department is now identifying with you. . . . It boils down to self-respect and pride. That's the A number one problem in relations with people. It's paramount.

While both of the officers quoted above attribute their positive attitudes towards the department to seeing blacks moved into administrative positions, for one this is because of "fairness," for the other "image." The black officer quoted below goes further in attributing to such advancement the reduction of race, altogether, as a category informing attitudes towards hierarchical relationships.

What I believe I see too is that cops are now judging bosses more or less as to whether they're "sweethearts," not whether they're black or white. That doesn't mean that a few of the white cops still don't say "Fuck him, I'm not taking orders from a nigger." But I think in comparison to 15 years ago this kind of attitude is rare. I'll give you an example. If a white guy was transferred to a precinct 15 years ago and he found out that he had a black sergeant or lieutenant, his initial attitude woud have been quite different than if he knew he had a white boss. See, years ago most black bosses weren't given much respect by white cops. Today, this is not really so. Bosses are evaluated on what kind of men they are; you know, what kind of bosses they are; how they treat the men, not so much color.[4]

Occasionally these feelings are coupled with the belief that the department has finally abandoned long-standing practices which restricted both the role and duties of black policemen in the past. The following story related by a veteran detective focuses on one such restriction and infers how its persistence today would effect police race relations for the worse.

I was in Brooklyn in TPF and an old black man walked up to me and showed me a retired police officer's shield. And in my conversation with him it was brought out that he was either the second or third black officer hired by the department. And he stated during those times, when he was an active police officer, that black officers could only be assigned to black areas. And he stated that in most instances it was actually stated to him that the only place blacks were good enough to work was in a black neighborhood. [He continued.] You know this is not the case now, at least not to the degree it was in those times. . . . He told me of other things. . . . He told me of other things that existed at that time, things that would really cause problems if they existed today. Because these situations no longer exist I think that's the reason why relationships are better.

The police department, of course, did not elevate black superiors to high administrative positions or modify the duties and assignments of black cops in order simply to facilitate improved working relations between white and black police. This was, quite clearly, an unanticipated consequence of these changes. But the department did act decisively in the area of police race relations in the early 1970s and incidentally, at about the same time young militant blacks were being drawn in the service, by intensifying its human relations training programs.

Human Relations Training Programs

Early in 1971, as part of a broader effort to reduce racial frictions and prevent polarization between black and white police, the NYPD instituted a series of human relations training programs for patrol officers. One of the first programs developed at the precinct level, was the Human Relations Workshop. This was similar to the workshop conducted earlier by the National Conference of Christians and Jews with the police and community. The only difference between the two was that the participants in the workshop were police personnel and the problem solving was oriented toward possible differences between white and black patrol officers. A broader program, introduced a year later, was the Intra-Organizational Human Relations Workshop which was conducted by the department's Community Affairs Division. Funded under a grant from the mayor's Criminal Justice Coordinating Council, this program was designed to provide a forum for the open exchange of views and opinions between black and white members of the patrol service. By bringing uniformed members of different patrol precincts together for 20 weeks in a workshop setting, it was felt that points of mutual concern to both groups could be explored and arbitrated, thereby preventing a racially polarized and functionally ineffective department.[5]

The police department maintained that many of its members had profited from attending the workshop. However, a few of our respondents did not agree. They felt that the program itself had failed to reach and convince some policemen that racial problems did in fact exist on the job at the time. The department faced another problem: an initial lack of enthusiasm on the part of policemen to attend the workshops. To overcome this reluctance and to insure a somewhat balanced attendance at these meetings, it is reported that some police commanders simply selected "volunteers" from their respective precincts. According to one "volunteer,"

> Going back to one particular program they had in Long Island, I can remember that participation didn't come about voluntarily. The C.O. had to eventually pull guys out of the precinct to attend. This was the toughest part initially. You could see by a lot of attitudes that the guys didn't give a fiddlers-fuck in the beginning. They thought this was strictly bullshit.

There were, however, other policemen who recognized that a need existed for some type of human relations training program. These men agreed that racial tensions were growing in some police precincts in the late 1960s and that the department should resolve the problem. One officer, who had participated in the Intra-Organizational Workshop Program, explained how the "workshop" concept eventually succeeded in reducing racial tensions and conflict between those men who attended. He said,

> It brought a lot of guys closer together, understanding where each of us comes from, our feelings, differences and that sort of stuff. . . . You clear the air, wipe out suspicions as far as how whites and blacks feel toward each other. Also, you find out why you feel a particular way. Personally, I think they were somewhat successful. I feel today some relationships are better because of these discussions, not excellent but better. You still got some problems, but I think they'll be worked out.

One of the stated goals of the workshop program was to encourage policemen to discuss openly their grievances, real or imagined. It was anticipated that a new sensitivity and respect for the views of others would be gained by those officers who participated and that these attitudes would be communicated to others in the precinct. But stated goals are not always achieved in the manner anticipated. One officer, for example, suggested an ironic ending to a dialogue session he attended early in 1971.

> Some of the guys left the meeting and on the way out they started talking about how fucked up it really was. . . . You see, they already had something in common. Then they started bullshiting on the way downstairs, started with the ethnic jokes. This kind of loosened things up a little. It's aggression on both ends, but it's a safe sort of aggression. It's covered up so to speak. So these guys began to feel more relaxed with each other. Then the next time they got together they really got into the problems.

This same officer then spoke of the importance of continuing these programs in the future as well as expanding and extending them to include those members of the department who still have difficulty relating to policemen of other racial backgrounds.

> The problem is that the department seemed to lose interest in these programs. You can't do that. You've got to continue them and you've got to get to the rest of the cops who can't get along in the precinct. This should be done even if it means taking the men off the street for a while. . . .

The department's interest in interracial workshops did, in fact, decline somewhat toward the late 1970s. But this was not because it deemed these programs a failure. Rather, it was due largely to the growing stability of intergroup relations themselves. This is not to say that mutual racial antagonisms disappeared entirely from within the patrol ranks by the late 1970s, but that rigidity of positions, extremism and open conflict, characteristic of the early 1970s was gradually giving way to negotiation, mutual concessions, and an acceptance of differences on both sides.

College-Level Training for Police

Besides human relations training, higher education for police also was advocated in the early 1970s. Because of the growing complexities of police work, politicians, academics, and police leaders alike began to look toward college education to help qualify officers to meet the demands of their jobs.[6] Agencies of the Federal government were the first to take a decisive position with regard to the issue of requiring higher education for policemen. In a series of commission reports on law enforcement and the administration of justice, the government concluded that this nation could not expect improvement in the quality of its police services until higher educational requirements were established for all police personnel.[7] Responding swiftly to these and other related recommendations, Congress enacted the Law Enforcement Education Program (LEEP) in 1968, providing Federal assistance in the form of loans and grants to students planning careers in law enforcement and to police officers interested in pursuing higher education. During its first year in operation, LEEP provided financial aid to over 20,000 students across the country. By 1975 that figure jumped to 100,000. In all, between 1969 and 1975, LEEP disbursed close to $200 million in educational benefits to policemen and pre-service police students.[8]

As college enrollment increased among police in the early seventies so did scholarly interest in the area of police education. By the mid seventies dozens of studies and reports had been released which supported earlier contentions that college training could, among other things, overcome the undesirable, often disruptive effects of prejudices which not only isolated police from major segments of society but which divided white and black cops into separate and opposing camps.[9]

It is important to note that only a few policemen in this study questioned the need for more college-trained officers in the department. Indeed, most felt that the requirement of pursuing a higher education during the administration of Police Commissioner Patrick Murphy has paid off for the department.[10] Consider, for example, the following comments:

I was in the Capp Program. Some of the courses that dealt with race relations were extremely helpful. The discussions in class broaden the knowledge base of all cops. They tend to force individual patrolmen to deal differently with minority people than they used to. A case in point: I don't see a lot of blacks coming into the station house brutalized anymore. . . . I think this has a lot to do with cops generally being more educated now. . . . That, to me, is a key factor if you're speaking of relations between blacks and whites.

White cops that I know that went to college now relate better to people in the street—at least the ones that are somewhat serious about school. . . . I think education has forced a lot of these guys to finally open their eyes. They're going to different schools; they're taking courses in race relations, sociology and what they're learning seems to be rubbing off. They act better, more professional now.

A few of the men claim that higher education, especially in the liberal arts, exposes policemen to new ideas about society and its racial minorities. The result, they argue, is to overcome negative images that are attached to members of these groups and to better relations not only between police and people in the street but between black and white police themselves. This is illustrated by the following quote:

I think education in the past few years has had a lot to do with racial feeling on the job. One thing that can be pointed to in particular that I observed is that so many cops have decided to go back to school. . . . This is important because it shows that a lot of these guys want to expand themselves. . . . School (is a place where) issues like race can be viewed from different positions. For example, some of the old beliefs about blacks are discussed and shown to be untrue. Let me give you a forinstance. Fifteen years ago I couldn't go down to the basement (in the station house) to eat with these guys because I was black. The thought was that blacks had body odor or something. Most of this type of garbage thinking doesn't exist today and I'm not saying that this is just because of education, but it definitely had something to do with it. Those guys who are in school just don't hang on to these attitudes anymore. . . . You see, you clear the air in school, you have better relations at work.

Many of those placing a high value on education felt it was more appropriate to younger than to older members of the department.

Younger police perhaps would be more receptive to new ideas about society and its social problems than their senior counterparts, and, as a result, adjust more easily to working with black partners in ghetto neighborhoods. The following comments touch on this:

> I don't have to tell you about the old school. I personally think that the younger cops today are more educated and have much broader minds. . . . I ran across quite a few white cops who feel quite at ease working with black guys, much more so than some of those guys who came on the job 20, 30 years ago.

> Also, animosity has disappeared to a large degree with the disappearance of the old timers. It's the old timers who had real funny notions about blacks. They were really set in their ways. These guys simply didn't have the education of many of the younger cops today.

These comments suggest of course still one other view, namely that it is not simply LEEP or college programs that account for today's more stable and amicable relationships between black and white police officers, but rather a shift in the values of two different generations. This argument would have it that as the older generation retires, race relations improve, and one could reasonably argue that this would have happened without LEEP or the emphasis on police education. Not everyone, however, takes as sanguine a view of progress, as we shall shortly see.

NOTES

1. See William B. Helmreich, *The Black Crusaders: A Case Study of a Black Militant Organization* (New York: Harper & Row, 1973), p. 27.
2. In 1971 alone, ten policemen were killed by black extremists, five of them black. See Nicholas Alex, *New York Cops Talk Back: A Study of a Beleaguered Minority* (New York: Wiley, 1976), p. 151; also see note 11 on p. 174 of same.
3. As reported by James I. Alexander in *Blue Coats-Black Skin: The Black Experience in the New York City Police Department Since 1891* (New York: Exposition Press 1978), p. 83.
4. William M. Kephart also noted that more than half the white policemen in Philadelphia resented taking orders from black sergeants and captains no matter how qualified the black bosses were. See *Racial Factors and Urban Law Enforcement* (Philadelphia, Pa.: Univ. of Pennsylvania Press, 1957).

5. This general goal was extracted from department pamphlets and official memos issued to members of the service attending human relations workshops. More specifically, the goals as enumerated in one pamphlet entitled, *Human Relations Workshop, Objectives and Components,* were as follows: that participants would experience or gain a greater degree of empathy for each other, experience a breakdown in stereotyping and, profit at the same time from the reduction of tensions that might exist.

6. See James B. Jacobs and Samuel B. Magdovitz, "At Leep's End?: A Review of the Law Enforcement Education Program," *Journal of Police Science and Administration,* Volume 5, Number 1 (March 1977), pp. 1, 2.

7. See The President's Commission on Law Enforcement and Administration of Justice, *Task Force Report: The Police,* 1967, p. 126.

8. James B. Jacobs and Samuel B. Magdovitz, op. cit., pp. 8, 9.

9. See, for example, the following articles and books: Alexander B. Smith et al., "Authoritarianism in College and Non-College Oriented Police," *The Journal of Criminal Law, Criminology and Police Science,* Volume 58, Number 1 (March 1967), pp. 128–132; Irving B. Guller, "Higher Education and Policemen: Attitudinal Differences Between Freshman and Senior Police College Students," *The Journal of Criminal Law, Criminology and Police Science,* Volume 63, Number 3 (September 1972), pp. 396–401. In this study Guller examined the effect of college on freshmen and senior police students attending John Jay College in New York City and found a significant *inverse* relationship between years of education and "dogmatism" among police. In his conclusions, Guller suggested that exposure to college promotes positive self-esteem among police officers, while diminishing punitive attitudes toward others; Roy R. Roberg, "An Analysis of the Relationships Among Higher Education, Belief Systems, and Job Performance of Patrol Officers," *Journal of Police Science and Administration,* Volume 6, Number 3 (September 1978), pp. 336–344. Within the context of improving police performance and behavior, several current research efforts have provided some tentative support of the assertion that college training does reduce the incidence of civilian complaints and charges of misconduct against individual officers. See, for example, Bernard Cohen and Jan M. Chaiken, *Police Background Characteristics and Performance,* Lexington, Mass.: Lexington Books, 1973). In this study the investigators discovered, among other things, that police officers who attended college were less likely to receive disciplinary charges than those who did not attend college.

10. In an *Open Door* letter to all members of the department, dated March 1973, Police Commissioner Patrick V. Murphy emphasized the need for more college trained police officers. Murphy stated that he was encouraged to see that so many members of the service were availing themselves of the opportunity to attend college courses offered in the precincts. He noted that about 30 percent of the department had some college education and that the figure was increasing yearly.

Chapter Four

———•••———

Forces Against Improved Relations

I've been to a dance where comments were made and got back to me. . . . I asked the wife of one of the white cops to dance. Imagine that!

A number of the men interviewed, a minority of them, rather strongly rejected the notion that working relations between black and white police have improved significantly in recent years. These men, nine of the 46, testified that conflict and division along racial lines continue to exist in their commands, a continuance they largely attribute to the persistence of antiblack sentiments and practices on the part of white *patrol* officers.

Racial Exclusivism

A few of these respondents placed the problem squarely in the lap of white policemen and some blacks who, they argue, still prefer racial exclusivism as a working arrangment. One policeman went so far as to state that most white cops in his precinct deliberately avoid contact with black police and in so doing intensify racial division and strain among the men. He went on to say

There are of course situations in which whites and blacks get together, but in most cases there is still this dividing line. They purposely avoid riding with black cops and they generally eat by themselves. This is the result of prejudice; simply that.

Yet, according to one of these nine respondents it is quite natural for members of one group to prefer working with others of the same ethnic group; evidence of these associations should not automatically give rise to charges of racism by either group.

> In all the commands I've been in I found the same situation to exist. White cops generally tend to hang together, so did black cops. But this is a natural thing for people to stick together, because they feel more at ease, not necessarily because they dislike each other. Look, ducks float on water because they're ducks, it's natural. But there are other problems.

It is also quite possible that social convention, defined here in occupational terms, dictates to some extent one's choice of a working partner. A white policeman, for example, may have no personal objection to working with a black partner, but may feel nevertheless that if he is seen in the company of blacks too often, other whites in the precinct will begin to ask questions. To the extent that such situations manifest themselves in one's command, it may simply be easier, as the policeman quoted below reports, to work with members of one's own group.

> I'm not saying that all white cops are prejudiced. A few of the guys don't mind working with blacks, buy maybe they feel a little funny about it. Say a guy chooses to work with a black cop for whatever reason, when there's 20 other white cops on the roll call. There might be questions asked. How does it look? He might even have snide remarks passed if he's done this before. So it's easier to avoid all the possible bullshit.

But such an explanation is an exception. Most men in this group steadfastly maintain that white uniformed police deliberately limit contact with black officers not because of the prejudicial attitudes communicated by their white peers but because they themselves are biased against blacks. Although only a few offered reasons for this prejudice, all seemed pessimistic about the possibility of improving intergroup relations in the near future. The following comments are typical:

> I don't really feel that anything can be done to change their attitudes. Prejudice will always remain with them. Feelings start at home,

develop at home. By the time a guy comes on this job his attitudes are already set and nothing is going to change them. The deparment can't eliminate problems of this sort, short of getting rid of these guys, and that means 75 percent of the force. No amount of training is going to help.

Well, you know the way I look at the situation, the mean age of white cops in this department is about 35. When you subtract 35 from 77 what do you get? 1942. These were the kinds of attitudes prevalent then. Kids grew up and accepted the attitudes of their parents then. That's what most white cops still live with today.

Deep-seated, antiblack sentiments whether a product of child hood experiences, later socialization in the police department, or a combination of both—are communicated to black policemen who feel that because they are not members of the dominant racial group they are not trusted by white policemen in their precincts. This causes bitterness in all of these men and, for some, concern for their safety in the street. For example,

A lot of these prejudiced cops look at all black cops as being different. They have doubts about the black cop's loyalty, whose side he's on. . . . This is not the kind of relationship that I would call amicable. It's a dangerous job and you shouldn't have this feeling that you can't trust someone just because his skin color is different.

Prejudiced white policemen are also accused of attaching to black policemen racial stigmas that some people in the old South had held. The officer just quoted went on:

You also have too many white guys who look at black cops as blacks, not as cops. These guys generally don't feel that we're qualified to perform certain police functions. They look at the black cop as someone who has to be led around by the hand to do the job.

Strong racial feelings also find expression outside of work, particularly at social functions attended by white and black patrol officers. At such gatherings, commented one officer, it is especially important that the black policeman conduct himself along lines of traditional racial etiquette. The black policeman who indicates that he does not know his "proper place" at these affairs, or who openly disregards such norms, will most certainly hear about his transgressions the next day.

I've been to a dance where comments were made and got back to me . . . I asked the wife of one of the white cops to dance. Imagine that!

It should be mentioned, however, that most social gatherings attended by white and black police do not involve wives or girl friends. They are usually affairs to honor recent retirees or members who have been promoted to higher rank, and there is no reason for racial friction. This does not necessarily mean that racial feelings are entirely absent during these ceremonies, nor does it mean that they do not intrude upon and influence patterns of interaction among the participants. At many social functions attended by uniform members of the service, blacks gradually gravitate to tables occupied by other blacks, whites to the other tables. This, again, may not be the result of racial animosities since much mixing is evident during the early evening but because of the fact that white and black patrol officers often hold different beliefs, values, and interests and tend to gravitate toward others who they feel share these same qualities. However, this behavior is much less evident at social affairs attended by detectives. Indeed, black and white detectives mostly play down or ignore the race of the people they socialize with. As a rule, detectives who work together in the same squad or unit tend to sit together for the entire evening. Here, the sharing of occupational values, beliefs, and personal interests—a condition that develops naturally as detectives experience interracial contact in the work setting—plays an important role later in shaping patterns of interaction during off-duty social gatherings.

In sum, racial exclusivism has been and still is commonly found in uniformed patrol precincts. Whether of benign intent or not, exclusivism operates to support existing racial beliefs and stereotypes, which in turn lead to further polarization of the groups and even to occasional incidents between members of different groups.

Racial Incidents Between Police

Black policemen in New York City have the same legal status, authority, and official responsibilities as white policemen. Both are authorized under the Criminal Procedure Law of the State of New

York to make arrests when crimes are committed in their presence, and both are required by department regulations to carry their weapons at all times while in their geographical jurisdiction.[1] Adherence to these requirements presents no special problems in terms of relations between blacks and whites, except when the black policeman is off duty or when he is assigned to work in civilian attire. That is, black policemen occasionally become involved in situations in which they are forced to draw and sometimes use their weapons. A problem that has led on more than one occasion to heightened racial tension in the department is the failure of civilian-clothed black policemen to properly identify themselves as police officers to other officers who may have arrived in the meantime while taking action in the street. In the past, this has resulted in the accidental killings of nonuniformed black policemen by white officers—killings which prompted bitter charges from the leader of one black police organization that white policemen "shoot first and ask questions later."[2]

Our respondents are unclear as to where the blame should be placed for these "mistaken identity" shootings. Some feel that the department is at fault since it failed to take adequate steps to insure the safety of black civilian-clothed policemen in the street. Others argue that no amount of training or special instruction could prevent these tragedies because the shootings themselves were symptomatic of more fundamental problems underlying relations between blacks and whites today.[3] These men maintain that white policemen, whether in uniform or not, act upon racial stereotypes which automatically assign "police" status to any civilian-clothed white holding a gun on a black. But when the civilian-attired person holding the weapon happens to be black, a "criminal" status is assumed. These beliefs and the accompanying fear of taking police action while dressed in civilian clothes is well dramatized in the following comment offered by a police officer who, back in 1978, had single-handedly captured a team of robbery-murder suspects in the Bedford-Stuyvesant section of Brooklyn. What concerned this officer most was not the actual capture of two armed felons, but the police sirens cutting through the hot summer night and the realization that the responding officers would see him, a black man, dressed in civilian clothes, in a slum neighborhood, holding a gun in his hand. As he later related to a reporter, "I was scared that they might [take me for a criminal and] blow me away."[4]

One black policeman in this study recalled a similar incident in which he narrowly escaped being shot by two white uniformed officers who, while investigating a neighbor's report of a stickup in the building in which he lived, initially mistook him for one of the armed felons. He went on to point out that relations between black and white cops can be set back substantially after such an incident, especially when later official inquiries disclose that color was the sole criterion used by the white policemen in distinguishing the "good" guys from the "bad":

> You know as a black man and as a black cop that these shootings wouldn't have happened if the cops had been white. Look what nearly happened to me. Because I'm black I was easily mistaken for a criminal and I almost got it. . . . It's going to take a long time to do away with this image. Every once in a while you're going to have an incident like what happened in Brooklyn. And it's going to set back relations for a while. I've noticed that after one of these shootings things in the precinct are quiet. Guys don't look at each other. They try to avoid each other.

A detective claims that his personal knowledge of police shootings under "mistaken identity" circumstances not only forced him to reevaluate his feelings about white policemen, but also diminished his effectiveness as an officer:

> I've read enough about these incidents that I've come to see white policemen in a different light. . . . It also makes me apprehensive. It affects my total dedication to my job. There are certain areas in which my efforts might be curtailed because of the innate fear on my part of being killed in the line of duty.

But this extreme reaction seems to be an isolated one. A young black detective states that the wave of accidental shootings of black policemen a few years back has simply forced him to become more cautious, more aware of the possibility that he too could be mistaken for a felon and shot while taking police action dressed in civilian clothes. Other policemen report similar reactions:

> Sure, it had a very definite effect on me, even though I might know the guy isn't shooting at me because he thinks I'm a police officer.

I still can't draw my revolver in certain instances. I know I stand a good chance of getting shot, so I'm more careful in the street.

I'll tell you what it does to me. It makes me very conscious of the fact that I could easily be mistakenly shot in the type of environment I work in. Its effect on me, I'm just more cautious, that's all. It's like red light-green light.

One officer attached considerable significance to the difficulties facing black detectives who often take police action while dressed in civilian clothes. Accustomed to dressing casually while engaged in field assignments in black, high-crime areas of the city, he stated that now he is forced to dress the part of a detective while on duty:

I started wearing a suit to work, something I was not accustomed to doing because of the work I was doing. I felt maybe this would help insure that I was a cop in the minds of white policemen.

This officer's statement implies that the black non-uniformed policeman must make a special effort to ensure that he is recognized as a member of the department by white policemen. Yet, even then, there is no guarantee that he will be accorded the appropriate response by white officers. He said,

My partner and I were returning to our office when a 10−13 [assist patrolman] was transmitted. My partner and I proceeded in the direction of the call. When we reached the scene we observed several hundred people in the street. The first thing that came to my mind was this is a real one [a police officer was actually in trouble]. The second thing was to get my shield out. [We were both dressed in suits]. My partner and I got out of the auto and saw two [white] uniformed cops trying to subdue a female and a male. When I reached the scene I put my arms around the female from the rear. The cop yelled, "Who the fuck are you?" I said, "I'm on the job," and showed him my shield, which was in my right hand. The cop started yelling, "She's got a knife, she's got a fucking knife." I looked over to my right and observed the other cop trying to subdue the male and it looked like he had a long wooden pole in his hand. The next thing I know I feel and see a nightstick around my neck. I said to myself, "Oh, shit, I'm in trouble now." I automatically relaxed and fell to the rear. Then I heard the people yelling, he's the police, over and over again. Then I felt someone grab the cop's arm, saying, "What the fuck are you doing?" When the cop released me I turned and said, "What the fuck are you doing." The next thing I know another cop grabbed me from the rear and pushed me up against a car. After that it was chaos.

Another detective recalled a similar incident he experienced while assigned to a high-crime, Harlem precinct:

One incident I recall, my partner [who was white] and I responded to a shooting over on 125th Street, in front of the ———— Bar. We got there before the uniformed guys. At that point we had two suspects lined up against a car when three or four radio cars pulled up. There was a lot of confusion, people rushing out of the bar, people coming from all over the place. I remember being grabbed by a white [uniformed] cop. I didn't have my shield out and he told me not to move. Some of the other cops had gone over to assist my partner bringing one of the guys we had lined up into the radio car. Mind you, my partner and I were the only ones dressed in jackets and ties, but they grabbed me initially and pushed me up against the car until I thoroughly convinced them I was a cop. By then my partner had also told them who I was. I got a bit nasty after that, not because I felt that I was being roughed up, but because neither cop apologized to me. One of the guys, all he said was, "Well, how the fuck was I supposed to know who you are." This left a bad taste in my mouth. And I'll tell you this, my partner was so pissed off, he told me to make a beef about it, the way things went down.

However, despite the occasional flaring up of racial incidents in the department there seems to be a positive feeling among most of these men toward white policemen with whom they have worked regularly in the past. Incidents such as the ones described above may seem important for the moment. Indeed, they may even provoke retaliatory measures. But, as we shall see, they are not apt to jeopardize or upset established successful working relationships.

There have been a few times when the air has gotten heavy over some racial incident. . . . Most of the guys who are already close realize that these incidents will occur from time to time and they just don't let them interfere with their personal feelings.

Most black cops have seen it before, and a few might take exception to it. It definitely would not have any effect between partners or friends. They understand what causes it. The knowledgeable police officer knows what causes these incidents. If it got to the point where 100 percent of the individuals were involved, then it would cause problems. Now it's not a problem between partners. I've heard about a few of these incidents. The way I look at them personally, they're individual matters. They certainly aren't going to influence the way I might feel about a white guy that I respect for different reasons. Should I stop being friends with him because of some stupid incident that happened in another precinct?

The incidents of mistaken identity shootings depicted in this section have no doubt alienated some black policemen from their white counterparts. But they did more than that. They also provoked strong political reactions from black police groups in the city—reactions which eventually led to drastic policy changes in the department. For example, not long after a series of tragic, and in two instances fatal, shootings in the early 1970s, in which white officers mistakenly fired upon black civilian-clothed cops taking police action, the Guardians Association publically threatened to call all black plainclothes officers off their assignments unless the police commissioner acted decisively to correct the situation.[5] The department did act decisively. Beginning in the spring of 1974 police officers at all levels began to receive formal training on how to verify the identity of another member of the service in civilian clothes and how to handle potential confrontation situations in the street. Since the inception of this program not only have racial incidents between black and white cops declined, but according to a recent study, not one black or white cop has been shot by another member of the service under "mistaken identity" circumstances.[6]

Confrontations between civilian-clothed black police and white officers was, however, only part of a wider racial problem that was reported by these nine men. Black civilians, we are told, were also being subjected to prejudice and discrimination at the hands of white policemen.

Prejudice Directed Toward the Black Public

Black-white relations between policemen can be strained further when anti-black police sentiment is expressed outside the station house, in black communities. Many of the men who complained about the way black cops are treated by their white colleagues, also expressed deep anger and resentment at the insensitive, rough treatment black citizens often receive at the hands of white policemen. One officer, who alleged that even seemingly nonprejudiced white cops deal harshly with blacks, offered a rather interesting explanation for such behavior. The white policeman, he asserted, is under constant pressure from his white colleagues to "act tough" in the street, even when he is not personally inclined to do so. The officer pointed out that

> A lot of white cops feel they have to rough people up or talk tough to them even if the people aren't shitheads. This they feel is expected of them by their peers. So even if a cop isn't a bigot or tough guy by nature, he feels he'd better act the role in front of his white [police] friends.

"Acting tough" in the streets and station house is indeed an occupational norm that most police officers come to accept upon being assigned to a precinct command and one which evokes considerable peer pressure to conform with. This behavioral code serves, among other things, to protect the police officer by defining his position and intentions to others who are evaluating him as an officer. However, this behavior may be reinforced by expectations of how he thinks certain minority groups behave. The result in some instances may be physical abuse of innocent persons who become victims solely because of their membership in a particular social category. An example of this sentiment is described below:

> When these guys are out in the street presented with what they interpret as stressful situations, their innate response is to behave according to what they learned as a child. As a child the white officer was unconsciously taught to fear blacks. Now he's simply responding to what he has learned. So he doesn't realize he's abusing people. He's simply looking to protect himself. Basically, he's afraid. . . . But that's one reason why relations aren't that great in some precincts.

This form of "social adjustment" on the part of the white policeman has its effect, in turn, on the blacks in the community and finally, on the black policemen themselves. That is, the black policeman may be accorded the same negative label attached to white policemen by members of the black community simply because he is a member of the police organization. The detective quoted above continued:

> The one thing that really irks me though is when I'm personally presented with a situation and I'm not looked at as a black cop but as a cop representing white authority. Some people don't see us as black men. That really blows my mind. For example, my partner and I went to an apartment the other day to interview some people. We presented ourselves as detectives to a black woman who opened the door. This woman slammed the door in our faces, saying, "I don't want to talk to no damn police." To her we had to act like niggers, kick the door down before she would respond. . . . It shouldn't be like that. But you know where these people get their attitudes from. White cops. I guess a lot of black cops are confronted with this type of situation and I guess it affects their feelings about whites.

It is not only occasional acts of physical abuse directed against black citizens but the constant flow of remarks and subtle innuendoes which assign negative characteristics to *all* blacks living in the ghetto that disturbed our respondents and continue to hurt black-white relations on the job:

> The white cop basically looks at ghetto people the way he was brought up. "They're all fucking mutts," he'll say. When turning out, you always hear white guys saying things like, "Well, back to the fucking jungle." I personally resent these remarks. I feel that if a white cop feels this way he shouldn't be here and he definitely should keep his remarks to himself. My family lives in the ghetto because they can't afford anyplace else. Therefore they must be animals too. To be honest I have a lot of trouble dealing with these guys. And you see these same guys fucking with people in the street. There's no fundamental respect for anyone here in Harlem.

Not only are some white officers believed to apply a double standard in their dealings with blacks on the street, but in their actual perception of interracial arrests. While often unaware of their own motivation in the arrest situation, they are quick to question those of a black officer. The policeman quoted above continued:

> These are the same guys who wouldn't sit still one minute if a black cop brought in a white woman under arrest. All sorts of questions would be asked.

The belief that some white policemen confine the use of abusive and demeaning language to ghetto sections of the city evoked strong feelings of resentment from a veteran patrol officer:

> There are only a few [white] guys I've enjoyed working with. Most white guys I don't care to work with, but sometimes I have no choice, so I get to see how they operate. I feel these guys are prejudiced and they have a tendency to bring these feelings out when they respond to a job. . . . I might ride up on a scene when one of them is abusing or insulting a black person. I tell him after that he shouldn't talk to people like that. I tell him also that he wouldn't pull that kind of shit on Park Avenue. . . . This happens too many times as far as I'm concerned. . . . When it's over I go my way, he goes his. That's the way it is here. It's not all of them, maybe a bunch. I've been here ten years and I've worked with most of the guys. As I said, I sense that things haven't really changed all that much.

Aside from stirring up feelings of contempt and frustration, what other reactions might the black policeman experience when he witnesses black citizens abused by white police? One extreme response takes the form of rejection of *all* white policemen in the department.

> I ask you, how am I supposed to feel good about white cops when I constantly see them fucking with people. You see, relationships are not that simple. I might like a guy initially and then I see him constantly fucking with people. How am I supposed to continue to feel good about him? I stay away from him and other white cops because I feel that behind my back they're all doing the same shit in the street.

However, another policeman offers what appears to be a more common reaction to this kind of provocative behavior, and the logic behind it:

Well, I would probably talk to the cop privately like I said before. Of course that depends on the situation. . . . What more can you do, make a formal complaint? It would only be squashed by some boss anyway. You definitely can't start any shit in the street. Then you got real problems. Cops start taking sides. This can lead to a real ugly situation. Besides, I feel strongly that the public should never see cops fighting or arguing. There are people out there that don't like us no matter what color we are and they will use anything they can to divide us.

Perhaps one of the most persistent sources of conflict between black and white cops is the feeling that white police take the law into their own hands in the black community. They feel that white police abuse black citizens; they are insensitive to their problems and treat them differently from white citizens just because they are black. Actually, there *are* differences in the way white (and some black) officers respond to certain citizen groups, though it may be, as other writers have argued in the past, that these differences arise from social class lines rather than racial lines.[7] Such factors, for example, as manpower allocation, or time spent on an investigation or even the way in which a patrol officer deals with a particular citizen may well depend more upon the perceived *social* status of the individual than upon race. Police situations and, in particular, investigations involving complainants of apparently "reputable" character are generally afforded greater priority and attention than those involving lower-class, marginal, or obviously deviant individuals, regardless of color. What may have triggered comments to the contrary from a number of our respondents is the fact that, for the most part, these men, from the time they entered the police department, have been assigned almost exclusively to black areas of the city where color, because of its overriding visibility and uniformity, acted to obsure other social factors that influence the way white police officers respond to citizens and job situations.

There is, moreover, a certain amount of tolerance for abusive treatment of black citizens which seems to be built into the system despite the presence of strong retaliatory inclinations on the part of some black police. The black officer realizes, for example, that there is little he can do to prevent such occurrences. He knows that he cannot interfere or openly criticize a brother officer in public, for to do so would signal a division in the ranks that could be exploited by hostile individuals or "troublemakers" in the community. In short, all cops are acutely aware of the need to present, when working together, a united front in the eyes of the public. But this does not mean that incidents involving white cops and black citizens are either ignored or easily forgotten. Depending on the frequency and seriousness of these incidents, they can divide individual black and white officers, if not entire groups, into opposing camps, perpetuating in the process mutual antagonisms and negative racial stereotypes. Incidents between the police and blacks, which are perhaps unnecessarily provoked by white officers, can also create role and status problems for some black officers by forcing them to choose sides. This, however, is a "no-win" situation for the black officer since no matter which side he chooses to align himself with he will be subjected to charges of disloyalty from the other. The white officer who happens upon the scene of an incident between a white policeman and a black citizen faces a similar dilemma, except that the resolution to his problem is made easier by the fact that he is unlikely to be subjected to charges of disloyalty by the black citizen. However, should he side with the black citizen, which has happened on occasion, he subjects himself to an even greater risk of being labeled disloyal by his white peers. Some people assume that in encounters between white policemen and black citizens the black policeman arriving on the scene will probably side with the black. There is no such expectation that the white policeman will do so. Perhaps this largely explains why the white officer invariably defends the actions of his brother officers even when they are clearly in violation of the black citizen's constitutional rights.

Needless to say, the problem areas identified in this section do not exhaust the concerns of black policemen who frequently find that they must work alongside their white counterparts. They have been selected because of the frequency with which they were mentioned and because they constitute, in our estimation, both potential and real barriers to the complete integration of blacks in the department. It should also be noted that although black detectives and others assigned to plainclothes specialty units may also share some of these same experiences and views, the conditions themselves are confined mostly to patrol precincts and involve the activities and actions of uniformed police personnel. In sum, then, it can be said that the patrol situation itself serves to displace loyalties and to generate internal barriers that divide policemen along racial rather than occupational lines.

In the chapter that follows we consider an entirely different set of perceptions of intergroup work relations in the department and the logic behind these views. Here too there is strong support for the argument that organizational structure determines in large part how black and white cops get along on the job.

NOTES

1. In March 1981, the New York City police department modified the rule that members of the service must always be armed while within the confines of their legal jurisdiction. Accordingly, members may now leave their firearms at home or in the station house under certain circumstances such as when they are going to sporting events or beaches, while they are on vacation, while they are engaged in off-duty employment or in a social activity where it would not be advisable to carry a weapon. Source: *Interim Order Number 8, March 19, 1981.*

2. See Nicholas Alex, *New York Cops Talk Back: A Study of a Beleaguered Minority* (New York: Wiley, 1976), p. 169.

3. In fact, beginning in 1972, the department did institute steps to prevent encounters between uniformed police and civilian-clothed on-duty and off-duty members of the service from becoming tragedies. Specifically, police were instructed at both formal and informal training sessions in certain standardized procedures that were to be used in encounter situations. In addition, the use of colored headbands for civilian-attired police personnel was instituted and members of the service were instructed each day as to the appropriate identification color. Source: *Chief of Operations Memo, Number 10, August 31, 1973.*

4. See Thomas A. Johnson, "Many Black Police Feel They're Between Two Guns . . . and a Black Police Chief May be 'in the middle' Most of All," *The New York Times,* July 18, 1978, p. B1.

5. See James I. Alexander, *Blue Coats-Black Skin: The Black Experience in the New York City Police Department Since 1891* (New York: Exposition Press, 1978), pp. 98–104.

6. Ibid.

7. See Gunnar Myrdal, *An American Dilemma* (New York: Harper & Brothers, 1957). Also see, Nicholas Alex, *Black in Blue: A Study of the Negro Policeman* (New York: Appleton-Century-Crofts, 1969), p. 9; Donald J. Black and Albert J. Riess, Jr., "Patterns of Behavior in Police and Citizen Transactions," in *Studies of Crime and Law Enforcement in Major Metropolitan Areas,* Volume 2, Section 1 (n.d.), p. 136; Albert J. Reiss, Jr., "Police Brutality-Answers to Key Questions," in Arthur Niederhoffer and Abraham S. Blumberg (eds.), *The Ambivalent Force,*

2nd ed. (Chicago, Ill.: Dryden, 1976), pp. 333–342; Alexander B. Smith and Harriet Pollack, *Crime and Justice in a Mass Society* (San Francisco, Cal.: Rinehart, 1973), pp. 44–49; Rashi Fein, "An Economic and Social Profile of the American Negro," in Raymond Mack (ed.), *Race, Class and Power* (New York: D. Van Nostrand, 1968); James Q. Wilson, *Varieties of Police Behavior* (Cambridge, Mass.: Harvard Univ. Press, revised 1978); John Gandy, *Law Enforcement and Race Relations Committee in Metro Toronto* (Toronto: Social Planning Council, 1979).

Chapter Five

The Variable Nature of Police Race Relations

So I say cops, all cops in the street, have to be more or less on guard.
(Cops) have to stick together, protect one another.

A third group of black police officers—17 men in all—were
inclined to reject the notion that relationships on the
job could be explained exclusively in black-white terms.
They felt that such simplistic generalizations masked the complex nature of human interaction and in the process ignored
other basic determinants of attraction and rejection in the work
setting. As some of these men see it, interracial relationships
tend to vary considerably according to one's location or assignment in the department. For others basic similarities—and
differences—in such areas as occupational ideology, personal
values, and interests constitute more powerful determinants of
friendship and acceptance than either race or assignment.

Assignments

Many of the policemen who were interviewed felt that getting
along with colleagues of a different race depends in large measure
upon where one is assigned. There was a general acknowledg-
ment, for example, that interracial relationships between *detectives*

performing similar functions are generally superior to relationships between black and white uniformed *patrol officers*. It should be noted that in all but one case, the views expressed here are those of police detectives who had been assigned to investigative units for at least four years prior to the interviews, and in some cases for more than 15. These years of separation from the patrol force might perhaps constitute a biasing factor in the responses. Is it possible, for example, for a detective who has been virtually isolated from uniform patrol conditions for so many years to offer an accurate assessment of racial conditions on this level of the organization? The question was addressed by a black colleague who had reviewed an earlier draft of this section. His initial point, part of which is reported below, seems well taken.

> I feel that it would be impossible for a detective who has been in the bureau for some time to make an accurate comment. I think that some of these men were reacting only to personal experiences. I don't think they're qualified to make statements comparing relations here (in the detective bureau) with the patrol force with any degree of accuracy.

The merits of the officer's comment were given serious consideration and it was decided to interview as many detectives from this group as possible for a second time. Accordingly, eight respondents were asked specifically to consider the fact that they had worked for some years in virtual seclusion from uniformed patrol personnel. The following quotations are typical of the replies offered by these men and, except for the first, appear to lend more direct support to their initial observations and accounts:

> I don't know. I guess I never gave it much thought. It's just a feeling I have that relations are better in the (detective) bureau. I guess, it's just, you know, an overall feeling.

> I've only been in the bureau a few years so I guess I feel qualified to compare the two. Besides, most of my friends are uniformed cops, guys I worked with for some years. They talk on the matter from time to time, nothing heavy, but they express their feelings to me.

Another detective offered a similar explanation:

My thought would be that you can get a pretty good idea about racial conditions today. I hear about incidents between cops. I ride the elevator up to the office with uniformed guys. I overhear conversations, comments made in passing. Also, whether guys talk to each other or not, what they talk about. . . . You get a feeling about things. You can surmise. I have friends, too, uniformed cops. We talk after work, stop and have a taste. Sometimes what isn't said is important. If things are sour you will hear about it from your friends.

There is, of course, no way of knowing for certain whether or not the responses reflect "actual" differences in racial conditions between detective and uniformed commands in the city. What may be gained from the interviews, however, is a better understanding of why certain racial conditions are believed to exist at one level of the organization and not at another. We begin by examining some recent changes in the organization and structure of detective work.

The Changing Structure of the Detective Bureau

In the early 1970s the detective bureau in the New York City police department underwent significant internal reorganization. Prompted in part by increases in the caseload, and the size of investigative units, the bureau changed from one which had been organized for some 50 years around the principle of "generalization" to one organized around the concept of "specialization."[1] As part of the reorganization plan, separate and distinct speciality squads outside the normal precinct chain of command were set up in convenient locations throughout the city.[2] Within these new units detectives concentrated on one particular type of crime. For example, criminal cases that resulted in the death of a victim were automatically channeled to district homicide squads for investigation. Specialization, it was felt, had several important advantages over the traditional "precinct squad" or "generalist" concept. The most obvious was that detectives could now concentrate their time and energies in the investigation of a particular type of criminal activity, and through continuous work in a specific area, gradually develop skills and information indispensable to department efficiency.[3]

Prior to the introduction of specialization most detectives worked out of precinct squads and handled a wide variety of criminal cases. Police officers who were newly assigned to these squads typically began at the bottom as "white shield" detectives but could advance in time to third-, second-, or even first-grade status. Substantial pay increases accompanied grade advancement in the bureau. Promotion to first-grade detective, for instance, resulted in a salary nearly equivalent to that earned by a uniformed police lieutenant and carried with it a high level of prestige among all members of the service.

Promotion for detectives has traditionally depended in large part upon performance ratings. In considering a detective for advancement, precinct squad commanders generally placed great weight on "quantitative" aspects of performance; that is, on the actual number of arrests made during a specific rating period. Other factors such as having "sponsors" or "personal contacts" on the job could, of course, help insure that a particular detective moved up fast or jumped ahead of others on the eligible list, although sponsors have often been reluctant to extend themselves for "marginal" performers. Thus, detectives who desired to move up in grade were encouraged by their immediate superiors and sponsors to produce large numbers of arrests. This type of reward system had, unfortunately, a number of major drawbacks; chief among them was that it encouraged among the men assigned to a particular squad a strong sense of individualism.[4] Detectives who aspired to advancement in grade found themselves involved in a "numbers game," competing with other detectives in their office to see who could amass the greatest number of arrests by the end of the year.[5]

Not only did the differential emphasis on the "quantity" of arrests, before the policy of specialization was adopted, foster the growth of individualism among detectives, but it is believed to have contributed toward racial polarization in some precinct squads by dividing detectives into two opposing groups; those who chose to align themselves with the department's reward system and play the "numbers game" at the expense of black groups in the community, and those who did not. Although this division was clearly not always along racial lines, some black detectives obviously perceived it as such. One said,

I've been in the bureau since the early sixties and there was one major problem that I can remember. This came up between those guys (mostly white) who were up for grade money and some of the black detectives. These guys naturally made a lot of collars—loitering, needles, things like that—to build up their arrests. There was a lot of competition between detectives then. Everyone was pretty much out for himself. . . . I remember there were a few black guys who inwardly resented the fact that blacks were being collared for bullshit charges so guys could get grade. One of the black guys who didn't appreciate this conveyed his feelings to a couple of the white guys one night. This created a lot of hard feelings between them. It didn't change a fucking thing though.

Individualism, which had for so long characterized the activities and relationships among precinct squad detectives, was soon to disappear, however. With the shift to specialization in the early seventies, the police department temporarily did away with the grade system and its emphasis on "quantity" arrests.[6] Detectives assigned to specialty units under the new system handled significantly fewer cases and were normally responsible for working only those investigations specifically designated to them. Case clearance replaced traditional criteria for judging a squads' effectiveness and served, in addition, as an important indication of an individual's worth to the organization.[7]

Since specialty detectives now had considerably fewer cases to work, and since they were no longer expected to make arrests other than those resulting from case investigation, personnel evaluations began to focus more than in the past on *qualitative* aspects of individual performance. The ability to demonstrate "social" as well as "technical" skills took on increasing importance in some specialty commands among those detectives who desired to retain their positions or to move up into more prestigious units such as Homicide. Detectives who were newly assigned to specialty commands soon discovered that they either had to develop these skills on their own—if, of course, they did not already possess them—or team up with other members of their squad who, regardless of color, were proficient in these abilities.

Central to the discussion here is the fact that specialty squads such as Homicide, Robbery, and Burglary were considered by most detectives in the city as "choice assignments," and investigators attached to these units were regarded by some as the elite of the bureau. Retention in a particular squad became, for many detectives in the early seventies, a goal in itself. Investigators who did not perform satisfactorily while assigned to one or the other specialty squads faced the very real possibility of being transferred to less "visible" precinct investigative units, or worse yet, being reassigned to uniform patrol commands with a loss of salary, prestige, and status.

One respondent, who attempted to explain how the shift from generalization to specialization in the early seventies improved relations between white and black detectives, touched on some of the points discussed above. He said,

> There was a lot of competition between detectives for grade money. Each guy was more or less out for himself. . . . It's completely different now. From what I've experienced so far, since specialization came in, it's more of a team effort now. For example, you catch a case now and generally it's up to you and your team to solve it, but you get help from other guys in the office too. But mainly it's up to you and your partner to work the case. That's the way it is in my office. Guys saddle up with other guys who they feel are capable, guys who want to work, who can get along with people. . . . Color's not that important anymore.

Competitiveness, as a traditional organizational concept, did not entirely disappear with the advent of specialization, however. As one respondent indicates, its form simply changed. Now there is competition between specialty squads, rather than within them.

> Things are okay now, at least in the bureau. I've been in a few commands in the last six or seven years and, job-wise, there are few racial problems. I do feel that there may be some jealousy and competition between different offices. For instance, in my office most guys feel that they are different from guys in other offices. Both black and white guys from my office may slight guys from another office.

Retention in a particular specialty unit was probably as important for detective supervisors as it was for the men themselves. Just as detectives were evaluated largely on their ability to clear assigned cases, detective superiors were rated on their squad's overall clearance record. This meant that detective bosses began to think more in terms of acquiring, retaining, and rewarding men, who, regardless of color, could "get the job done." Consider, for example, the following comment:

> Well, before specialization you had precinct squad commanders and sergeants who weren't as concerned about evaluations as they are today. This was because if their men screwed up or didn't produce collars and the sergeant or lieutenant got transferred to another squad, it wasn't all that bad. It really wasn't a "step-down." Now if a boss gets transferred from say a Homicide Squad to a P.I.U. [Precinct Investigative Unit] it is definitely considered a "downer." If a boss is looking for a decent job when he puts his papers in [retires], he stands a better chance of getting the job if he can say he worked in Homicide or Robbery for some years than if he worked in a P.I.U. . . . So now a lot of bosses are looking to stay in key spots, and the bosses from P.I.U. are naturally looking to "move up" to a specialty spot. So what does all this mean. It means that a boss is going to be looking to get the best men possible in his office, no matter what color they are. If a guy's black and he gets the job done, clears his cases, certain favors will come his way. . . . That's why I say it's not really a racial thing. Nowadays it's a question of who can get the job done. At least that's the way I see it where I work.

This is an interesting observation in light of earlier testimony accusing white police superiors of distributing rewards and favors based primarily upon friendship rather than on merit. Here it is suggested that, with the move to specialization in the early seventies, detective superiors in some squads abandoned these customary practices and adopted in their place a more rational, bureaucratic orientation which emphasized individual qualifications and capabilities over racial considerations.

Closely related to the above is the belief that racial feuding in a detective squad can seriously hamper cooperative efforts among the men, effecting in the process a unit's overall case clearance record. Add to this the label that might be attached to a unit commander or squad supervisor who appears incapable of controlling his men, and it is not surprising to find that most supervisors of detective units seem to go out of their way to discourage expressions of racial conflict in their commands. As one detective put it,

I can't really speak for uniformed cops, but I can say that in my office there is an unwritten policy against racial fighting. This has been conveyed to the men in very indirect ways. Racial fighting is a "no-no." Personality clashes, that's a different story. You go into the boss and you get your team changed if it's serious enough. If there's a problem over some racial feeling, you will definitely hear about it. I know my boss wouldn't tolerate this type of thing. I guess he feels that once it starts, it would spread like fire and there goes the clearance. . . . You can't work under that type of condition. Besides, it's damn embarrassing for the boss. You gotta remember he gets rated too.

It goes without saying that the effectiveness of any branch of the police service depends in large part upon the ability of its members to work together in a spirit of cooperation and harmony. Conflict of any kind, and especially intragroup conflict is not only harmful to morale but can impede the achievement of organizational goals. It would follow therefore that conflict, whether racial or otherwise, would be least tolerated at those operational levels in which cooperation is viewed as most essential to the successful completion of organizational tasks. If, in fact, this is true, then one should expect to find a greater emphasis in promoting a tension-free, cooperative atmosphere in detective commands than in patrol precincts where most routing assignments (e.g., issuing summonses, tending to the sick and injured, giving advice and directions) can be carried out with little or no help from other officers.

Not only are changes in organizational structure perceived as having influenced patterns of race relations in the detective bureau, but in some cases structural elements themselves are seen as accounting for differences in the way black and white officers assigned to different branches of the service get along. Two elements identified by the men here are the physical and social environment in which policing is carried out.

The Environment in Which Detectives Work

In attempting to explain why interracial relations are better in detective commands, a number of men expressed themselves in terms of the elite status held by police investigators as compared with uniformed patrol personnel. Specifically, they spoke of the higher pay detectives receive, of the fact that detectives work in civilian clothes, of the absence of close supervision, and of the benefits of a more flexible work schedule. These men regarded detective work as inherently more interesting than routine patrol[8] and referred to the age-old jealousies which existed between the two groups. In short, from the standpoint of these officers, black and white detectives work together with little or no display of racial friction mainly because they have more to lose should racial problems develop to the point that they adversely affect the unit's productivity and case clearance.

Besides having more to lose than patrol officers, important differences are also said to exist in the work environments in which investigative and patrol duties are routinely performed, differences which, the men claim, can influence racial patterns on each level. Detectives, for example, spend a good part of their working day under "relaxed" office conditions, preparing and reviewing case reports, interviewing witnesses and complainants, contacting various outside agencies and subunits within the department and conferring with colleagues and superiors. In addition to this, space arrangements in detective squads are so situated that members generally have direct access to their colleagues. Since privacy is not a consideration in most routine investigative operations, there are no partitions which normally separate work areas. This arrangement tends to facilitate the continual flow of interaction among detectives and affords them appreciably more time than their uniformed counterparts—generally confined to radio cars in teams of two—to exchange information about each other.

One detective, reflecting on the relaxed atmosphere and extended interracial contact found in his office, explained how these conditions are conducive to the development and growth of positive feelings among the men. He pointed out that

> It's an entirely different atmosphere. You get a chance to interact with just about everybody for a long time, at least as long as you're there. . . . In my office you sit around, discuss cases and things that are important to you. You are in the office most of the time and you have time to learn about each other. The more you're with someone under office conditions, the more you speak to him, the more you learn about him and the more he learns about you and

where you're coming from. You more or less learn about his background. You eventually find out why he reasons the way he does.
Very little is kept secret. Also, there's more kidding around here,
and that way you get to know the other guys better.

This is clearly not the case at the uniformed patrol level. In those
precincts in which black officers have traditionally been concentrated, the demands of the job are such that the men find themselves completely occupied for the entire tour of duty, responding
to one assignment after another. In short, the patrol situation, by
its very nature—that is, its quickened, hurried pace—often diminishes both the frequency and type of contact needed to form attachments and friendships across racial lines. Although the following respondent's account tends to exaggerate work demands at the
uniformed level, the distinction this officer is attempting to draw
between the nature of patrol and investigative work is clear:

> On patrol you're more individual, two individuals just working as
> partners. You may not hardly have the chance to talk to each other.
> . . . Uniform guys work in a "go-go-go" atmosphere. You come
> to work, change your clothes and go to work. Eight hours of in-
> teraction between cops and citizens, not among cops. Eight hours,
> you change your clothes and go home. There's little time to talk
> here, too much happening in the street. Working in uniform you
> can work with the same group of guys for years and not really get
> to know them. And you find yourself liking a guy on the basis of
> how he wears his hair. It's funny, here you have more time, more
> opportunity to get to know one another. Here, if you dislike some-
> body you will thoroughly know the reason why.

Another detective draws upon a similar distinction between the
demands of routine patrol duty and typical investigative functions
in accounting for what he sees as differences in patterns of interracial relations between these two branches of the service.

> Relationships are generally very good among detectives where I've
> worked. As a matter of fact they've always been very good. I do
> believe there are differences between detectives and patrolmen al-
> though I've seen some pretty tight camaraderie in uniform pre-
> cincts; also, precincts where animosity exists among fellow officers
> in uniform. . . . First of all our job dictates that we work close to-

gether. Because of this I feel that personalities are brought out more. The true personalities of the uniformed officers are not brought out that much even though they are in close contact in the radio car. [Why is this?] Well, detectives use all their ability to arrive at a conclusion on a case. As a detective you're questioning people, spending a lot of time trying to get information from them, talking to people for hours, not under stress conditions. You're usually cajoling them into becoming witnesses or maybe to give you information. What happens is your "real" personality cannot help but come out. Your partner learns a lot about you and you learn about him. You find you have more in common than you thought. You begin to respect each other.

At the patrol level, in contrast, where the pace of work is speeded up, as it often is especially in high-crime, ghetto sections of the city, and where cops often work within a climate of strong emotional pressure, the type of contact needed to build friendships and attachments across racial lines may be absent. Hence, a uniformed patrol team may spend considerable time working together without ever really getting to know the more private aspects of their partner's personality and relationships may develop only on a "surface" level. The detective quoted above described the situation:

In a radio car you may not have a chance to expose your personality, your true personality. That's because the functions of patrol are not investigative. They are basically "quick" dealings with people, where tempers flare and things said and done do not reflect the real personalities of the individuals involved. Then you're sent to another job. You don't get a chance to really learn about your partner. You're always wondering what kind of guy he really is.

Another policeman also felt that differences in patterns of interracial relations found in detective and patrol commands could best be understood by examining both the type of work performed at each level and the conditions under which the work is carried out. Although this officer admittedly had not worked in uniform for some years, he reflected nevertheless on the kinds of situations patrol officers are likely to encounter during a typical tour of duty and how these situations might lead to dissension and conflict between the groups:

It's my opinion that relations are good in my office. Personally I feel they are good. I would think that conditions downstairs [meaning the patrol precinct] are not like that. . . . First of all working conditions are different even though the area might be the same. We are a specialized squad, where we deal with homicides. Guys downstairs deal with everything. Friday and Saturday nights it's a zoo. When do we ever have to deal with that? I would be inclined to speak more or less the same way if we were working in the 5-0 [a relatively quiet, low-crime precinct]. You still have your junkies, drunks, psychos, pocketbook snatches, burglaries. . . . The guys downstairs turn out for roll-call and maybe if they are lucky they get a glimpse of one another two or three times during the tour, whereas we are constantly in touch with each other, talking, joking, communicating with each other. We aren't out there all night dealing constantly with the kind of shit these guys have to deal with. That kind of work produces tensions. A white cop may say something derogatory in the heat of the moment and the black cop will take it wrong, like a direct insult against him personally. And now you got an uneasy situation. . . . You see, it's more of an emotional thing in uniform. When you get to a scene, for instance, it may be heated, emotions may be high because of something that happened before. People see a white cop in uniform, a force, a system and someone may overact. . . . That's basically why relations are better upstairs. We are not on the street responding to jobs all the time, so we don't have to deal firsthand with that kind of stuff.

Another detective points out that, unlike the patrol force, communication and cooperation in the detective bureau often extend, out of necessity, beyond the individual's immediate working team. It is not uncommon, for example, to have separate criminal investigations lead to the identification and arrest of the same suspect. In these situations detectives from different teams or even different squads may have to work together on a particular case thereby getting to know one another better in the process. He put it this way:

Sometimes cases overlap. Detectives might have to work together because one guy did a couple of homicides and he gets identified by both detectives. You have no choice in these cases. You work with another guy who may be white. You get to know him. You pool your resources. You spend a lot of time together and many times you become friends.

As suggested in a number of comments in this section, encounters between uniformed patrol officers who are dispatched to a scene and ghetto citizens are often marked by uncertainty, tension, and apprehension for all concerned. White patrol officers, for a number of reasons which will be considered later, may overreact in quite ordinary situations. They may become disrespectful and abusive toward black citizens even when they are in the company of fellow black officers. Beyond this, there are other potential sources of intergroup conflict at the uniformed patrol level. One of these is the use of routine pedestrian stops or "field interrogations" in black neighborhoods. Since police seldom observe crimes in progress, patrol officers occasionally initiate their own encounters with "suspected" law violators. The decision, for example, to stop and question a citizen in a car or on foot is regarded by police agencies as a legitimate means of uncovering evidence that a crime has been committed, is being committed, or is likely to be committed in the near future. While the agency may justify this practice as being responsive to the expressed needs of law-abiding citizens for increased protection, black policemen in particular may resent this practice. But it is not the actual stopping of people or the limited intrusion upon their private lives that has aroused the anger of these black officers. Rather, it is the "unregulated" manner in which this activity is carried out. They contend, for example, that it is almost always white police who conduct these so-called "routine" stops, that these practices are confined almost exclusively to black neighborhoods, and that they are not monitored by the department as carefully as they should be because they do in fact occur in politically "less visible" areas of the city. Black policemen charge that blacks who are stopped for questioning are more often than not treated in a discourteous manner, subjected to humiliating searches often while in the company of friends, neighbors, and family and seldom ever told of the purpose of the stop. These men consider such activities provocative, discriminatory, and above all else, damaging to relations between white and black officers themselves.

When white police make routine stops which are based upon "minor" or "contrived" violations, and when, during the course of these intrusions, police weapons are unnecessarily displayed—or used—relations between white and black patrol officers can become even further strained. One detective who claims to have personally observed numerous instances in which guns were thrust in the faces of so-called "suspicious" blacks, gives us some idea of how black policemen feel about such practices. He explained,

> You see, this happens every day here. White TPF cops, the same guys everyday stopping people on the street for no reason, stopping cars and sticking their guns in the windows just because the car is filled with blacks. . . . You see them stopping gypsy cabs, giving them summonses. Not one summons for no rear light, but fifty summonses for every kind of violation imaginable. This guy's out hustling to make a few bucks, he's not sticking up bars. So maybe his car isn't in the best of condition, maybe his rear lights are out. But the guy is hustling to make $30 and now he's got to pay $50 in tickets. Meanwhile around the corner some guys are sticking up a grocery store, but the white cops are giving a summons to the cabbie.

Another policeman who sensed that relationships were somewhat strained at the patrol level, offered an interesting insight into the problem. According to this officer there is something about the police uniform itself that affects the white officer's conception of how he ought to behave in ghetto communities.

> I get the feeling that most of these guys are probably okay when they're not working. But as soon as they put on the uniform they become monsters. There's a certain change in attitude towards black people that develops in the street. It's like Harlem all of a sudden becomes their own private plantation and they are the overseers.

As this respondent suggests, the police uniform not only affirms the white officer's sense of power over people living in the ghetto, but it also influences his actions and reactions in the street. To the extent that the white policeman views the uniform as a symbol of unassailable authority, it may, for example, prevent him from "backing down" during a confrontation with a citizen, even though he himself was wrong to begin with. Consider, for example, the following comment from a veteran patrol officer:

> Because he's in uniform. . . . and once emotions start flying he feels he can't back down. He's got to carry through with what he started. Let's say he's insulted someone or shoved someone around. He can't

back down now even though he started it and he's wrong. How would that look in uniform?

The police uniform does, in fact, help shape the patrol officer's definition of his role in the black community by forcing him to modify his own self-image and behavior in accord with certain stereotypes thought to be an integral part of the police subculture. An officer may feel, for example, that because he visibly represents the authority of law, he not only has the right but the duty to demand and expect deference during his encounters with citizens. This can cause problems with black citizens and in turn with black cops who may not share the feeling that the white officer attaches to the police uniform nor the opinion of the role he performs in the black community.

An understanding of the symbolic meanings attached to the police uniform is essential in the analysis of police race relations for another reason. That is, it helps explain why detectives who work in the absense of such powerful symbols do not, as a rule, feel the overriding need to conform to these subcultural stereotypes in public. Indeed, the absence of a "military-style" uniform and its trappings not only alters the visual image of the detective but makes his appearance seem less threatening. It thereby reduces the anxieties associated with contact between police and citizens and diminishes the potential adversary nature of such contacts.

But one must look beyond the significance of the police uniform as it relates to the question of police behavior. Historically, detectives have operated under a "collaborative" rather than a "conflict" model of policing. This is due in large part to the fact that one of their primary functions is the solving of crimes and the clearing of cases, a task which relies heavily, if not entirely in many instances, upon citizen support and cooperation. Consequently, detectives have developed a vested interest in dealing with people in a friendly and supportive way regardless of how they may feel about members of a particular status group. And it is this orientation toward citizens in the black community, perhaps more than anything else, that has prompted most black detectives interviewed in this study to present a favorable report of their white colleagues and of interracial relationships in the detective bureau in general. As one investigator summed it up,

I personally don't have much respect for white (uniformed) cops. When I worked undercover three years ago I noticed a tremendous difference between white patrolmen and (white) detectives in terms of how they handled people in the street. In most situations the outcome depended on the initial approach of the cop. Detectives as far as I could see had a much better rapport with people. . . . When they got to a scene they were prepared to react in a certain way— as investigators. . . . There's a certain amount of mutual respect which develops for a person's ability to handle people professionally.

The implication thus far is that working relationships in the department cannot be explained in simple "black-white" terms. Indeed, we have seen that other factors, both directly and indirectly related to the organization and demands of police work, can affect the way black and white police feel about and behave toward one another. Yet even these are by no means the only explanatory variables. In the following pages we consider still another set of factors that are thought to influence relationships in the work setting.

The Job as a Basis of Solidarity

It is widely believed by social scientists that human beings are united by many factors which cut across racial lines. These may include social class, sexual identity and preference, age, individual preferences, special interests and values, and, of course, occupational affiliation and ideology. It would seem reasonable, therefore, to expect that the views of at least some policemen in this study reflect a belief in the importance of the job itself as a basis of cooperation and mutual support.

The Uniform

The police uniform, as we have seen, serves a number of important symbolic functions for both members of the department and the community they serve. For black and white cops specifically, conflict and polarization can result when these meanings differ. When they converge, however, cooperation, mutual support, and feelings of solidarity are likely to emerge which neutralize the importance of visible racial differences.

For some police officers the significance or meaning of the blue uniform lies largely in its ability to distinguish the "good guys" from the "bad." As an example,

> Once they put on the uniform there is a solidarity between the men. This is inculcated in the police academy. When a cop gets into a jam in the street he looks for another uniform. It's that simple. Whenever I find myself in a situation where either I have to take police action or I observe another cop taking police action, and it's obvious that he needs help, I see it as a cop coming to the rescue of another cop. I don't see any color line. I believe that saving his ass is more important and I'd like to believe his saving my ass is important too. The only line that is drawn in the street or that *should* be drawn is between cops and criminals.

Certain behavioral expectations are indeed attached to those who wear a police uniform. For example, as we were just told, there is a common assumption held by police that when a uniformed cop is in trouble in the street, other cops will automatically come to his assistance. This is so not only because the uniform signals a sense of common occupational identity among some officers but because it serves to bind all officers into a system of reciprocal obligations. Thus, despite a policeman's personal feelings about a colleague of a different color, one thing he can always count on is help should he find himself in trouble. One said,

> Look, if a black cop is in trouble another white cop will come to his aid and vice versa. There is a sense of brotherhood with the uniform on. . . . It's interesting, if you're walking down the street and you see a man in uniform fighting or even being hassled, you rush over to help him. You may find that he is only a special guard for some department store or something, but you rushed over because he was in uniform. You see, years ago it was rare that a civilian would strike a cop, never mind shoot at him. Now, there's more and more of that. So you become more aware, I guess, that another cop can get hurt and that cop may be you. You really don't have time to ask questions first.

Just as the police uniform is thought to signal a sense of common identity and solidarity among some policemen, from the point of view of some people in the black community, it symbolizes the enemy regardless of the person wearing it. One officer who felt that relations between black and white police have recently changed for the better, attributed this improvement to the special problems facing all uniformed policemen assigned to high-crime ghetto precincts today. He explained,

> Most blacks here are decent people who don't break the law. But there are also enemies out there. And you can't always tell them apart from the friends. The cop in areas like Harlem has to be able to count on his partner. When you're in the street there's no color. Maybe years ago there was, but not today anymore with all this violence. You have a uniform on and that's all some people see. Take a brick that's thrown through your windshield. It's not really aimed at your white partner. . . . Some of these young kids are easily brainwashed by the wrong people. They take up a cause against us. The uniform here is all they see when they throw a brick or take a shot at a radio car. So I say cops, all cops in the street, have to be more or less on guard. They have to stick together, protect one another.

The Police Role

Beyond this, there are policemen who align themselves with others, who, despite color differences, appear to identify with traditional police roles or who share a common set of goals. For instance, the manner in which a criminal suspect is treated once he is brought into the station house or squad room for questioning is one such definition that can divide policemen into opposing camps. This is indicated by one of the responses:

> There are some younger black cops who feel they are black first and cops second. I'm not saying that these guys are right or wrong, but I think that this might make for poor relations. Let me give you an example. A black officer who sees himself as a black man first is likely to get upset seeing another cop [white or black] bring in a young black kid and hook him up to the wall and later cut him loose because he has the wrong guy, and not give a shit. If he makes his feelings known there can be problems with some of the other guys. Then there's the "cop first" guy who will bring these kids in, hook

them up and not be concerned with whether they are the wrong guys. These guys get along great with most of the other cops.

According to another patrol officer, race was never considered relevant in choosing a partner. What was important was how the man felt the job of policing ought to be done.

> It's very much a matter of dealing with individual personalities. Working relationships are a matter of techniques of working. You can't operate with people whose techniques are radically different from your own no matter what color they are. . . . I've always been extremely careful to pick a partner who felt the same way I did about the job. It didn't matter so much whether he was white or black.

Above all, policemen tend to place great importance on demonstrating loyalty among themselves when they confront those perceived as the enemy. The manner in which a policeman responds to a call for assistance from another member of the service can, for instance, either strengthen his identity as a "fellow officer," or discredit it entirely. Consider, for example, the following incident that happened to a detective shortly after he was transferred to a Harlem-based squad:

> A couple of years back I remember I had a chance to prove myself, so to speak. I was new in the office and maybe some of the guys weren't quite sure where I stood. Well, one night we were out investigating what appeared at the time to be an abandoned taxi. There was no one inside the cab and the motor was running. We had had a rash of cab stick-ups at the time and we figured maybe the driver was inside this abandoned building, dead or something. One of my partners (who was white) stayed out front while I went inside the building with [my other partner] who was also white. At that time it looked as if something was up. We were on the second floor when I heard my partner outside calling for help. As it turned out the driver of the cab had come back with his friend and saw my partner looking into the cab, and they started some shit with him. I'm sure they thought he was alone. Well, we got down the stairs, and we took care of things with these two guys so to speak. We wound up locking these two dudes up for assault [on a police officer]. I guess you might say I demonstrated whose side I was on that night. From that time relations were really good. Guys who were cool to me before opened up and it's been the same ever since.

Yet, this policeman's comments suggest that different images and expectations are attached to black and to white officers who are newly assigned to a police command. Whereas it is mostly taken for granted that the white policeman's loyalties will be to his fellow officers, the black policeman may have to prove to his white colleagues that he is a cop first and a black second.

The Public as Common Enemy

The occupational world of the policeman does in fact generate a form of mutual dependence and solidarity among the men.[9] On the job most policemen feel compelled to present a united front against the criminal, especially one who may want to inflict physical harm upon them. But all policemen perceive another enemy in the street—the general public.[10] In their everyday dealings with the general public some of the policemen interviewed claimed they have found that people cannot be counted on to be fair and impartial. They accuse the public of being too quick to criticize police actions in the absence of objective, first-hand information, and too quick to register formal complaints against them. Occasionally, accompanying these charges are accusations against the department itself which seems to punish even honest mistakes made by police in their dealings with the public:

> Problems with the public, well that's another story. They can't be ironed out without some cop getting hurt. One thing I found out about the public, they can always be counted on to be unfair with police. They always seem to act without the facts. If a cop, God forbid, makes a mistake, forget it. The public pursues these mistakes to the end regardless of the color of the cop [involved]. You see the department is also at fault here. It doesn't permit honest mistakes, it punishes them. So cops naturally have to stick together.

In addition, these cops see that the public often acts through the department to get other cops in trouble. Thus, it is not only the general public that the black cop views as a potential troublemaker and threat to his security but the department as well. In this sense, then, the situation of the black policeman is perceived as being basically similar to that of the white policeman, a belief which can draw both groups together and force them to seek refuge within their own occupational milieu. Depicting a rather typical situation confronting policemen who deal with the general public, a veteran detective explained why he views the public as a potential enemy:

> It's been my experience for some time not to trust the public. They're really something else. When it comes to canvassing apartments or asking people in the street for information on a homicide, no one ever sees anything. They're all asleep. . . . Actually there were about fifty people in the street when it [a homicide] went down at 10:30 [p.m.], but when you ask, no one was out. But when an incident involves a cop shooting some civilian, every one comes forward with information, what they allegedly saw. People start to come out of the woodwork. The phones don't stop ringing. Just a while back we had an incident involving a black, off-duty cop. He was going home with a friend |in Harlem| when he was approached by four punks. One of these punks put a linoleum knife to his throat and took his money. The cop managed to get to his gun and he wound up shooting one of the punks, who died later. This all happened about four in the morning. How many people could have been in the street at four o'clock? But you want to see how many people were lined up waiting to speak to some boss about what they wanted to believe happened. If I entertained just some of their statements I would have been inclined to lock the cop up for murder. You had to hear some of the stories. You know, originally no one came forward with any statements until the word filtered back to the street that the guy who did the shooting was a cop. Then everyone came in with something to say. All I can say is Thank God the cop was 100 percent correct in the actions he took that night.

Our respondents are acutely aware of the possible dangers facing them in their everyday contacts with the public. They believe that they are dealing with, at best, an apathetic citizenry from whom they derive little or no support in crisis situations. To the extent that these men have personally had negative experiences and have come to see themselves as a beleaguered minority, they are apt to identify more with their occupational group and accept the definitions of the public expressed by their white colleagues.

Shared Values, Beliefs, and Interests

It has been argued earlier that racial factors tend to diminish in importance as policemen come to share similar definitions of their occupational role. But can shared definitions override the effects of racial differences when they involve areas external to the policeman's occupational world? Several members of the study population, obviously speaking from personal experiences, seem to feel they can. For example,

> There are guys in my team who are family men. I'm talking about black and white cops. They don't screw around after work. These guys rarely "stop off" [for a drink]. On the other hand there are some guys who do screw around and "stop off." When either of these groups of guys are together they talk and find out they have something in common—maybe their wives have something in common too. . . . Some kind of feeling develops between them. Again, I'm not saying that because a black and white cop has the same feelings about how to run their personal lives they are going to be ass-hole buddies and start getting together with their families, although, I've seen this happen too. What I'm saying essentially is that there's something they can share together, something they have in common.

Shared interests that are totally unrelated to the job are also thought to constitute a crucial factor in breaking down the social barriers between white and black policemen. Discovering they have interests in common, policemen may begin to interact more frequently. This in turn can result in the strengthening of friendships between the men. An officer, who, for example, has an interest in a particular sport may seek others out who share his interest, believing perhaps that if they are attracted to the same things they must be similar to himself in other important ways as well.[11] As one policeman put it,

> You kid around a lot too, bullshit a lot. You get the wives together. . . . You find you have other interests in common. Before you know it you're not just tolerating Clyde, who's black, but you're going out to play golf with him.

Besides sports, an outside interest that seems to have softened the effect of racial differences on the job today, by providing both an intellectual and a social framework for people to meet on common ground, is college education.

Education naturally changes your opinions. It brings guys together. They go to school together, meet in classes. They discuss the instructor; they get together to study for exams. This is especially true for cops who are serious about their education. They may feel that this is a dead-end job and they find they have something in common that's more important than their color, which, by the way, becomes less visible with time.

Another is one's marital situation. Divorced or separated policemen who work together, for example, often find that their "particular" situation can become a basis for mutual support and lasting friendships, despite racial differences. A detective emphasized this point:

> I've seen a lot of guys in my office get real close, I mean go places together (after work). There's two that I know of who just went through divorces. They both really love their kids and their wives are bitches about letting them see them (the kids). I overheard them talking about their problem one night so I walked over to stick my two cents in. So both of them politely got up after a while so as not to embarrass me and they go out on a case. I'm married and I threw a little dig in about it being their fault if they cared for their kids so much. I guess they didn't want to hear my shit, so they left. Anyway, these two are pretty close now.

Two respondents went even further than others in this group in rejecting the notion that working relationships can always be explained within a racial context. For both of these men, feelings of attachment or rejection toward fellow officers were *individual* matters that had little or nothing to do with skin color. They said,

> I personally feel that relationships are individual matters. I get along pretty well with most of the guys in my squad and I definitely don't judge people by their color. There are some guys who I feel are stinkers (both white and black) and I'm sure they feel the same way about me. But I have a feeling that they view me this way because of personality reasons.

> To start with I've never experienced any real problems. That's because relationships are based on individual personalities. Either I like a guy or I don't. If I like him, I'll work with him whether he's white

or black—it doesn't matter. If I don't like him, I don't like him and I won't work with him. . . . There's good and bad relationships in every precinct, but mostly they're on an individual basis. This is because of the human factor. Some guys just can't stand each other's guts, and it doesn't always have to do with color. So there's really no general answer to your question.

However, when pressed into explaining what they meant by "personality differences" both of the officers quoted above referred alternately to job values and to personal interests and beliefs. The second officer, for example, put it this way:

Well, I'm not sure how important these are but I think that when you work with different guys you find out a lot about them. . . . Well, you might find out that a guy feels the same as you about junkies, numbers guys, drug dealers. You may not talk about these feelings but you find out anyway while you're working with him. So you find that you have this in common. . . . One (white) guy I hit it off with was telling me one day about barracuda fishing in the Islands. Well, I'm a nut about fishing. . . . So we both decided to take a trip that spring to (the Islands) and do some (barracuda) fishing. That's how our friendship got started—a fishing trip. Today we're the best of friends.

As many of the observations and personal accounts in this section tell us, the nature of human relations in general and specifically the forming of attachments and friendships across racial lines is indeed a complex process that depends not only upon racial considerations but upon a variety of structural, situational, and personal factors operating both within and outside the work setting. Many of the men speak, for example, of improvement in the way white and black cops get along on the job today. Yet, they are in general agreement that, except for the direct attempt on the part of Commissioner Murphy to institute a program of interracial workshops at the command level, the other factors that drew the two groups closer together in the 1970s all evolved independently of any direct effort or involvement on the part of the department to promote reform in this area. And, as we have seen, even these events themselves (e.g., the assaults on black and white patrol teams) did not succeed in eliminating conflict between all black and white cops. Lingering beliefs about the innate inferiority of black people in general coupled with "traditionally accepted" ways of dealing with racial minorities, sustained in some precincts and among some patrol officers a visible separation of the groups along racial lines. This division was intensified at times by reciprocally formed negative images of white cops held by some of the younger, more militant blacks who got caught up in the black movement in the late 1960s and early 1970s and who clearly were no longer going to tolerate racial abuses.

Perhaps the clearest example of how structural elements influence racial patterns can be found in our examination of the differences between work levels or assignments. For example, on the patrol level internal factors such as work demands and physical environment operate to produce the potential for conflict between white and black cops. Yet these same two elements operating on the detective level clearly serve to minimize the importance of race as a factor defining group boundaries. If anything, it can be said that such elements lessen the likelihood of intergroup hostility and conflict. According to the testimony of the men quoted in this chapter, the quality of intergroup relations on the job is also a function of the extent to which white and black cops, regardless of where they are assigned, come to share or agree upon common definitions of their work role. The logic advanced here is that role (or goal) concurrence among members assigned to a particular unit or command leads invariably to greater interaction between the officers, reduced interracial conflict, and eventually to the mutual discovery that they share other common characteristics between them. And it is this sequence of events, we are told, that accounts for the more harmonious intergroup relations that are evident in most, if not all, of the city's detective squads and specialty units.

In Part III of this book we continue our examination of the black policeman's working world, this time focusing on those factors that are thought to have shaped his views of, role in, and relationship with the larger black community and its various subgroups. At the center of this discussion is the critical issue of relations between the police and minorities and the need for *all* police to establish and strengthen ties with disaffected urban groups and individuals.

NOTES

1. See Peter W. Greenwood et al., *The Criminal Investigation Process, Volume 111: Operations and Analysis,* (Santa Monica, Cal.: The Rand Corporation, October 1975), p. 8.

2. The department, however, still maintained precinct detective squads which handled criminal investigations that were not referred directly to specialized units after preliminary investigation by members of the patrol services.

3. See V.A. Leonard and Harry W. More, *Police Organization and Management, 3rd ed.* (New York: The Foundation Press, 1971), p. 266.

4. This statement is based in large part upon my own observations and experiences as a precinct squad detective in Harlem prior to specialization in 1972.

5. Although arrests by detectives sometimes were the result of case investigation, in busy high-crime precincts, the bulk of arrests made by detectives were initiated by the detectives themselves. In the Harlem-based squad to which I was assigned prior to 1972, these arrests involved, for the most part, violations of drug and drug-related laws including loitering for the purposes of using drugs.

6. Interestingly, the "grade system" for detective advancement was reinstated on a limited basis in 1977, approximately two years before the detective bureau reverted to the "precinct-squad" concept.

7. Criminal cases are typically cleared when an offender has been identified, taken into custody and formally charged with a crime. However, cases are occasionally cleared when circumstances beyond the control of the investigator prevent the lodging of formal charges such as the death of the offender, the refusal of the prosecuting authority (i.e., the assistant district attorney) to extradite a known felon from another jurisdiction or to proceed with a formal complaint against a known offender.

8. See Peter N. Greenwood et al., op. cit., p. 8.

9. See, for example, the comments made in this connection by Nicholas Alex, *Black in Blue: A Study of the Negro Policeman* (New York: Appleton-Century-Crofts, 1969), pp. 86–89.

10. See David H. Bayley and Harold Mendelsohn, *Minorities and the Police: Confrontation in America* (New York: The Free Press, 1968), pp. 49, 55.

11. This argument is drawn in part from personal observations and interviews, in part, from George Homan's description and explanation of "social system" as found in Joseph A. Litterer's, *Organizations: Structure and Behavior, 2nd ed.* (New York: Wiley, 1969), volume 1, pp. 167–188.

THE POLICE
AND THE
BLACK COMMUNITY

Cooperation is piss-poor, and the reason is that people here don't
trust cops.

THE quality of the relationship between the police and the members of any particular community has essentially depended upon the extent to which cultural values and beliefs held by the two groups have tended to converge. The problem in many urban centers, and especially within racial ghettos, is that there has existed a sharp divergence between the values shared by police and those held by the community, and it is this discrepancy that in recent years has led to increasing conflict and open confrontation between the two. Conflicting values, however, are not the only determinants of relations between police and citizens. Face-to-face interaction also constitutes an important basis for any relationship. Individual experiences, it has been argued, often tend to become articulated into fixed images or stereotypes which can, in time, condition the way all police and citizens respond to each other. At the same time individual distinctions tend to become obscured as members of each group begin to alter their perceptions and respond to one another solely on the basis of the stereotypes they themselves have created. In understanding the nature of relations between the police and citizens in a particular community, therefore, one must consider not only the effect of conflicting value systems but also the effect of reciprocal images that have been formed over the years through repeated contacts between members of each group.

Part Three looks at a number of these social variables and processes in its discussion of the police involvement in the black community. A number of political and legal factors that are believed to have shaped police-black relations over the years are also examined. In Chapter 6, "Images, Attitudes, and Expectations," several of the traditional causes of conflict between blacks and police are identified. Next, the impact of adding greater numbers of blacks to the police ranks during the early seventies and assigning them to racially sensitive areas of the city is considered. Specific views are then presented on the issues of "integrated police precincts" and "working teams," views which ought to be considered before attempts are made to reduce conflict between police and members of the black community as well as among police themselves. Finally, we consider the adequacy of department programs aimed at reducing tensions between police and blacks and promoting cooperation between the groups.

In the final chapter, "The Police Role in the Ghetto" we address the various meanings the police function seem to hold for black officers as well as the way the police function is perceived by members of the black community. Particular attention is given to those problems black (and white) police routinely confront in attempting to reconcile their work role with the expectations and demands black citizens attach to the policeman's job in today's society. The focus then shifts to police relations with two subgroups occupying nearly identical positions in the black community: *black youth* and *black offenders*. Here we take a careful look at the problems generated by the opposite and extreme positions held by these groups, on the one hand, and by black police on the other.

Chapter Six

Images, Attitudes, and Expectations

You can get hurt here just by talking to the police.

As members of a public service organization interacting on a frequent and continuous basis with their clientele, police have become highly sensitized to the attitudes of people living within their precinct and can readily distinguish favorable from unfavorable ones. But occupational affiliation does more than just alert police to particular community attitudes; it also sensitizes them to the conditions which give rise to these attitudes. So it is with our police respondents. When asked to appraise the attitudes blacks have traditionally held toward the police, a clear, but decidedly unfavorable picture emerged. Virtually all of the men conceded that major segments of the black population in New York City, if not whole communities, held the police in contempt. They attributed this to the way blacks have generally been treated by the police over the years. White police (and to a lesser extent black officers) were accused by our respondents of overstepping the boundaries of their legal authority and engaging in practices which favored and protected the interests of dominant white society. Not surprisingly, the most frequent charge leveled against white policemen in their dealings with blacks was brutality. Our men allege that acts of physical and psychological abuse directed against black people in the past were commonplace in all of the city's precincts and contributed greatly to the hostility and distrust that many blacks feel toward the police today. One officer who grew up outside the ghetto had this to say:

> Police were hated in the past. There was a lot of physical abuse. . . . People weren't aware of their rights and were needlessly abused by the officers. . . . Blacks were treated worse than animals in the street. This I've heard from some of the older blacks.

A veteran detective who grew up in the area he now works in described past conditions in the ghetto:

> Police definitely presented a very negative image in the past which I believe has carried over today. Not among all blacks, but enough. The image I'm talking about was one of brutality. . . . In the fifties and sixties you saw cops beating blacks over the head with little provocation.

License to exercise authority over people, often to the point of physical abuses, was at one time (and no doubt still is) a means of job satisfaction among some policemen. In some instances it may even constitute an important reason for joining the department. Yet, many of our men view the problem of brutality strictly within a racial context, asserting that its causes can be traced directly to unfavorable images of blacks passed on to white police by racist parents and friends.

> A lot of white cops I knew grew up despising blacks because that was what they were taught at home. They looked at black people as scummers. They treated them like shit in the street because they were black, no other reason. They saw a black man in the street and wondered what kind of shit he was into.

Moreover, we are told, in past years no systematic effort was ever made by the police department to dispel the image of the "black as deviant" held by most white officers. Thus, it was possible for decent, law-abiding blacks to be considered to be the same as the criminal element and treated accordingly. An officer explained that

> There is no question that police harassed blacks in the past. They didn't understand black people and there was no attempt to teach

police about the different ways of blacks. You had white cops on this job when I first came on in the fifties who treated every black the same no matter who he was—the typical shithead as well as the law-abiding guy. They were all put in the same pot. There are plenty of black people who still feel uncomfortable around police because of this. Their attitudes are not positive. This results from memories of the past.

Criticism of white police focused not only on patterns of physical brutality and harassment but on other aspects of police interaction with black citizens. White cops, for example, were accused of adhering to a double set of standards in the way routine police services were provided in lower-class, black communities. This situation, we are reminded, figured prominently in shaping the attitudes of blacks toward *all* police today:

Police were not well liked in the black community and that's putting it mildly. Police treated blacks differently than they treated whites. They were treated, I guess you might say, as inferior people who were born that way. What do I mean by that? Well, if a black had a problem or something he was not taken seriously by the white officer. His problem was definitely not given the same consideration as if he were white. For example, before I came on this job I saw instances in which white policemen just drove by people who were injured or needed some sort of help. Also, people who were robbed or assaulted, police just seemed to treat these cases as being less important. People here today remember, some of them anyway. They have very little use for police because of it, and that goes for black police too.

As expected, many also pointed to extreme differences in police enforcement practices experienced by ghetto blacks and more well-to-do whites. Ghetto blacks, they claim, were routinely singled out, arrested, and charged with violations that would have been ignored in white communities. The following comment from a veteran police officer assigned to a precinct in Harlem is typical:

Police were despised. . . . I've worked in both black and white neighborhoods and I can say as a point of fact that years ago black people were arrested and charged with crimes that most whites would have been let go for. Cops—both white and black in those days— did things in black communities that they never would have gotten

away with in white neighborhoods. . . . Black people were aware
of this and there are still some who remember and hate the police
for it.

Widespread police abuse of authority, differential enforcement
of the law, and provision of police services were only some of the
complaints blacks expressed against the police that were to find
expression in the riots and general unrest that swept through our
nation's cities in the mid-sixties. Ghetto blacks were not only fed
up with being treated as inferior, second-class citizens by the police, they were also deeply angered and resentful of the failure of
government to act upon these and other social unjustices in a deliberate and meaningful way.

As the decade of the seventies approached, the clash between the
police and blacks began to take on a new seriousness. The spon-
taneous disorders that had characterized the national scene just a
few years earlier, offered, perhaps, the clearest evidence of just how
great was the division and conflict between police and the black
community they served. The feeling of complacency that had for
so long characterized police response to this growing friction was
finally being called into question, and police officials in departments across the country began searching for ways to bring the
two groups closer together. In the remainder of this chapter we
consider the perceived effect of two such efforts on the quality of
police-black relations in New York City today.

The Influx of Black Police

Over time, white police have come to share a set of occupational
values and beliefs about minority groups that set them apart from
significant segments of the black community. The recruitment of
greater numbers of blacks into the lower ranks in the early 1970s
was part of a larger effort designed to narrow this distance. The
assumption was that young black policemen by virtue of their cultural ties to other blacks would bring different conceptions of the
police role into ghetto neighborhoods, creating in the process a
broader base of community support for the department.[1] Although such assumptions reflected progressive thinking at the time,

it was not altogether clear how ghetto residents actually felt about being policed by members of their own race. Since white police were viewed by many blacks in the ghetto as the "enemy," it was quite possible that the newly hired black officers would be viewed in much the same way.

There were other problems too. Many black policemen resented department efforts to limit their assignments to high-crime, slum precincts. They felt (and perhaps rightly so) that such practices were discriminatory to the black officer who, by virtue of his skin color and presumed affinity to the black community, must work under more trying, hazardous conditions. The obvious question, then, is, would a black policeman, or for that matter any officer, who viewed such assignment practices as discriminatory or unfair, perform at a level equivalent to an officer who was not especially troubled by having to work in these areas? In the pages that follow we consider some of the possible implications of assigning black police predominantly to precincts situated in crime-ridden, black communities. We are especially concerned with the reactions of policemen to the political motivation of the department, as expressed in such assignment practices, and their perception of how they have been received by members of the black community while occupying positions of authority and control.

Assignments in Black Precincts

When asked what they thought about the practice of assigning black police to black precincts, contrary to the feelings of many black police, a number of the 46 men agreed that it was "good policy," and the department was entirely justified in implementing such a practice. Black policemen, they argued, know intuitively how to approach other blacks without arousing unnecessary fear or anxiety and take a greater interest in community problems than do white policemen. Unlike the average white officer, the black policeman generally stops and talks to people in the street. While on patrol he makes himself visible and available should his services be required. Consequently, we are told, he has gained the respect and trust of most black citizens who come to him with their grievances, look to him for assistance and support in times of trouble, and rely generally on his advice when problems arise. A detective enlarged on this:

> The people see the way the officer arrives on the scene or handles a routine call for assistance, speaking instead of shoving or pushing—the treatment of people the way an officer might want his family treated. They just appreciate a black officer coming on the scene where there is no fear involved.

Other policemen offered similar reasons for supporting restricted assignment practices.

> I believe black cops should be assigned to black areas. You know the culture, background of the people. You can service them better because of this. Personally, I don't believe it's discriminatory. I don't mind working here. The black community wants the black officer here.

> It's practical, especially as a rookie or a young black patrolman, because he can identify with the people. Black policemen will be less inclined to insult and abuse the black community member and more apt to understand the problems facing black people because of his ethnic affiliation.

One respondent suggested that the presence of additional black policemen in areas such as Harlem has finally begun to blunt the edge of bitterness blacks once felt toward the department by effectively neutralizing the discriminatory behavior of prejudiced white policemen. He claimed that

> By assigning the new black cops to black precincts, the department is helping to remove the stereotype of the police in many ways. Sometimes white cops act uncool and unconsciously racist. The presence of more black police has helped to correct the situation. If a black cop is there in the street white cops are unlikely to treat blacks—especially black women—the way they used to.

Another policeman who acknowledged the importance of the above factors in shaping the black citizens' attitudes toward black police, suggested a further dimension. He felt that being a black policeman in an area such as Harlem entailed more than just working there eight hours a day. It meant becoming involved with people in the community after the tour of duty. Off-duty socializing, he concluded, not only went a long way toward drawing the community closer to individual officers, but it also served to promote a sense of rapport between blacks and the department. A portion of his response was as follows:

> As I said, after my eight hours I'm not rushing to go anywhere. It's not eight hours and then I'm hauling ass to go home every day. I stick around sometimes. I feel that this is important. A lot of black cops stick around and socialize after work.

Another area that might be explored if one is to understand and appreciate why some blacks seem to prefer to deal with black policemen has to do with perceptions and expectations of public behavior in black, slum communities. It has been shown in a number of studies that police are likely to be more apprehensive and alert to signs of danger in high-crime, ghetto precincts than in other areas of the city.[2] Both individually and collectively they tend to associate these areas with an abnormally high incidence of violent crime, especially violence directed against the police.[3] Black citizens and particularly black youths living in slum communities serve as constant reminders of the potentially dangerous and explosive nature of even "routine" encounters between the police and citizens.

Judging from some of the comments we received, it appears that white policemen are considerably more sensitive than black officers to the possibility of harm coming their way in ghetto communities. But this is hardly surprising. Recruited as they traditionally have been from middle- and working-class backgrounds, white policemen on the whole are not familiar with lower-class culture. This, in turn, inhibits their ability to distinguish between behavior which by ghetto standards is normal, and essentially harmless, and behavior which is unusual and potentially dangerous. Moreover, white policemen as a group are subjected more than their black colleagues to negative definitions of the work situation in ghetto communities—assessments that can and frequently do override the effects of everyday, routine encounters with black citizens on the street.

Although most of our respondents would probably concede that there is less risk of encountering violence in more affluent areas of the city, many agree that white policemen tend to exaggerate the prevalence of danger in slum communities and because of that take steps to avoid what they regard as "unnecessary contact" with blacks. As an example of one response to this,

> I don't know all the reasons why a lot of white cops are more afraid of working in black precincts, but they are. I suppose a lot has to do with all the killings and shootings here. But I think that they exaggerate the danger here. Compared to all the violence that happens, only a few cops have been seriously hurt. . . . This fear personally prevents many of these guys from doing their job properly. If a cop is afraid, he's going to get off the street as much as possible, or he's at least not going to have that much to do with the people in the community. The people here just don't see the white cop who's on a foot post and even when he's riding, he hardly ever stops and raps with them.

To the extent that the black perceives this avoidance as deliberate and indicative of the white man's feelings toward blacks in general, he is apt to respond by expressing in various ways his preference for black police.

Some white policemen may be unhappy working in black precincts for other reasons too. They may, for instance, view their assignment as a form of punishment, an expression of the department's displeasure with their performance. If this impression leads to deliberate avoidance on the part of the white officer the effect on the community can be the same. One said,

> They feel that the white officer does not want to work here. They feel that he looks at this assignment as though it were some form of punishment and because of this, he cannot or does not want to deal squarely with the situation he confronts. They see this and they respond to it by turning to the black policeman.

While basically in agreement with the practice of assigning blacks to precincts located in black communities, a few of the men nevertheless expressed concern over what they felt was an "unwritten" department policy which makes it almost impossible for black cops to transfer to white areas of the city. Assignment policies, they argued, should be sufficiently flexible to accommodate the diverse and changing needs of individual police officers; members of the department, regardless of color, should not be required to spend all of their time in any one particular precinct or district. One officer who felt this way justified his preference for "assignment rotation" on the grounds that occasional movement between precincts and districts resulted in a well-rounded, more effective employee:

> It's not discriminatory, but don't keep him there for 20 years if he doesn't want it. He should be allowed to transfer to other precincts if that is what he wants, and he should be allowed to experience different places and different people and round out his overall experience. You know this goes for all policemen, not just the black cop. I feel that a more rounded officer is a more effective officer, no matter where he works.

Another policeman complained about what he felt was a long-standing department policy of sending additional black officers into ghetto precincts during times of civil disorder and then to remove them when the situation returned to normal. What disturbed this policeman most was the feeling that he and other black officers in the city were being "used" by the department to quell racial disturbances that they did not in fact start or contribute to in any way. He stated,

> If you ask the average black officer where he wants to work, he will usually say that he prefers black areas. I feel that this is generally a good policy for many reasons. . . . But I would resent being sent into an area because there is some racial flareup. I don't think it's fair to send minority policemen into minority areas during crisis situations, for example, the Mosque incident. Why send me to put out flames that someone else started. Other guys feel the same way, ask them.[4]

Whatever individual reservations these men might have toward concentrating black cops in black precincts, their attitudes toward such a practice remain, on the whole, supportive.

A second and somewhat smaller group of policemen expressed uncertainty over the practice of systematically assigning black officers to black precincts. Their comments reflect acceptance of the practice on the grounds that the black community benefits by having black officers stationed there and, at the same time, rejection of the arrangement because it is patently unjust to those policemen involved. For example,

> Anytime you assign a man strictly on his race, it's discriminatory. If you ask me whether it's bad policy from the point of view of the black community, the answer is no. It's good for the community in many ways.

> I don't think it's fair to the men. Department-wise, I feel that everybody should be assigned equally. You shouldn't have to work in an area because you are black and not be able to work in Forest Hills or Bayside. It's more dangerous working in black areas; therefore, it's not fair. There is a higher percentage of being hurt in a black area. . . . But for public relations, I think it's good, in the same sense that I think an Italian would work better in an Italian neighborhood. You know the people and you understand them better. You speak their language and you eat their food.

A policeman with a little under seven years of service with the department expressed his uncertainty in the following way:

> Putting black cops in minority precincts may be discriminatory to the cop, but it may also be viewed as a practical administrative strategy. Why? Because there is less community resistance and static putting a black officer in a black area than putting a white officer there or putting a black officer in a white area.

A third group of policemen rejected the policy, based on the assumption that effective police service is related to skin color. For example,

> I don't believe there is any difference if you're a cop in uniform. People will come to you with their problems no matter what color you are. Most people I find don't differentiate between the black and white cop when they have a problem or need some type of help.

When asked why he objected to the practice of confining black police to black precincts, a detective with over 12 years of experience responded,

> I believe that the administration thinks black officers are more effective with black citizens. I don't feel that this is so. I believe that any white officer can be just as effective as any black cop. I've worked with white patrolmen and white detectives who have been just as effective as any black officer. I always found that better detectives employed the "humane approach" regardless of color. Many blacks have commented to me that attitude is important rather than color.

Both of the officers, in responding to the question, missed the crux of the issue. There is no question, for example, that people in trouble will invariably welcome any officer who happens on the scene. But the fact remains that serious problems (e.g., someone attempting to break into an apartment) are experienced far less frequently than either routine problems or service calls. The question, then, is whether white policemen are, on the whole, not as capable to deal with the routine, day-to-day problems confronting blacks living in the ghetto. If they are not, as some commentators point out, then people living in these areas are indeed getting shortchanged when ghetto precincts are staffed mostly with whites.

Opposition to restricted assignments was also motivated by the belief that there is disproportionately more work to be done in ghetto communities. Some of our policemen complain, for example, of being "shortchanged" themselves by having to work in busy precincts while receiving the same pay as cops assigned to quieter sections of the city. They feel that

> I don't think you should assign mostly black officers to black areas when you have other officers who are getting the same pay.

Equally resentful of segregated assignment practices, but for different reasons, a detective responded,

> It's discriminatory. It's simply unfair to the black officer who is assigned here strictly on the basis of his color. Supposedly, you can deal better with the people in the community. However, I don't go along with that. Cops should be trained to handle any situation in any neighborhood. They feel that you have to saturate black areas with black cops. Well, white officers should be trained properly to work here. Besides, I feel cheated somehow if I have to lock up blacks all the time.

One policeman took the position that in a society of rapid change such as ours, black cops should be assigned to precincts throughout the city on a more-or-less random basis. To do otherwise, he maintained, makes the task of adjusting more difficult for black cops who eventually find themselves working in predominantly white precincts and for whites who may never have confronted blacks in positions of authority.

There are precincts that have only three black officers. The ———— precinct has only five black officers. When you get out of a car in the ———— precinct to give a summons to someone, the person you are giving the summons to can't believe he is getting one from a black officer. He has never seen black officers before. So just because the officer is black, he should not be assigned to black areas in my opinion.

Here the objection to restricted assignment practices is based less upon the feelings that ghetto precincts present greater personal dangers to the officers or that they are more physically demanding than on the possible psychological costs to the black officer's identity in the larger society. That is, the longer the black officer is denied opportunities to work in white areas of the city during a presumably progressive era, the greater will be his feelings of status frustration and sense of marginality.

A few respondents challenged the police department's assignment of black cops to black precincts on the theory that they had an affinity toward the people in the community. These men spoke of the fear and suspicion even their presence evoked among blacks and of the general disrepute into which black police fell.[5] One Harlem-based officer remarked that some blacks in his precinct wanted nothing to do with the black officer, that they saw him as an enforcer of the "white man's" laws, hired and assigned to work in the ghetto in order to keep blacks "in their place." This same officer also felt that some of the negativism directed toward black police resulted from conflicting definitions of the black officer's professional role in the community. Some blacks, he went on to explain, view the black policeman as a "newcomer" to the job and thus not entitled to full recognition and acceptance. The black officer, of course, rejects this definition.

Some blacks also are unaccustomed to playing subservient roles to other blacks and that includes the black cop. They resent his authority over them and they refuse to have anything to do with him. This leads to trouble on both sides.

Related to the feeling that he holds only "newcomer" status is the question of the black officer's authority to regulate conduct in the black community. Some feel that this is not automatically built into the black officer's official position, but must be earned over time.

> To me it's amazing. There are white cops in this precinct who deserve anything but respect. They are holy terrors in the street. But they are white and the people generally respect their authority. . . . It's as if I have to prove myself, prove that I'm a cop too and have the same authority as the white cop.

One detective brought up the often-belabored point that some ghetto blacks feel that the black cop sold them out when he joined the department. Especially despised by these members of the black community, according to this officer, is the black policeman who joins extremist groups (e.g., Black Panthers) under the guise of kinship and loyalty to the black cause, but who is secretly working for the department in an undercover position. He stated that

> The black cop is frequently held in contempt particularly in the role of undercover officer. The community simply feels that one of them has violated the trust of their ethnic group by exposing ethnic secrets.

In addition to being accused of "selling out," the black policeman is susceptible to the charge that he is an "Uncle Tom." One officer explained what he meant by the term:

> Some blacks don't want to deal with the black cop because they see him as an Uncle Tom, a person who stands by while the white cop abuses and shows disrespect toward other blacks.

A detective, in explaining black negativism toward black police, added an interesting note to the discussion. He stated, in effect, that because black police are aware of the real needs and problems of lower-class blacks, they make discriminations which tend to discourage certain groups of people from raising questions or making complaints that, in their eyes, do not constitute "real" police matters.[6] This, he felt, has alienated some blacks from the black officer and encouraged them to turn to white policemen in times of distress.

> The black cop is more aware, he more fully understands the reasons why some blacks make complaints to the police. A lot of these complaints are strictly bullshit. They just take up a lot of time. Most detectives that I know feel that they have more important things to do than stand around entertaining bullshit stories, or talking to so-called complainants simply because they feel they have something to say and want to say it to a detective.

This officer then pointed out that blacks who drink to excess sometimes fall into this category:

> If a drunk staggers up to a black cop he is often heard to say, "Get the fuck out of here." The white cop may listen; his patience may be longer. The black waits until he gets drunk to make a complaint and then he comes up to the officer and hobbles away saying nothing. They just come up to bug you. . . . This may explain why some blacks turn to the white cop. He may be more *outwardly* sympathetic.

The negativism directed toward the black policeman may derive from other, but somewhat related, sources as well. There is a feeling among a few of the men, for example, that the recent economic gains made by all New York City police during the Lindsay administration provided black cops with the means for a more affluent style of life. Ironically, they add, these same gains also served to weaken the black officers' attachment to the ghetto and its special problems. A veteran officer explains,

> I would have to say that at one time, blacks probably preferred to deal with black officers. There were stronger bonds between them. The black officer accepted other lower-class blacks, naturally, because he was one of them. This is not always the case now. Many

blacks look at the black officer with suspicion. This is because, like other minority groups who have advanced themselves in our society, he no longer cares about residents in Harlem or their conditions. He only comes here to work. It basically becomes just a job for him.

The notion that in the process of moving up the social ladder black police have come increasingly to disassociate themselves from everything that once symbolized their identification with the ghetto and its people may not be mere conjecture on the part of these officers. Reference group theorists, following the lead of Robert K. Merton and others, have pointed out that socially mobile blacks do in fact tend to assume the value orientations and aspirations of white middle and upper class groups. In one important study of ethnic mobility, for instance, the researchers found that high-status black positions were not only associated with acceptance of white attitudes but with *weak* involvement in racial matters and *weak* identification with the black community.[7]

A few respondents appeared more circumspect in their explanations, holding both their brother officers and members of the community responsible for the persistence of antiblack police sentiment. One policeman, who at first took some of his colleagues to task for their insensitivity toward lower-class, ghetto blacks, then turned on the larger black community in an apparent attempt to balance the blame. He said,

> The public is mixed up. They want protection but they complain when some of these characters get their tail kicked. They want homicides solved but they don't want the police around doing any questioning.

This officer went on to state that even the increased hiring of black cops and their subsequent assignment to ghetto precincts has failed to alter the mood of most blacks toward the department significantly.

> They want black representation in the community. They ask for more black cops and then they accuse these officers of being traitors. With feelings such as these, it's not surprising to find that the overall attitude of blacks hasn't really changed that much.

There is, in addition, a feeling shared by a few of the men that rejection of black policemen is linked to the negative symbols attached to the police uniform, rather than to the black police themselves. Implicit in this argument is the notion that some members of the black community see only the uniform and the interests it is presumed to represent; obscured in the process are both individual and group distinctions.

> You figure he's in uniform, he's a police officer whether he's white or black. This is the way many blacks view the policeman. As I said before, a pig is a pig, whether he's white or black.

> I would have to admit that a lot of blacks don't care for uniformed police of either color. They have as little to do with us as possible, except, of course, when they are in trouble, when someone's knocking down their door.

However, another policeman offered a qualification to this view. He argued that one must be careful about making accusations against any one group of people since negativism toward the police may not be uniformly held throughout the black community.

> The way I see it most middle-class blacks look down on the black officer as do upper-class whites to the white officer. But they respect his authority and accept his services willingly. Lower-class blacks barely tolerate the black officer or any officer for that matter. The only time these people care, I mean really care, is when someone is behind them with a hatchet.

As the accounts in this section suggest, not all policemen support the position that precincts located in high-crime, black communities should be staffed mostly with black police. In fact, a number of convincing arguments were offered to justify a position against just such assignment practices. Perhaps the most valid argument has to do with the actual nature of police work in ghetto communities. One can hardly dispute the claim, for example, that areas such as Harlem and Bedford-Stuyvesant do present greater personal dangers to the men than more advantaged sections of the city, or that police work in ghetto precincts entails greater personal stress being placed on the officer as a result of the type and frequency of calls for service from the public. It would seem then that the argument calling for more flexible assignment policies is a legitimate one at least from the point of view of those officers who find themselves locked into hazardous precincts indefinitely.

There is, moreover, the problem of the black or white police-man who, for any number of other reasons, is bothered by having to work exclusively in crime-ridden, slum communities. To keep this officer in such an area because it seems politically advanta-geous may, in the long run, be counterproductive to the interests of the department since under such conditions the officer is apt to perform his duties in a less than enthusiastic manner.

How then should police be selected and assigned to precincts populated largely by ghetto blacks? What qualifications (racial or otherwise) ought to be considered in choosing an officer for as-signment to these areas? And finally, how might police best be de-ployed once assigned to a ghetto precinct so that friction between the police and blacks is kept at a minimum? In the pages that im-mediately follow these questions are considered with the idea of developing strategies that would promote more cooperative rela-tions between police and racial minorities.

Selected Qualifications for Assignment to Black Precincts

Despite recent efforts to hire larger numbers of black cops, it is doubtful that the racial makeup of the department will reflect the city's black population within the next few years.[8] What this means, in effect, is that communities, such as Harlem, will continue to be policed and serviced by a mixed or even a predominantly white force. With this in mind, the respondents were asked to identify particular qualifications or characteristics that police officers should have who are assigned to ghetto precincts.

Surprisingly, the largest number of policemen—many of whom had earlier expressed support for a policy of segregated assign-ments—felt that ghetto precincts would be best served in the long run if factors other than, or in addition to, race were considered in assigning police to these areas. Many of these men indicated a strong preference for police officers who had a basic understanding and acceptance of ghetto culture, who were flexible in their approach toward racial minorities and who, above all, expressed a desire to work in the ghetto. As one policeman remarked,

> If I were the C.O., I would personally interview the men I intended to have in my command. I would want those officers who indicated to me that they were interested in working in black communities.

Another qualification thought by many of our respondents necessary to assure the success of the police in ghetto communities is a college background. The following replies are typical:

> I think I would be most interested in their background, you know, their educational experience. I feel that the more educated men are the most understanding men, regardless of color. These men have more understanding of the problems facing the black community. And my questions to them would involve community problems and how they felt about them. So I wouldn't say that it would be strictly a black or white issue.

> Ask for and demand the best officer possible. Only those officers who volunteered. . . . How much formal education does he have? I would choose the guy with the most education. I would look at his educational background. If he had a college degree, I would definitely consider him over another cop who didn't have any college.

Because of the frequency with which this particular qualification was mentioned, it would seem a fair assumption that black police, on the whole, perceive a rather strong connection between higher academic training and superior police performance in ghetto communities. Although we did not inquire more deeply into the reasons for this supposed relationship, it is strongly suspected that black policemen who consistently reported higher education as being of central importance in the provision of quality police services may have had some direct contact with officers who attended college. Perhaps first-hand contact with these men at the work level has allowed them to draw distinctions between police students and other members of the department whose educational background was more limited.

A few policemen, while acknowledging the advantage of a college education, nevertheless felt that assignments to ghetto precincts should be based primarily on compatibility with members of the community, as has been discussed earlier. For these men, compatibility had more to do with having been raised under conditions similar to those found in slum communities today than with either racial similarity to the clientele being served or to years of formal education. One policeman put it this way:

> I would choose officers who understood the nature of minority people. And this would have to be someone who grew up in a lower-class neighborhood, whether he's white or black. This person went through it already. He's experienced what most blacks are experiencing now. He would best understand the problems of black people. Hopefully, he would treat them the way he wanted to be treated when he was growing up. Of course, education is important, too. I personally believe that it instills a sense of feeling and understanding in some officers in these areas. If I had to choose, though, between two officers, one who had some college and one who was born and raised in a ghetto neighborhood, I would choose, I think, the guy who came from a lower-class area, all other things being the same, of course.

In addition to such criteria as desire to work in a ghetto community, college education, and compatibility with the community, other characteristics thought to be related to superior police performance had to do with individual personality traits themselves. The following list represents, in decreasing order, the frequency with which these traits were cited. (In a few instances the men mentioned as many as four items; most, however, mentioned only one or two):

Understanding of and sympathetic toward minority people
Not short-tempered or overly excitable
Not afraid of blacks
Possessing common sense and good judgment
Open-minded
Capable of listening
Not prone to labeling people
Fair-minded
Capable of anticipating trouble
Knowledgeable about job
Honest about feelings

While most of the characteristics are easy to comprehend, as they were expressed, a few are not. Thus, the true definition of some traits require some clarification:

Not prone to labeling people: not going around with "those people" attitudes.

Understanding of and sympathetic toward minority people: receptive to peoples' wants and attitudes and questions, understanding ethnic backgrounds and customs of people you are working with. Can't go around laughing at people and the way they behave.

Honest about feelings: an "honest" person. I would rather work with an honest person even if I knew that he didn't like blacks. Just don't pretend that you do and then curse them out behind my back.

In contrast, a small minority of (younger) policemen did express the feeling that ghetto communities would be best served and tensions greatly reduced if precincts situated in these areas were staffed mostly with black officers. Not surprisingly, the arguments advanced by these men were consistent with views expressed earlier. Basically, they felt that the average black policeman was more attuned to the subtleties of ghetto culture, more sensitive to the problems facing black people, more interested in promoting genuine cooperative relationships, and more dedicated to the professional ideals of the job as they relate to policing racially segregated communities.

In addition, as the following response makes explicit, the black policeman is thought to be more interested in helping reduce the incidence of criminal victimization in black communities. Consequently, when *he* makes an arrest, he is making it for different reasons than does the average white officer.

> I would have predominantly black cops, about 80/20. I think the average black cop has more understanding of the community and more willingness to serve the people in different ways. He is more interested, therefore, he performs a better service. . . . He makes arrests, but for different reasons. He wants to make the community a safer place in which to live. A lot of white cops simply use the job to "hunt."

The Question of Integrated
Police Teams

Much of the research (including our own) that has examined the issue of integrated or segregated social structures uncovered evidence which tends to show that sympathetic attitudes develop among members of diverse racial groups as contact between the groups increases.[9] While this finding may be applicable to a particular level of interaction, say, in working relations between white and black police officers, the question here is whether such benefits can be extended out into the community itself. There is a feeling, for example, that despite the positive effects inside, fully integrated precincts might be viewed by some blacks on the outside as an indication that the department lacks confidence in the ability of black police to do the job adequately. Moreover, if black policemen are constantly assigned to work with white partners, they too may come to feel in time that they are being controlled by the department and that their assignment is an expression of the department's distrust of blacks in general.[10] There is also the possibility that integrated police teams may initially bring out the worst in some officers. A young, inexperienced black cop may, for example, want to prove to his white partner that he is "one of the guys" and may demonstrate these feelings by being unusually tough on blacks in the community. Or, if he is senior to his white partner, he may want to show him "how to handle blacks."

While some of these opinions may have been held by blacks in the past, there is no evidence, at least from the present study, to support their widespread existence today. On the contrary, when asked for their views on "integrated police precincts" and "working teams," the majority of men fully supported a policy which would assign, when practicable, a black and white officer to work together. Asked to justify their position, they spoke mostly in terms of the benefits that would accrue to members of the black community from such an arrangement. Some recalled, for example, that even routine confrontations between white police officers and black citizens can escalate into highly charged, violatile incidents. The presence of black policemen at a scene, it was pointed out, could help prevent these potentially explosive situations thereby preventing injuries to both sides. As one policeman, with over 15 years of experience in a Harlem-based precinct, put it,

> I would divide the precinct in half. An integrated precinct stands a better chance of controlling possible disruptive situations as compared with a mostly white precinct. In many situations, I've seen white cops act strictly out of fear. Fear controlled the situation and things happened that shouldn't have happened. On the other hand, most black cops tend to act calm, they understand the situation. . . . There's another thing, too. With an even number of black cops, there is less danger for all concerned, particularly for the cop. For example, if a white cop has to knock down a dude and then arrest him, oftentimes the people in the community will attempt to take the person away. When a black cop is there, this doesn't happen.

A further advantage to the "integrated team" approach was suggested by a patrol officer who viewed this arrangement within the context of enhancing the department's image in the eyes of the black community. Implicit in this, as well as many of the other comments contained in this section, is the feeling that white police, if left on their own, would not be as effective. As the officer said,

> By having an equal number of black and white cops, you would be cutting down on the racial image of police. What do I mean by that? Well, during times of incidents and street conditions, if a black and white officer respond to a job together, the situation has a better chance of being handled properly without unnecessary problems. It would then cut down on the black peoples' dislike of police. It would also cut down on brutality charges and civilian complaints.

Another respondent spelled out the potential benefits of having ghetto communities patrolled by police teams of blacks and whites within the framework of a learning experience for both groups of officers. As a result of increased contact with black policemen, this officer envisioned a favorable shift in the behavior of white cops toward blacks in the community. He thought that

> Every white cop should have a black partner because the black cop can unconsciously train the white cop to be cool in certain situations. By flooding the precincts with black cops, you are accenting polarization. With integrated precincts, one officer can train the other.

The white officer will subtly learn the attitudes and behavior of black ethnic groups from the black officer.

Two respondents pointed out that "mixed" patrol teams, because they employ the talents of policemen of diverse racial and experiential backgrounds, contribute different ideas and insights into solving job-related problems in the ghetto. There is also the added benefit that the department's credibility would be enhanced when people in the community saw police officers of different racial backgrounds working together on an equal status basis.

> It also gives different approaches to problem-solving. Being white with a different background and vice versa. A consolidation of both. Two black officers would probably give similar suggestions on how to handle a specific problem they ran up against. With an inte grated team, one guy has one approach based upon his background and experiences and the other guy has another approach as opposed to an all-white or all-black view. You have a balanced view which is superior to an ethnic view.

> Yes, there is a very definite advantage to an integrated team as I see it. In an integrated team, you have the best of both worlds. Both have cops' experience, but the white officer is bringing in his values and the black officer is doing the same and each is learning from the other. It's good for the cops and good for the community. They get a chance to see two people working together as a team. Two people from different racial backgrounds trying to solve some of the community's problems together.

A further perspective on the issue of integrated teams was provided by a policeman who had recently been transferred to a Harlem command. This officer noted the tendency for some of the younger black policemen to be too lenient with black law breakers, who were not arrested when they probably should have been. Yet, this same officer was equally troubled with some white policemen in his precinct who he felt acted far too punitively in situations that could have been handled "out of court." An integrated-team approach, he concluded, was the most practical solution to these "extreme" styles of policing in the sense that it provided both the community and the department with a system of "checks and balances." A portion of his response went as follows:

You won't have anyone behaving in a racist way and you won't have an all-black theory of "letting them slide." The white officer will control letting most things slide and the black officer will control the white officer's aggressiveness.

The reactions of a few policemen to the prospect of integrated teams are of interest here because they illustrate the doubts and potential problems that such an arrangement could evoke. For example, one officer expressed the feeling that a department order requiring black and white cops to work together on a systematic basis would almost certainly come up against strong resistance from those police commanders who did not view the arrangement as contributing toward the reduction of crime in their precincts. Thus, without the support of those occupying positions of direct control over the assignment of patrol teams, such a policy, even if instituted at higher levels, might not be fully implemented at the operational level.

Further, and perhaps more important from the standpoint of those policemen who would be directly affected, the forced institution of "mixed" working teams might tend to create serious morale problems, especially among those officers who have worked together comfortably in the past and who suddenly find themselves split up. One need keep in mind in this regard that individual policemen tend to develop different work styles over the years and generally seek out partners who share their views about how the job of policing ought to be done. Forcing men to work together on the basis of some untested "racial" formula rather than allowing them to select partners based upon mutual compatibility would, it was feared, result in lowered morale, reduced motivation and productivity and possibly increased racial dissension within the ranks. Two felt that

> You have two guys who can't stand each other's guts and by putting them together you create a worse situation for the men and the people in the community. These men aren't going to do a thing for the C.O., not a fuckin' thing.

> Primarily teams should be compatible with each other regardless of their individual backgrounds. You start sticking guys together for

some political end and they don't see eye to eye, you got problems, morale problems. And that leads to men "going dead" in the street.

In short, these men agree that under normal working conditions patrol officers should be assigned together on the basis of compatible work styles. A "happy" team is a productive team. To assign policemen otherwise, and especially because it was thought to be politically expedient at the time, would only be self-defeating in the long run.

Another point which may have some bearing on the issue of assignments was raised by a detective who had worked with cops of both races during his 16 years on the job. According to this officer, good arrests constitute an important measure of a squad's or team's overall effectiveness, and many "quality" arrests are made by policemen working in civilian clothes. The question this officer raised and then attempted to answer was whether the color of the men working as a team, out of uniform, had any effect on their ability to apprehend felons effectively and safely in racially segregated communities.

> For example, I had an occasion to make an arrest in the street with another black officer. The individual that we were attempting to arrest (also black) began to run before we had an opportunity to clearly identify ourselves. Once we caught up with him and made it clear that we were officers, he immediately calmed down and began to cooperate with us. He then stated that he thought it was a rip-off. On another occasion, the exact opposite happened. Myself and another black officer in civilian clothes spotted an individual in a crowd of about 30 to 40 people. My partner and I left our car and walked approximately one-half block into the middle of the crowd right up to this individual and told him that he was to walk with me and my partner to the car. This was done successfully. The crowd was black. If it were me and a white officer, it could never have come off that way.

As this detective points out there are certain tactical advantages to be gained from the assignment of two black, plainclothes policemen to work together in a black precinct. The fact that the two officers are black allows them in many instances to blend in with the surroundings more easily, thus minimizing problems associated with approaching and arresting suspected felons. Yet, in other situations, teaming two black, nonuniformed policemen together can create special problems in which taking a criminal suspect into custody is not only more difficult but more dangerous as well. Consider, for example, the possibility that the suspect in the first situation mentioned above had a gun or other concealed weapon and was determined not to be ripped off—the fear he later communicated to the arresting officers. In this situation it might have been less apparent to the suspect that the two individuals approaching him were, in fact, police officers, than if one or both of the men had been white. There is the additional danger, then, that the suspect, thinking he was about to be victimized himself, might have used his weapon to inflict injury upon the approaching officers. Yet, being black clearly afforded the police officers in the second situation a tactical advantage in apprehending the suspect without risking unnecessary injury to themselves or others nearby. Depending, of course, on the nature and seriousness of the crime alleged to have been committed, it is unlikely that the suspect in the second situation would have remained in the middle of the crowd had either or both of the approaching officers been white.

Moreover, as has been mentioned earlier, black policemen working in civilian clothes routinely run the risk of not being recognized as police officers by other members of the department. There is always the possibility that they may be mistaken for felons themselves and shot before their true identity is established. In this connection the following comment reflects both the advantages inherent in an "all-black" team approach to policing black communities while dressed in civilian clothes and the fears of black, nonuniformed policemen working in these as well as white areas of the city:

> Basically, I'm in favor of integrated teams, both in uniform and out of uniform. There are definite advantages to both. But there are maybe more advantages to having two black detectives or plainclothesmen working together. They can get in and out of places quicker without static. They can come on a guy they're looking for without being recognized as the "man" more easily than a black and white team. You have problems here too, though. And I have to answer this by bringing up a sensitive topic. It's a fact that more

black cops are shot by white officers when they were chasing someone with their guns drawn. This rarely happens to white cops working in plainclothes who happen to be chasing someone or who have someone up against a wall. It's tragic, but it's a fact of life here. Black cops just take a greater chance that they will be shot when they take their guns out in the street. That's why I say it's a difficult question, there's pros and cons to working in civilian clothes in any area in the city [if you're black].

The issue of "integrated police teams" is indeed a difficult one that must be examined from both the departmental as well as an individual point of view. In assigning officers to patrol in mixed teams, the department must consider not only its own specific interests and needs but those of the wider community and the individual officer. It must also weigh such a policy against other, possibly more effective, ways to make assignments. The problems and divergent needs articulated here represent just a few of the issues that must be addressed before such a policy can be put into operation. In the conclusion to this book an alternative to the "forced" mixing of patrol teams is considered in some detail.

Police-Community Relations Programs

As the comments in this study reveal not all black policemen working in precincts situated in ghetto communities feel that the attitudes of people living in these areas have changed all that much in recent years. Indeed, negativism on the part of black citizens seems to persist despite the steadily growing number of younger, presumably more understanding, sympathetic black police and, as we shall see, despite efforts on the part of the police department to expand its community relations functions.

Most policemen in this study, when asked, tended to minimize the effect of department community-relations programs, some claiming that they were designed simply to create an "image" of police sensitivity and concern toward the black community and its problems. One officer, who speaks for many of the men, charged that the department actually undermined individual efforts to establish a relationship with blacks because it continued to adhere to

archaic rules and regulations which limit interaction with the public to matters of "official" police business.[11]

> The department has done very little. Community-relations pro-
> grams just fool the people into thinking that the police are con-
> cerned. They haven't really changed the average black person's at-
> titude. . . . I personally feel that the department as a whole has
> hindered those officers who are trying to do something. If a cop
> seems like he's concerned, he's looked at as if he's some sort of a
> sissy. . . . Also, you know this mentality about staying out of bars
> and things like that. Don't get involved unless you're taking some
> sort of police action. This only hurts in the end. The only time a
> cop is supposed to be talking to somebody is when he's making a
> collar or getting information on a homicide. . . . Even with all this
> talk about sensitivity and police-community relations, I wonder
> sometimes if the department is really concerned about how people
> feel.

Another, and perhaps more pointed, complaint directed against
the department's community-relations effort is that it has only been
successful in gaining the cooperation and support of a handful of
law-abiding blacks in the community. Uninfluenced, for the most
part, have been the masses of alienated blacks, people who are most
affected by police policy decisions and operations in their precincts, people who are most distrustful and suspicious of the police and who, in the estimation of some of the men, are the least
able to articulate their problems and concerns. This is supported
by the statement that

> What they are doing in the community-relations thing, they are
> working with people who are already pro-police, people who want
> to cooperate. But the average citizen is not being contacted, and
> the police cannot operate effectively with the cooperation of only a
> minority of law-abiding people.

A few policemen were more specific as to which groups were
not being reached. Some, for example, felt that the department has
traditionally concerned itself with the problems facing adults in the
community, thereby neglecting black youth who may be more
flexible in changing their attitudes towards the police. As one officer concluded,

You have got to start with the kids. Just start by talking to them. Say something positive when you drive by. Stop and bullshit with them. What can it hurt? What can you lose? Unfortunately, too many cops just don't see their job as becoming involved with these kids. . . . I believe that you have got to convince these kids that you are interested in them, that you are not just out there riding herd over them. These kids are impressionable, some of them anyway. They need to see that the policeman cares. . . . If you ask me if I have a preference, in all honesty, I would prefer if the department spent a little more time and money on the kids. You can have all the community meetings in the world, but if you don't somehow reach the kids, then you have won the battle but you are sure going to lose the war. I'll say this, if you can win the kids over, you have won the war, because the older people will follow.

This is an important observation. For, as some of our respondents see it, without the trust and cooperation of neighborhood youth, long-range efforts to improve the quality of relations with the larger black community may fail despite successful attempts to win over its older and more stable members.

Not all of the comments, however, reflect unfavorably on recent department programs aimed at drawing the police and black community closer together. One officer spoke about the positive effect one such program had on people living in the precinct in which he worked:

In my precinct they were giving away bicycles to the kids. There were also plenty of outings and bus rides. These are not really community-relations programs per se but I believe that they are still doing a lot to make life easier for the cop in the street. . . . Well, some of the parents of these kids have come up to me in the street and told me what they thought of the bike program. They thanked me even though I personally had nothing to do with it. In fact, to be honest about it, I wasn't even aware that the precinct was giving away bikes. . . . The point is that I really feel that these people have a better attitude about the police here now, the kids especially. If I were in some kind of trouble now I think they would help me. And a few years ago they really didn't give a damn what happened to you.

One must be careful, however, not to overstate the importance of programs that are designed to encourage people to "fall in love with the police." If, as a byproduct, such programs do promote greater appreciation and acceptance of the police, all well and good. But it would appear that a more important overall goal of the department should be to improve the quality of police services in the ghetto.[12] Quite obviously, the program depicted in the officer's comment, while it initially may have succeeded in enhancing the department's image in the eyes of some community members, did not, in and of itself, address the more fundamental problem of, for example, community apathy. Still, there are some men who, like the officer above, feel that "public relations" efforts are crucial if the department is to narrow the gap between itself and people in the black community. Police, they say, could begin by spending more time with ghetto kids while on patrol, listening to their problems and grievances, and attempting to find out "where they are coming from." As one officer put it,

> There are individual efforts that are being made to reach the kids. I personally am a great believer in talking to kids. Quite a few guys have been communicating with them. They go out of their way to rap. They feel that they are doing the right thing. Listen, a lot of these kids aren't going to make it no matter what. But I think a lot of them can be reached. It just takes a lot of patience and interest. You know the simplest thing in the world when you get out of a radio car is to act friendly.

Part of the overall effort of the department in the seventies to improve relations with the black public involved "humanizing" its image by introducing some basic changes in equipment, training and dress. Police operating on the patrol level especially were told to improve styles of grooming, neatness of uniform, and keep their weight in line. Those officers who failed to live up to these new standards were often subjected to informal sanctions, and if they failed to conform, formal sanctions were brought in many cases.

There also was an attempt during the 1970s to reduce the incidence of police misconduct, much of which occurred in precisely those communities in which the people were most estranged from the police. Potential and actual behavioral problems were handled largely through innovative training programs and through the threat that the department would no longer defend a police officer found guilty at a departmental hearing of having violated specific civil rights codes. With regard to corruption, a problem long plaguing police agencies in this country, the department moved swiftly in the early 1970s, in response to the Knapp Commission report, by introducing new regulations which were designed not only to reduce the opportunities for corruption but also the temptation to engage in dishonest activities.

Overall departmental efforts to create a more professional image and to instill in the individual officer a new sense of pride in his job and respect for the laws and rights of *all* citizens appear to have paid off initially when new officers entered the ranks in the seventies. Not only were these officers trained to be more attentive to their own personal appearance but, according to some of the men, they were instructed to act with greater physical restraint in their dealings with minority citizens. Thus, one said,

> I think a lot of changes have come and a lot of blacks now see us in a different light. I think these changes have come about as the result of the younger officer. When I first came up here cops wore ragged uniforms. . . . They behaved very poorly toward black citizens and especially toward people they locked up. Beating of prisoners now is less than when I came on the job. I really don't see it anymore. When a prisoner came in handcuffed years ago, 50 guys jumped on his back wanting a piece of him. This rarely happens any longer. The younger cops have come on the job when it was no longer fashionable to beat people and abuse them. The younger cop just feels differently about the way he treats people and I think it's rubbing off a little on the people in the street.

Widespread and systematic corruption is also thought to be a thing of the past according to some of the men, as are other forms of serious police misconduct in the black community.

> Personally, I think it's the younger cop who has made a change in the way people see us. They're not abusing people publically. They're not taking money from people. They're not shaking down or harassing people anymore.

References to "younger" policemen as being more professionally oriented in the seventies may not be conjecture on the part of these respondents. It might be recalled that departmental efforts to alter its image, to cut down on police violence and incidents of brutality and to eliminate corruption from within the ranks all evolved in the early 1970s. These young officers who joined the department during this period of rapid internal transition received intensive exposure to new directives and procedures which were aimed at eliminating undesirable attitudes and habits. Besides this, the racial make-up of the department at the time was also undergoing change with the influx of black and Hispanic cops, many of whom aligned themselves with the minority community and supported public attempts to bring about changes in police behavior.

As we know, however, many of the "idealistic" internal changes in police practices were short-lived. The growing crime rate in the seventies, coupled with a laxness in police supervision and a declining militancy of black police themselves, resulted among many officers both white and black in a gradual return to some of the earlier habits and styles of policing. This is perhaps no where more evident than in the testimony of those men in this study who sense that even the assignment of young, black policemen to ghetto precincts and the expansion of police-community relations programs in these same areas have failed to substantially reduce the fear, mistrust and contempt that has long characterized black feelings about the police.[13] But then the development of an improved attitude toward the police may not lie exclusively or even largely in increasing the proportion of blacks assigned to ghetto precincts or in augmenting innovative community-relations programs with select citizen groups. Rather, it might be accomplished by increasing the understanding and sensitivity of *all* police toward their changing role in racially segregated communities, to insure impartial enforcement of the law as well as protection of all citizens from those officers who are prone to abuse their authority and power. For, as we shall see in the following section, the cost of adhering to traditional police roles and methods in today's overlegalized and permissive society is even greater isolation between the police and the communities they serve.

NOTES

1. See Nicholas Alex, *Black in Blue: A Study of the Negro Policeman* (New York: Appleton-Century-Crofts, 1969), p. 24; also see The President's Commission on

Law Enforcement and Administration of Justice, *Task Force Report: The Police,* Washington, D.C., 1967.

2. For example, see David H. Bayley and Harold Mendelsohn, *Minorities and the Police: Confrontation in America* (New York: The Free Press, 1968), pp. 87–108; also see W. Eugene Groves and Peter Rossi, "Police Perceptions of a Hostile Ghetto," *American Behavioral Scientist,* Volume 13 (1970).

3. See David H. Bayley and Harold Mendelsohn, op. cit., p. 107.

4. In the Mosque incident, which occurred on April 14, 1972, a white police officer responding to a signal 10-13 (assist patrolman), forceably entered the Muslim Mosque located on West 116th street in Harlem, New York City and was apparently shot and killed with his own gun by a member of the Mosque.

5. In *Black in Blue,* Nicholas Alex presents a similar finding with regard to lower-class blacks residing in black communities. See p. 144.

6. Note also the following account offered by a black secretary from the Philadelphia Guardians Civic League: "I've gone into communities and had blacks tell me they'd rather have a white officer on patrol than a black one, because the white officer will listen." "Black Cops' Role," *The New York Post,* June 10, 1971, p. 2.

7. See Seymour Parker and Robert Kleiner, "Status Position, Mobility, and Ethnic Identification of the Negro," in Marcel L. Goldschmid (ed.), *Black Americans and White Racism: Theory and Research* (New York: Holt, Rinehart and Winston, 1970), pp. 55–66.

8. This conclusion along with the underlying reasons accounting for black underrepresentation in the New York City police department was offered by the Guardians Association of the NYPD in a proposal to conduct a full-time law-enforcement and training program for minorities of underprivileged circumstances. The proposal was dated March 1, 1971.

9. See, for example, the following: E. Works, "Residence in Integrated and Segregated Housing and Improvement in Self-Concepts of Negroes," *Sociology and Social Research* (1962), pp. 294–301; W. C. Haggstrom, "Self-Esteem and Other Characteristics of Residentially Desegregated Negroes," *Dissertation Abstracts, 1963,* Number 23, pp. 3007–3008; Bonnie Bullough, "Alienation in the Ghetto," in Marcel L. Goldschmid, op. cit., pp. 66–74; William M. Kephart, *Racial Factors and Urban Law Enforcement* (Philadelphia, Pa.: Univ. of Pennsylvania Press, 1957).

10. As reported in Nicholas Alex, op. cit., p. 17.

11. See also, Herman Goldstein, *Policing a Free Society* (Cambridge, Mass.: Ballinger, 1977), p. 135.

12. See Louis A. Radelet, *The Police and the Community* (Encino, Cal.: Glencoe, 1977), p. 27.

13. The negative perceptions these officers have of the public's view of the police are largely supported in the literature on police. Compared with the larger white population in this country, the black community is still generally dissatisfied with the police. Black citizens tend to perceive inequities in the provision of police services and believe, among other things, that the police provide inferior and inadequate protection in black communities. For a compilation of both past and recent studies concerning public attitudes toward the police, see Scott H. Decker, "Citizen Attitudes Toward the Police: A Review of Past Findings and

Suggestions for Future Policy," *Journal of Police Science and Administration,* Volume 9, Number 1 (March 1981), pp. 80–87 and Daniel J. Bell, "Police and Public Opinion," *Journal of Police Science and Administration,* Volume 7, Number 2 (June 1979), pp. 196–205.

Chapter Seven

- • -

The Police Role in the Black Community

Nobody in the black community wants to be thought of as a stool.

O UR concerns are with the way black police perceive their
role in ghetto communities, with the expectations black
citizens attach to the police mission, and whether or not
these coincide. We also discuss some of the problems black (and
white) police routinely face in attempting to meet the demands of
the black community for greater police protection as well as the
reactions of the men as they come to realize that they are somewhat ineffectual in dealing with many of these problems.

First, and contrary to our initial expectations, the great majority
of black policemen in this study defined their role in the black
community in traditional police terms. That is, they saw their primary duties as fighting crime, apprehending felons and maintaining order rather than providing extra-legal, non-enforcement services to the public. Second, and also contrary to our expectations,
black policemen, for the most part, did not perceive themselves as
more effective crime fighters than white police. In fact, when asked,
this same majority of men rejected the notion that a relationship
even existed between a policeman's race and the quality of law enforcement he provided.

Barriers to Effective Crime Control

It is widely accepted by police in New York City that one of the critical problems facing cops who work in the ghetto is the widespread lack of citizen cooperation in matters pertaining to the control, apprehension, and prosecution of criminal offenders. The policemen we surveyed gave a number of reasons which, when considered together, tend to explain why people living under a constant fear of attack and property loss often do not rally behind the police. These are based on a misunderstanding of the police role and the constraints placed upon police, fear of criminal retaliation, and an enforcement priority system which concentrates on serious crime while leaving petty but high visibility offenders on the street. The effect of these factors on citizen attitudes and expectations is compounded by the reciprocal nature of this alienation. That is, policemen themselves tend to react with increased indifference to the people under pressure resulting from the community's lack of cooperation and from the official constraints imposed on them by the legal system and the department itself.

Much of the problem, we are told, stems from a general and widespread misunderstanding on the part of the black public as to what the police can and cannot do in terms of protecting people from personal attack and property loss. Our men contend that many blacks living in the ghetto see the police as failing to fulfill their law enforcement responsibilities and respond both individually and at times collectively by refusing to assist in police investigations. It might be noted that detectives in this study voiced even greater concern and disappointment than uniformed patrol officers over the black public's unwillingness to cooperate in criminal investigations. Yet, one might expect this type of response from detectives since, as a specialized group, they are subjected more than uniformed officers to organizational pressures to make arrests and clear cases.

Reflecting on what they believe to be the public's unrealistic expectations concerning the police role today, several detectives recalled instances in which they were personally accused of failing to meet their obligations to the community at large. The following account, for example, typifies the experiences of many police, both white and black, who find themselves in the position of having to assume responsibility for the inadequacies of the larger criminal justice system:

> There is very little cooperation from the public as far as I'm concerned. I don't know all the reasons, but I can tell you what I believe from working in Harlem for the last 12 years. Many people—not all—don't have trust in the police. And this is because mostly they don't understand our job. They blame us for all the things that go wrong in the street and courts, the guy who's out in the street and maybe should be in jail. . . . How about the guy that molested those two kids a couple of months ago? He was released a couple of days after we locked him up; something to do with the evidence at the hearing. Well, you know I got 50 calls from the mother of one of the boys and from people in the building screaming about why the guy is out. They're blaming me for a situation which I have no control over. . . . I personally believe that people hear stories like this one and they don't want to cooperate with us because they think that somehow we don't give a shit. They just don't understand that we have nothing to do with what goes on in court.

When asked why police appear to be ineffective in ghetto communities, another detective made essentially the same point.

> Cooperation is piss-poor, and the reason is that people here don't trust cops. But you also have to add, the majority of the public does not want to get involved. It's not all that the people don't trust cops. It's probably the most important reason, but they also don't want to get involved, most people.

The failure of people in the ghetto to acknowledge the restrictions imposed on the police is only one of the factors believed to influence the level of cooperation police generally can expect in these areas of the city. As has been mentioned above, many of the men also spoke of black citizens' fear of reprisal should they testify in court or otherwise assist in police investigations.[1] One detective commented very frankly along these lines:

> There is very little cooperation from the public. As a black policeman, I can understand their problems. And I realize at the same time that I can't deal with them as I would like to. I can't change

the laws. . . . People are arrested for serious crimes and in many cases they are out in no time; in some cases, even before the cop gets back from court. It's a joke, some of these cases. . . . You want to know about why police are not effective? Well, I personally believe it arises out of a misconception as to who is at fault when a murderer is released and possibly threatens a witness.

He continued,

Everyone is scared. There is such a fear on the part of the people here to become involved as witnesses and complainants. When they do cooperate, they either have to move out of the neighborhood or stay in their house. And what can the police do? What do you say to someone who points an accusing finger at you and blames you for not protecting him. . . . The way I see it, the policeman is only a part of the system. He can't be all things to all people. He can't offer protection to every victim or witness. So again I say, what do you say to someone when he asks what happens if the guy gets out and comes looking for him, or if the case gets thrown out of court? You certainly can't sit and hold his hand. So how do you get this guy to cooperate if he's a victim? People just don't want to understand our side of the story.

Such a response also suggests that the police are seldom in a position to mold the job according to their own needs. Personnel shortages combined with the sheer volume of serious criminal offenses committed in ghetto communities preclude the possibility of police offering protection to all but a few victims and witnesses. Consequently, many of those who may want to assist the police are reluctant to come forward with information or to testify in court.

The reaction of many policemen to the discovery that they are virtually powerless to perform to the satisfaction of the public is frustration with the legal system and apathy toward their professional responsibilities and duties. As an example of this,

Cooperation from most people here is poor, very poor. People will run over a dead body just to get out the door before the police come so they won't have to answer questions about what happened. . . . The policeman generally is not in a good position to be sympathetic to what he sees. He has a very limited knowledge of human behavior. His attitudes about people here develop from these kinds of experiences. He finally says to himself, if he's worked here long enough, "Why should I care when the people don't care."

One detective spoke of the experiences of police investigators who are routinely called upon to obtain statements from recalcitrant witnesses to shootings and criminal homicides:

> As an investigator, I find it difficult to perform my duties as I would like to. Cooperation from the public is poor. People just don't seem to care. They don't want to become involved. They tell you they didn't see anything, they didn't hear anything. Thirty people tell you that they were in the bathroom, all at the same time when the guy got shot. Meanwhile, the bathroom is big enough for two people, at most. A lot of detectives see this attitude when they go out to interview witnesses. They come back to the office with a "fuck them" attitude. This is the main reason, as I said before, why police are not that effective. It's not all their fault though.

Police indifference to ghetto crimes may be intensified by the efforts of victims, who often have to be "tracked down," to avoid testifying at a criminal proceeding.

> In the beginning, the people are angry about what happened. They say they will look at pictures and come to court if necessary, that there's no problem. But later, when an arrest is made, it's a different story. When you go out to get the complainant to go to court, he's never home. And when you do finally catch up with him, he makes some outrageous excuse for not being able to make it to court. Most people never really come out and tell you how they really feel. They say things like, my mother is sick down South and I had to go see her. I don't know how many times I've heard that story. But let's talk about how the cop feels. A lot of cops don't give a shit anymore, black cops as well as white cops. As I said, it's frustrating. They feel that they have cases to close and they get fed up with this kind of cooperation. So maybe they don't kill themselves the next time. Where's the reward, the appreciation?

While it is indeed frustrating for the community to learn that a judge has dismissed a criminal charge against a known offender because of insufficient evidence or legal technicality, it is even more disturbing perhaps to the individual officer who may have spent weeks or even months collecting evidence and preparing a case for trial only to find that an obviously guilty criminal is being released because the victim or complainant couldn't be located in time or, if found, decided not to prosecute the case after all. The following comment, for instance, reflects the feeling of utter despair experienced by detectives (and uniformed cops) who sense that their efforts to bring serious criminal offenders to justice are often thwarted by an indifferent, scared, or unappreciative public:

> Sometimes you really feel like giving up. For instance, I had a case a little while ago which involved a guy who was stabbed during a petty stickup. He was a working man who was on his way home when two junkies tried to take his money. After about two months, my partner and I made a collar. The guy [victim] was as happy as a pig-in-shit at the time. Anyway, the trial took almost a year to come up. When it was time to go to court, everyone wanted to drop the charges; the family of the victim, as well as the victim himself. Let me tell you, we broke our asses on that case just to make a collar. And after all this aggravation, they tell me that he wasn't really sure that that was the guy who cut him.

Actually, fear of criminal retaliation is probably no greater among black witnesses to serious crime than among white. However, one aspect of the problem may be unique to lower-class, black areas of the city. And that is the added concern of the black witness about how his neighbors and friends in the community are going to react should they discover that he has voluntarily cooperated in a police investigation. As one respondent candidly put it, "Nobody in the black community wants to thought of as a stool." Another policeman echoed this sentiment:

> A lot of guys think that the people here are only afraid of criminals. However, that's not the whole story. A lot of people are afraid of what their neighbors and even their friends will say. You can get hurt here just by talking to the police.

Related to the problems discussed above and apparently having some impact on the willingness of blacks to cooperate in and support police operations is the highly visible response of the department to "minor" criminal offenses and deviant street conditions.[2]

The New York City police department, like most police agencies in the country, has established a system of enforcement priorities, concentrating efforts on reducing crimes that directly threaten life and property, while expending less energy enforcing laws of a less serious nature.[3] Yet, there is some evidence from our interviews that people living in slum communities such as Harlem want laws relating to these lesser offenses and conditions more vigorously enforced. When they are not, they accuse the police of maintaining a double set of standards—one for the poor and one for the more well-to-do. As one officer who has spent the past 11 years assigned to a Harlem precinct put it,

> There is also what you would call a communication-gap between the black public and the police, and I believe it leads to mistrust on the part of the people toward the police. This is mainly because many of the blacks see the laws in areas like this as having little meaning to them. They see the police walking and driving by the junkies and pushers in the street and doing nothing about it. They think that the police don't care about what's going on. . . . "Why aren't these laws enforced here, they are in other communities? Why aren't these people arrested?" These are the questions they ask.

Although it is probably true that people living in Harlem are aware that such conditions flourish in almost every black slum community in the city, their appreciation of the reasons which create an image of police laxity in enforcing these laws may be much too superficial.[4] Yet, according to one officer, it is precisely this image which has prevailed in large part from the need to deal first with more serious criminal conditions that is the crux of the problem today.

> They think that because it's Harlem, the cops don't care. They don't understand that we have our hands full with more serious matters, that we must have some sort of a priority system when dealing with crime. There is enough *serious* crime here to keep the average cop busy eight hours a day.

However, even when arrests are made for minor criminal offenses there is a great reluctance to prosecute these cases since the judges and prosecutors themselves generally do not view them as "enforcement priorities." A policeman said,

The way I see it, there's no support for police to enforce these laws, either by the department or by the courts. The D.A. and the judges don't pay serious attention to these types of crime. And the people, they are not in court to see what happens when arrests are made. So they don't know.

In short, the frequency with which certain criminal activities are practiced in slum communities, coupled with the difficulty of suppressing and prosecuting them all may lead black citizens to conclude that they are being shortchanged by the police department. This can result, as one officer told us, in even greater distrust of the police and legal system.

There's a lack of support for police in most black neighborhoods. But this has a lot to do with the courts and the present system of law than with the police themselves. The people see the hustlers, junkies and pros' all over the place and question why the police aren't doing anything about them. They begin to question the policeman's motives and the law. They just don't trust us and the law and I guess when you get down to it, you really can't blame them.

In order to reestablish a sense of trust and confidence in the police, a few of our respondents felt that the department should take a tougher stand regarding the enforcement of certain so-called "victimless" crimes and that the police themselves should be given additional powers over common street hoodlums and deviant types.

You can hardly get a witness up to the squad. The legislature and the judicial system are at fault, not the cop in the street. Many of the laws—the gambling laws, drug laws—mean nothing to black people. The same with the prostitution laws. There could be more cooperation if the police were allowed to do their job and get these drug users and prostitutes and tin-horns off the street. . . . You're not going to get cooperation as far as witnesses are concerned because the people are getting no satisfaction in other areas. They see the police doing nothing and they assume, naturally, that they don't care.

Most of the men, however, argued that a show of force concentrated in one area succeeded only in forcing certain criminal types to locate elsewhere in the community. Of special interest here is

the following comment by a veteran detective which reflects critically on traditional department efforts to eliminate illicit drug activities in Harlem through the sporadic display of force.

> I personally don't think that would do any good. In fact, I can hon-
> estly say that I don't believe there are many cops who would sup-
> port this solution. Years ago, the police mentality was to handle
> problems of this sort by bringing in more manpower and by mak-
> ing a lot of arrests. I'll never forget the remark made by one [white]
> boss some time ago when a bunch of us were sitting around talking
> about some of these problems. "Give me a hundred cops with night
> sticks and I'll show you how to clean up the problem." To say the
> least, that was hardly a solution, but it was the way some cops
> thought. . . . The problem is still there, but only it's someone else's
> headache.

As has been said, divergent definitions of the police role, coupled with organizational constraints and enforcement priorities
which "play down" less serious but nevertheless socially disruptive
criminal activities, do in fact contribute to the public's low regard
for the police, to their general reluctance to cooperate in solving
serious crimes and, in turn, to the growing sense of apathy and
isolation experienced by many uniformed officers and detectives
working in the ghetto. But these are not the only problems facing
police today. Compounding this mutual alienation, according to
some men in this study, were the expectations of police profes-
sionalism and fairness on the part of those blacks who left the
agrarian South after the Second World War in order to escape the
pervasive problems of unemployment, racial discrimination, and
police prejudice.[5]

Upon arriving in Northern cities many, if not most, blacks found
that "city life" closely resembled the one they had left behind. More
often than not, we are reminded, the behavior of individual policemen toward blacks corresponded more with their own personal
prejudices and feelings than with the law. The eventual realization
that their exodus had failed to relieve the overt miseries attached
to subjugation and discrimination left many Southern blacks even
more suspicious of the fairness of America's legal system in general
and of the police in particular. According to one policeman, the
prospect of winning the trust and cooperation of some of the older
Southern blacks in the very near future appears bleak:

There is a different story with the older blacks. Some of these people who don't want to cooperate or become involved in any way with the police came up from the South after having been mistreated all their lives. When they got here, they received bad treatment also; mostly an "I could care less" attitude from the police. There has been some improvement in their attitudes, but not that much. Some of the people just can't forget the past. The scars go too deep, I guess. They just don't want to be bothered. I've talked with a lot of them and this is what they tell me. Maybe in the future, they will feel different, but right now they just want to be left alone.

Other respondents suggested that cynicism toward the police is not confined to people of any particular age level, or geographical region, but spread uniformly throughout the black community. There was agreement among these men, for example, that *most* blacks living in slum communities distrust the police and for that reason are reluctant to cooperate in criminal matters. The following negative accounts of the larger black public's perception of police are typical:

The black public in most instances looks at the cop as the enforcer—any cop. In a lot of instances, there might be a chance of a person approaching a black cop with some information. But mostly, the cop has the stereotyped image of the enforcer. People don't want to see him in any other way.

Not only don't they want to help solve murders, they don't want to become involved in any police related function. . . . I personally don't think anything can be done right now. People don't want to become involved with the police on any level. Police to them are "anti-society" groups.

The fact that people in the black community are often unwilling to assist in police investigations may, however, have more to do with their lack of real input into department decisions concerning police policies and operations at the precinct level than with where people come from. As one patrol officer cynically concluded,

All police serve the black community poorly, because the community doesn't give a fuck anymore. There is no community interest in police matters. . . . Basically people in the ghetto have given up. People don't give a shit about what happens. They feel that they have no say in how the precinct is being run, in how policemen behave in the street. They say to themselves, "why should I cooperate?" This feeling is shown in the way they react to a policeman responding to a job. People don't say, "Hey, I'm glad to see you," but rather, "what took you so long?"

It is also important to consider the frustrations many police experience that arise from the constraints imposed by the department and the legal system as a whole—constraints affecting the ability to deal with major as well as minor criminal offenses. When asked why they felt police are unable to deal effectively with the crime problem in ghetto communities, many of the men blamed the nation's highest legal authority—the Supreme Court. Recent Court rulings, especially those related to interrogation and search and seizure, they charged, have effectively neutralized police efforts to control serious forms of criminality by placing excessive limitations on the ability of the police to make arrests and to gather evidence. Consider the following comments:

Police can't deal with the criminal the way they used to. The courts are responsible for this condition. All these restrictions. And who do they hurt the most? Not the guy who just ripped off the grocer. This is the saddest part of all. It's the guy who owns a small business or who works every day to support a family that is likely to suffer the most. He's the one who is most likely to get ripped off by one of these guys walking around with a weapon in his pocket.

When it came to suspects, police were more effective in the past. The typical street criminal knows his rights now about being stopped by the police. The cop can no longer be aggressive in the street. He has to deal with the guy carrying drugs or even a gun in a very delicate way. And when he does stop someone who he suspects of carrying a gun or something and he locks the guy up, then he has to convince the court that he acted within the limits of the law. Maybe that gun could be used in a stickup or against another cop. The courts don't take these things into consideration when they release the guy because of an illegal search.

These men further contend that the Court's attempt to prevent abuse of police authority and to safeguard *individual* rights went too far in establishing rules that ultimately favored and protected the criminally guilty. One detective best summed up the situation as these men saw it.

> As I said many times before, the police have lost the battle; good people are scared to death, bad people do what they want, when they want.

Although the great majority of policemen felt that recent Supreme Court rulings prevented them from doing their job effectively, they were quick to deny allegations that cops routinely disregarded the decisions of the Court in their everyday dealings with people in the street. The general consensus was that today only a "crazy" cop would risk incurring civil or criminal penalties by deliberately violating an individual's rights or by giving false testimony concerning a criminal incident. A formerly "active" police officer, one who made a lot of collars in Harlem, spoke candidly of the possible consequence of such police violations today. He observed,

> You gotta be out of your mind to fuck around with people's rights today. . . . You hear some of the horror stories about cops being fined $50,000 because they broke into someone's apartment illegally. That don't make no sense. I personally wouldn't give a fuck what kind of crime the guy committed. If I wasn't 100 percent right I wouldn't go in. I'm not going to turn my house over to some shit head junkie or pusher just for a collar. That goes for using your gun too. If you're wrong, you got problems, big problems.

This officer speaks for most cops today who are not only disturbed over what they see as a radical shift in government and judicial response to allegations of civil rights violations but who are unwilling to place their jobs and personal holdings in jeopardy by intentionally violating an individual's constitutional rights.

But what about those policemen who unintentionally or mistakenly violate someone's rights? Our respondents maintain that in the eyes of the court they are equally liable to civil penalty as the officer who willfully engages in such conduct. Thus, to escape civil or, worse yet, criminal prosecution in cases where an "honest mistake" on the part of the officer results in harm or personal loss to a citizen, police may attempt to shift the blame to the injured person through the use of "cover-up" arrests. One explained,

> Well, in order to cover up a mistake in judgement the cop has to make a collar. . . . As I said before the system is at fault here, not the individual officer. It doesn't permit mistakes, it punishes them.

That is, if a policeman roughs up a citizen, for example, or otherwise violates his constitutional rights because he erroneously believed something to be true, rather than own up to the mistake, the officer, fearing punishment, may arrest the citizen on "trumped-up" charges or false evidence. The point here is that "cover-up" arrests or other illegal actions can reflect unfavorably both on the department and on those individual officers who are attempting to establish citizen trust and confidence in the police. In this regard the following statement from a prominent American Civil Liberties Union spokesman is well taken:

> If the police simply hit a man and then let him go, there would be an abuse of the authority conferred by the uniform and the stick, but not the compound abuse of hitting a man and then dragging him to court on criminal charges, really a more serious injury than the blow. One's head heals up after all, but a criminal record never goes away. There is no more embittering experience in the legal system than to be abused by the police and then tried and convicted on false evidence.[6]

A number of policemen also saw the efforts of their colleagues to reduce criminal victimization hampered by the department's reaction to the findings and recommendations contained in the recent Knapp Commission report on police corruption in New York City.[7] Specifically, they complained of drastic and unrealistic changes in department rules governing methods police have traditionally used to collect information and evidence on criminal activities. The following lengthy reply to the question, "What effect has the Knapp Commission had on police crime fighting efforts?" reflects the feeling conveyed by these men that in its attempt to eliminate corruption at the patrol level, the department simply traded one set of problems for another.

This group [The Knapp Commission] has had so much influence on department policy concerning corruption. Well, you know what I mean. Cops are really limited in what they can do in the street. Their hands are tied because of all this talk over corruption. You can't go here, you can't go there. Stay out of bars, social clubs. Don't make narcotic arrests unless a supervisor is present. Who ever heard of anything like that. . . . Now if you are seen talking to a policy man or other so-called undesirable character, IAD [Internal Affairs Division] calls you down and wants to know all about it. And chances are they are looking to hurt you. . . . These people [such as gamblers and bar owners] used to be great sources of information. Now they know that they don't have to talk to you if they don't want. There is no fear of the uniformed cop anymore. I mean when was the last time you heard of a uniformed cop making a policy collar. . . . So now you mind your own business and keep your eyes and ears closed. Who needs the aggravation anyway. The people downtown want to show that the department is not corrupt. So what did they do, they overreacted. They restrict your activities. The department winds up pulling on one side, the people on the other. The department cannot withstand pressure. They tend to go along with the press and what they believe is public opinion.

It should be clear by now that many black policeman see themselves as much as victims of the political-legal system in this country as do people they are sworn to serve and protect. They feel that their efforts to protect the public from criminal victimization have been all but neutralized by a series of legal decisions and high court rulings which favor the offender. They see their authority and autonomy over the street criminal slowly eroding in the face of directives aimed not at reducing crime, but at reducing the likelihood of police misconduct and abuse of authority. But most of all, like their white brother officers they feel beset by a public who is at best indifferent toward their efforts to reduce criminal victimization and maintain some degree of law and order in the black community.

Furthermore, like other policemen in the country, the black officer believes he is caught up in a political battle between those who champion the rights of the individual and those who support the rights of larger society. Should he support the former position and abide strictly by recent Court rulings, he risks being labeled inept by his superiors who feel they must maintain arrest quotas and by those segments of the black community who need and demand greater police protection. Should he support the position that the community must be protected "at any cost" he is eventually bound to overstep the limits of his legal authority, thereby exposing himself to the possibility of civil suit or even criminal action. This dilemma was described by a veteran patrol officer in Harlem as follows:

> The job today sucks. . . . Let me give you a typical case. Let's say you get a call that some guy is selling dope on 118th Street. You got a good description so you go over to 118th Street and there he is. So you give him a toss [search] and you find out that he's got no drugs on him. Now this dude's looking to sue you for sticking your hands in his pocket. . . . So the next time someone tells you there's some guy selling dope you tell him you can't do anything about it, that you'll give it to narcotics. Meanwhile this character just sold some dope to a kid who O.D.'s on it. So because you couldn't legally handle the job yourself, some kid's dead and now the neighborhood is screaming how the cops don't give a shit. . . . Anyway you cut it the cop loses no matter what color he is.

As we know, one of the purposes of drawing blacks into the police department in the early 1970s was to improve relations between the police and black community, warding off in the process the possibility of future racial disorders. Since these young black officers had already experienced the turmoil of the 1960s and were presumably aware of the causes of disorder, perhaps they would come to share a more service-oriented view of policing ghetto communities. Because of their close attachments to the black community and their shared identification with community concerns prior to joining the department it is also possible that they would be subjected less to the negative assessments of police work in these areas then their older brother officers. This feeling is largely borne out in the experiences and accounts depicted in the following section. Most of the men reporting here have less than eight years of service with the department. What is not so clear, however, is whether these men are referring specifically to their own personal experiences as young, black police officers working in the ghetto or to black police officers in general. Perhaps they are referring to a specific category of black officers who, because of their special attachments to the ghetto, have resisted or delayed full socialization into the police world.

Black Police as "Peace-Keepers"

The belief that black policemen provide more effective services to ghetto clientele, as has been discussed, is supported by a second, but considerably smaller, group of respondents. However, for nearly all of these men effectiveness was not linked to traditional definitions of the police role as expressed by the other officers, but to the task of maintaining order in the black community in as judicious a manner as possible. Several reasons were offered to support their contention that black policemen serve the black community more effectively than white policemen. For one, the average black officer was reared under conditions nearly identical to those found in the ghetto today. Consequently, they understand the psychological needs and motivations of other blacks and are better able than the average white officer, who comes from a totally different cultural environment, to manage most conflict situations without having to resort to the use of provocative behavior or excessive force. There sentiments were summed up in the statement that

> In terms of color, the black officer is much more effective. In most instances, he functions better. Black officers understand the problems in black communities better than most white officers. They have a better rapport with the people. Take a guy with a knife, for example. The black officer is in a better position to get the guy to drop the knife without having to use his gun. Black cops better understand the situation. The white cop may shoot much quicker. Also, white officers may feel that something is of major importance, while the black officer sees it as minor most often.

Another policeman reflected on the importance of the "peace-keeping" role in black communities and on the ability of the black officer to mediate citizen disputes due to his "cultural" ties to and understanding of the black community. He said,

> Ninety percent of the white cops cannot relate to the black community. This, however, is a natural reaction. The white cop finds

himself in a strange world. He lives in private homes, not in tenements. On the other hand, the black cop is much more effective. He does not panic as the white cop does in situations where he should not panic. For example, if a dude pulls out a knife or something. This dude is just trying to "put on a show" for his brothers. This is a means to release some of the frustrations of the environment. The black cop, understands it and doesn't panic. He raps with the dude. He understands.

For some of these men "effectiveness" was also closely tied to the degree of interest an officer develops in the community in which he works. Black police, we are told, evidence a greater interest in the affairs and problems of the black community, as do other police groups to their ethnic community. This, our respondents contend, is a natural product of belonging to a particular ethnic group and assimilating its distinct cultural values. The following comments are typical:

Yes, because black cops have a clearer understanding of black culture. . . . Black cops have different attitudes because they have been raised here and are part of the culture. They automatically have an interest in the people and the community and are generally accepted as the Italian officer is more accepted in Italian neighborhoods. Their presence is generally appreciated by most people.

White officers are not as effective as black officers. They do not have the interest that the black officer has for the people in the community because they don't understand the ways of black people and don't make an attempt to learn them. As if a white cop is Jewish and he's working in a Jewish neighborhood, in all likelihood he will service the people better because he understands their culture and speaks their language. He has a special interest in his people that no other officer can have unless he is also Jewish.

Thus, we are told, an effective police officer is one who takes a genuine interest in the community, who is sensitive to its cultural nuances, and who is capable of managing "culturally related" conflict situations without always resorting to punitive measures. The average white policeman working in a ghetto community apparently cannot be expected to meet these qualifications. Having been raised in a lower-middle or working-class environment and influenced by middle-class values, the white officer quite naturally experiences difficulty understanding and accepting the different lifestyles encountered in the ghetto. Thus, when white officers react punitively to situations they see as deviant or provocative it may not necessarily be out of malevolence toward the people but because the situations themselves are alien and unfamiliar to them.

> A lot has to do with the willingness of the white officer to understand and accept the ways of black people. And here we are again with the white officer who comes from a more affluent area. Many times he will react negatively to a group of people sitting on the sidewalk drinking wine or beer. That may be a violation of law. But he's got to understand that these people have no other place to socialize; no backyard and no air-conditioned apartments.

The white policeman working in the ghetto is also charged with maintaining a double set of enforcement standards. Thus,

> White cops in many ways are less effective in black communities. Regarding violations such as drunk driving, the white cop is more apt to make an arrest of the black, while he might let the white guy go and just take away his keys. This results from a basic attitude of prejudice and stereotyped feelings toward blacks and drinking.

He is accused of overenforcing the law.

> White officers have little or no compassion for black people, that is for junkies and the like. Their remarks are generally, "Fuck it, let's lock him up." Whites feel that Harlem is their own private hunting grounds, or their private plantation. They ride around on their white horses cracking the whip.

He is blamed for making arrests in situations which may not always call for legal intervention.

> Black officers are definitely more effective and do a better job because they are not going to lock up everyone in the street. They adjudicate less serious cases between individuals in the street rather than in court.

The black policeman, as has been discussed several times above, is thought by some to be more effective than his white counterpart because he is a "peacekeeper" rather than a strict "law-enforcer." His supposed ability to sort out the truly dangerous situation from the more benign, to apply a single set of enforcement standards in dealing with the criminal element, and to mediate even serious disputes outside the courts seems to support this belief. But as we know keeping the peace and maintaining order are only two aspects of the police function. Another is reducing criminal victimization through deterrence; that is, by creating an atmosphere in the community in which the potential criminal comes to believe there is little opportunity to escape apprehension and punishment.

It is widely accepted among police that the solution of serious crimes, and more importantly the successful prosecution of criminal offenders, depends largely on information supplied to the police. Not surprisingly, a few of the men in this group pursued this theme, defining effectiveness not only in terms of the greater ability of black police officers to serve as peace-keepers in the ghetto but to their greater ability to cultivate and use informants in their community. They said,

> The black policeman is generally more effective because he can find out more about what's going on in his precinct. This is because he mixes with the people. He stops and talks with them as a friend, not as a cop. . . . The black citizen just feels more comfortable in the company of black cops. He feels more at ease with them and he is more willing to open up to them.

> Well, there are some white cops I know who get along exceptionally well with people in the precinct. They manage to get a lot of information that's passed along to the [detective] squad. But generally, the black cop gets more. He may have friends and family living there. The black cop is able to get more information this way more easily than the white cop who doesn't socialize or live there.

The white policeman, in contrast, generally does not mix freely with blacks. Indeed, as suggested earlier, he may deliberately isolate himself from the black community because it is precisely in these neighborhoods that he anticipates hostility and violence the most. Yet, by isolating himself from people in the community the white officer greatly diminishes his chances of developing important sources of information. The first officer quoted above continued,

The white policeman rarely stops and talks to people except when he wants something. By then, it's sometimes too late. For many blacks, he is just seen as a face passing by.

But it is not simply the black policeman's "social" ties to the community that afford him a distinct advantage over the white officer in obtaining crime-related information; his visible ties to blacks also allow him, for instance, to return to the scene of a serious crime in civilian clothes, and elicit information without arousing suspicion and fear. That is, as a black policeman observed,

> It's a matter of going back to an area and talking to people after everything has cooled down. By going back, maybe off duty, sometimes people who were originally reluctant to say anything may now come across with some information. Because the black cop is not afraid of the area and because his presence would not cast suspicion on anyone in particular, he is more willing to go back and take a chance that he will come up with something. This, the white cop is unable to do. His presence immediately says to the people that he is not there to socialize, but to get information. His color immediately makes him stand out. It's understandable, there is more risk for everyone concerned, especially the person who is giving up the information.

In this section we have attempted to find out how black policemen view their role in black communities and to identify some of the factors thought to be linked both directly and indirectly to police effectiveness in these areas of the city. Whether or not the black officer is, on the whole, more effective than his white counterpart remains an unsettled question that must take into consideration different and often conflicting definitions as to what constitutes "effective" police performance. It may be significant in this regard that the great majority of black officers interviewed defined effectiveness in terms familiar to most white policemen; that is, they saw themselves basically as "crime fighters" rather than "peace-keepers." Moreover, these same men responded to the question of effectiveness within a non-racial context; most felt that police, regardless of color, were virtually ineffective in terms of protecting the public from criminal victimization.

While many of the respondents pointed to a lack of citizen support and cooperation as the greatest single deterrent to effective crime control in the black community, others saw their efforts in this direction severely hampered by recent Court rulings and department directives which they felt acted to reduce both their authority and autonomy over the criminal element. From the standpoint of these policemen, the courts and to a lesser degree the police department itself are the real adversaries of the larger, law-abiding black public. Inability to deal effectively with ghetto lawlessness was also indirectly attributed to the mounting despair and frustration experienced by police as they come to realize that many of the problems inherent in ghetto law enforcement are beyond their control. Frustration produced by repeated failure to gain citizen cooperation and to mold the job according to their own needs generates a psychological state of apathy among police which is then turned outward on to the black public in such typical expressions as "If they don't give a shit, then why should I."

In contrast, a number of younger men felt that black police were, on the whole, more effective in black communities. These men depicted the average black cop as being more attuned to the nuance of ghetto culture, and thus better able to deal with ghetto generated problems. White police, on the other hand, were seen as having little understanding of and compassion for blacks and therefore unable to respond to even routine situations in a non-threatening way. Effectiveness for some of these men was also linked to the issue of police informants. Because of their social and highly visible ties to the black community, black police were seen in a better position to assist the public in combatting serious crime by their ability to attract, cultivate and utilize sources of criminal information.

In the following section we continue our examination of police in the black community, focusing this time on the perceived role of the black officer vis-à-vis ghetto youth. Here our discussion centers on the relationship between location in society and the forming of certain attitudes and values toward crime as a way of life.

Dealing with Ghetto Youth

One of the most serious and perhaps pressing problems facing ghetto communities today is the growing involvement of black youth in criminal activities.[8] Young black males, it seems, are not only the most frequent perpetrators of serious crime in our central cities, they are in many ways its most tragic victims. Some sociologists and students of juvenile crime have recognized that reversing this trend would require the intervention of social institutions and agencies that come in contact with inner-city youth. Yet, if one looks closely at their activities, it would seem that the police are one of the few that have both the responsibility for developing positive attitudes toward our legal institutions and the capability of dealing with those youngsters whose behavior borders on or is in direct conflict with the law.

With the problems of ghetto youth in mind, interviews were conducted with a small group of black officers. They were asked about the extent of adolescent black involvement in serious crime and the role of the black policeman as an agent of social control (and change) in the black community, and one question was whether the black officer could, if provided with adequate resources and training, serve as an effective role model in ghetto neighborhoods in order to encourage black youngsters to conform to socially approved behavior. The general feeling conveyed by these men during the group discussion was one of pessimism and deep concern about the realities of ghetto life today. Only one thought that black policemen could favorably influence the black youngsters' choice of reference group and future lifestyle. The others felt that, while such goals were indeed important, if not crucial, to the future stability of black communities, they could not. In the forty-six interviews that followed, most black officers expressed the same pessimism. Problems facing these kids were perceived as "far too complex" and involving facets of ghetto life over which the average black officer or, for that matter, any police officer had little or no direct control. Most thought that the larger society stresses the importance of achieving success (wealth, power, and prestige) while it restricts the achievement of these goals primarily to white people. Consequently, the only "practical" avenue to success, as many black kids see it today, is though illegal activities. A detective put it this way:

> The black kid nowadays looks to where the money is. Bread is the name of the game and the only access to money is hustling.

What the kid sees in the movies and in the streets are material things in the form of success. He looks up to the guy in the street if he doesn't have a father. I don't think the black cop can do anything, there's just too much against him.

While these policemen are quick to acknowledge the many dis-advantages attached to being raised in a disaffected and socially limiting environment, they also agree that these disadvantages do not automatically mean approving illegal activities as a means of getting ahead. A policeman speaks for most of these men:

Kids in the street [want] money. This is a money society. When you really get down to it, what other chances do these kids have to make a buck. Not that I accept or condone what they do to get money, but that I can understand where they are coming from. They have learned to get money from hustling, and the way they see it they aren't dumb for doing it.

Our respondents concede that the street hustler represents a powerful image to the ghetto youngster. The flashy cars, fancy clothes, and expensive jewelry conspicuously displayed by most of these individuals symbolize a lifestyle that is not only attractive to the young black kid, but one that has been attained despite the severe economic and social restrictions imposed upon blacks by the larger white society. To many of these kids the street hustler has succeeded in achieving society's sought-after goals, while the black policeman is simply "getting by."

The kids have a fascination to watch these people [the hustlers and pimps]. The cops have too much to overcome. The kids see people and to them the pimps don't have the hassle in life. Besides, kids want these things naturally, I guess. They see the pimps in the cars. They are visible. The cop comes up and has nothing to show them, so how is he supposed to change them.

What can you say to a black kid who is constantly exposed to peo-ple driving Cadillacs and other expensive cars, "A Volkswagon is better?" Police cannot compete with the superfly dudes. This image represents money and power. The department represents the sys-tem to obtain goals legally. . . . The black officer can merely say, "I'm doing okay." This does not mean anything to the kids. The concept of society is built upon wealth.

Black policemen also believe that the street hustler has attempted to discredit the black officer by deliberately undermining his professional role and image in the community. One officer explained how.

> Black kids are set against the cops by these pimps and drug dealers. . . . They are taught by these people to despise us. They are also taught that we are the suckers in the community, not them. They will do almost anything to make us look bad in the kid's eyes. . . . The cop doesn't have a chance.

The criminal way of life in the slums of New York City is further encouraged as youthful blacks come to see that the street hustler acts with virtual impunity. The black policeman appears to be powerless to prevent his activities and he is at the same time unable to compete with him for status and position in the community. This dual problem was poignantly described in the following account of a Harlem detective:

> I feel that black policemen can't do anything with respect to these kids. The department doesn't allow them to. From my experience recently, the department passed T.O.P.'s (Temporary Operating Procedures). Cops were not allowed to stop known narcotic dealers unless a supervisor was present. The department seemed more concerned with corruption than with trying to uphold the law. This gives the pushers more leeway to do their thing. The kids observe. The kids observe the guy off the block that didn't finish high school driving a $20,000 Mercedes and a pocketful of money, beautiful girls, buying a home in Teaneck, Long Island or Mt. Vernon and not being harassed by the police. Whereas males and females that went through high school and college and come from the same block as the pusher have very little to show. So the notion of being a hustler and not being harassed by the police seems to be more glamorous than going along with the system. The police can't do anything because their hands are tied.

Recent scandals alleging widespread corruption and gross misconduct within a small but "elite" minority unit in the police department were also thought to have neutralized the positive image other black cops were seeking to project to black youths.[9]

In my opinion, there is very little chance of black policemen reaching these kids in the near future. A few years ago, there was a good chance that a black cop could have been some sort of a positive role model for these kids that get in trouble. You had the PEP (Preventive and Enforcement Patrol) Squad in Harlem. This group of black patrolmen had the respect of the community. Kids began to look up to them. If you remember, these cops made a lot of collars, good collars. They took drugs and guns off the streets. No bullshit arrests, just good collars. Then came the Knapp Commission and a lot of these cops were accused of stealing money and shaking down people. This did more harm to the image of the black officer than anything else. It's going to take a long time before the damage that a few of these cops did will be rectified.

When questioned further some black policeman expressed the feeling that there was very little they could do to influence young blacks since their primary function in the black community was fighting crime. In making this point one respondent also argued against the notion that police ought to become involved in "social work" roles. Social work, he felt, was not a "real" police function and police, therefore, should not be expected to engage in activities that other city agencies were responsible for.

As I said, social work belongs to other agencies. That's what they get paid for. Most officers feel that they have other things to do after they work, other than work with someone else's kids. They have their own kids and family to be with. As I said, it's not sound thinking to believe that policemen can do very much with these kids, nor should they be expected to do a lot.

Another agreed.

What is the cop supposed to do, take the kid home with him at night? I think it's asking a little too much for police to become involved in these programs. First of all, they are not trained to handle problem kids. They would need a lot of training which the department is not about to do. And what about the other agencies who are responsible for these kids. That's their function, not ours. I don't mean to sound callous, but I think that police in Harlem have enough to do without becoming involved in other areas.

A detective with over 15 years of experience in slum communities expressed the feeling that perhaps it is not always the individual black officer who's opposed to becoming involved with black kids on a more intimate level, but the policeman's wife and family who may have serious reservations about such arrangements, especially when they involve bringing "strangers" into the home.

> I thought about it a lot myself. Maybe some cops would be interested in that, but maybe the wife doesn't want strange kids coming into her house.

Concern with protecting family members from possible harm was, in fact, reflected in virtually all of the responses to the question, "How about bringing one of these kids home for a weekend?" The following typical comment expresses the reservations held by these men:

> I don't know if I would want to take the responsibility for bringing kids home. The way I figure it, it's just too risky. I don't know what I would do if something happened to one of my kids or my wife because I was trying to be a "do-gooder."

Other policemen felt that black youths could be helped, even if the police were restricted in the conduct of their occupation and suffered from a bad image. The department, it was thought, should not abandon efforts to develop among young blacks a more positive attitude toward our legal institutions and system of law. The point was also made that any successful attempt in this direction would require that police, both white and black, approach the problems facing ghetto youth from a "humanistic" rather than a "punitive" point of view. Black cops, especially, should start by projecting a friendly, nonthreatening image and by demonstrating not only by words but through actions that the police are concerned about their well-being. The following comments reflect these basic themes:

> I think the police could do something by changing their approach toward black kids in the neighborhood, particularly those kids who need the most supervision. First, they have to show them that they

are concerned. Black policemen are articulate enough to project themselves as concerned human beings and policemen at the same time. I suggest rap sessions with the kids. Get the kids to talk about what's on their mind, even if it's difficult for the cops to sit down and listen objectively. Black cops should get involved more in community-relations programs with the kids. They should especially seek out those kids who are antisocial.

Better community-relations programs with the kids. Playing ball with them, taking them out and showing them that someone cares. Also, by not locking up the kids for bullshit violations. But by doing this the cop is almost committing malfeasance. . . . Most kids are street kids. They are confronted daily with the superfly image in the street and movies. . . . They have to be shown that the policeman cares about them, that he can be a friend to them.

An important point here, and one which seems to have eluded most police officials and law-makers, is the comment made above concerning arrests for so-called "bullshit" violations. The enforcement of laws pertaining to minor criminal offenses committed by juveniles presents a serious dilemma for the black officer (and some whites) who often views these acts not as "real" crimes but as wrongdoings which are tied closely to the cultural codes of ghetto communities and only "technically" in violation of law. By locking them up for these "crimes" the black officer discredits his identity as a ghetto-dweller in the eyes of some people. They consider him, in effect, to be part of the dominant establishment, a member of the enemy camp, a traitor who is not to be trusted or counted upon. However, if he overlooks these "technical" violations and does not arrest a black juvenile offender, the black officer is violating the law himself. Of course, if his failure to act is reported to his superiors, he could indeed find himself in serious trouble. Thus, the policeman sometimes cannot release a juvenile who is suspected of having committed a minor offense if he is reasonably confident that someone will make the matter "public."

Besides overlooking certain minor criminal offenses, there are other ways policemen could strengthen their credibility and overcome the basic sense of distrust of black kids in the ghetto. A detective who claimed to have worked with "marginal" black youth in the past offered one suggestion.

If you want to change their attitudes you can. But the black cop cannot do it alone. He needs the cooperation of other cops in the precinct. My feeling is that you have to try to project a friendly image in the street when you come in contact with these kids. A friendly gesture, not an arrogant look or remark, is all that it takes in the beginning. The cop has to show them that he does not despise them. Of course, this is only a start. Another thing, these kids have to be treated with a little respect. Again, that involves all the members of the precinct, not just the black officer. Cops should receive training in human relations. They should try to picture these kids as belonging to one of their friends. It's tough to do this in many instances, but it's a start.

Projecting a friendly image is only one approach to the problem, however. Will the policeman's influence over the behavior and career choice of ghetto kids be increased as a result of a few weekend outings or rap sessions? One officer suggested that what is required is a "dual" approach to the problem; one that combines the virtues of promoting greater understanding of the police and legal system with a program that focuses more directly on ways to discredit the ghetto youngster's most visible and accessible source of identification—the career criminal.

There's no question that black police must improve their image with the kids. Becoming involved with the kids in their world is important, too. But this is not the only answer. There are kids here who are very impressed with these guys in the street. I'm talking about the guys driving around in big, expensive, flashy cars, with lots of women and a pocketful of bread. What they don't realize is that most of these characters wind up in jail eventually or maybe they wind up shooting dope in some vacant building. I have found that one way to get through to these kids—to make them have some respect for police—is to introduce them to ex-junkies and other hustlers who have been through it all, the streets, prison, the whole works. Show them the other side of the picture. Not every kid is going to buy it, but for some, the description these guys give of prison life is like shock therapy.

Another detective reflected on the importance of discrediting the lifestyle of the ghetto street hustler by pointing out that the final fate of the hustler contradicts, in nearly all instances, his everyday image of "being on top."

I see the question as meaning, can I, as a black police officer, offer the kids in the street myself as a model to follow. . . . I don't think that this is the entire answer. I think the answer is to show them that the hustler and drug dealer are on top today, but broke, or possibly dead tomorrow. You got a kid without a father who comes out on the street and sees a man driving around in a brand new Caddy and possibly owns two or three others. How is it possible for me, as a black officer, to impress this child to be like me rather than the man in the Caddy. This is the reason I feel the other way about it. Bring them up to the office, up to the squad, and show them the pictures and the files and the actual hundreds of cases of drug dealers and hustlers who are killed each year or sentenced to long prison terms or just plain end up on the street broke, junkies, whatever.

In this section of the book we have considered several ways in which black police perceive their role vis-à-vis ghetto youngsters. As the great majority of comments suggest, black policemen do not feel that they can promote respect and support for our legal system among youthful blacks by offering themselves as alternative role models for the older, more materially-successful street criminal. Largely by virtue of their occupation and social standing in the community, black policemen see themselves, for all practical purposes, as powerless to compete with the street criminal whose behavior and lifestyle represent an escape from the economic deprivation imposed upon blacks by the larger society. In and of itself, this finding should come as no surprise. Some sociologists have suggested that most traditional forms of delinquency and criminality emerge under precisely those conditions in which access to material success through legitimate means is blocked and where opportunities to learn and perform deviant roles are both available and rewarding.[10]

What then can the police do to help alter existing patterns of delinquency and criminality in ghetto communities? Certainly, the police alone, or even in conjunction with other social agencies, cannot alter the structure of society to produce greater opportunities for black kids to achieve rewards legitimately. But, perhaps in conjunction with other social agencies, they can help discredit the criminal way of life by presenting to these kids a more realistic picture of what becomes of those individuals who engage in systematic criminal activities.

In the final section of this part of the book the focus shifts to another subgroup within the black community—the black offender. We are concerned with a number of aspects of the interaction between the offender and the black policeman. Specifically, how does the black offender define and react to arrest by a black policemen? Does the black offender, in the course of being taken into custody, present special problems to black policemen? And, if he does, how are these problems resolved in the work setting?

The Black Offender

It has been suggested in at least two studies of urban police that the black offender can and frequently does create special management problems for the black policeman.[11] This view, however, received only partial support in the present study. When asked whether the black offender gives the black cop a more difficult time than the white cop in an arrest situation, fewer than half of the 46 policemen responded in the affirmative. Most of the men felt that the white officer was more likely to experience problems from the black who is being taken into police custody. However, even many of these men agreed that the situation was not cut and dried since the approach and demeanor of the officer involved played a decisive role in structuring the outcome of most arrest encounters. As one detective explained,

> Generally, black cops have less trouble, but it's also an individual thing. Why? Because it depends on how the contact is made. In an arrest situation, lets say that they [the police] are disrespectful or brutal, they are going to get a lot of resistance and trouble, especially from the younger blacks.

A similar position was taken by a uniformed patrol officer who observed numerous arrests while assigned to work undercover in a special narcotics unit. He explained,

> I would have to say a black cop probably gets more cooperation and receives less trouble because of his affinity to his own ethnic group. They all came out of the ghetto. Yet, in the years I worked undercover, I observed things in the streets, cops making arrests, stopping people and so on. Those cops who got the most trouble

were the ones who made the arrest a personal matter, as if the person committed the crime against them personally. Those cops who acted cool, or neutral . . . who approached the offender not like he was some sort of freak or degenerate, rarely had any trouble. This goes for white as well as black cops. The way I feel, it's all in the way you handle yourself in the street, how you treat people, how you talk to them.

Of course, the behavior of the offender also affects the outcome of the encounter.[12] The policeman occupies the position of strength and authority and any affront to that authority can escalate the possibility of violence for the offender. It is suggested above, however, that there are normative guidelines which structure the role each participant plays during an arrest. No matter what the color of the participants, if these rules are followed there will be little trouble for either. But even this assumption is open, as we shall see, to further qualification. For many of the men who personally felt that the black policeman experiences a more difficult time from the black offender, such qualities as demeanor and approach did not seem to matter all that much. The fact that the officer was black and in uniform at the time was sufficient in many instances to trigger some form of resistance from the offender.

One explanation offered for this reaction on the part of the black offender centered upon the conflicting definitions of the arrest situation established by both the black offender and the black policemen. The offender in certain instances may define the arrest situation in purely racial terms and attempt to take advantage of his visible and presumed social ties to the black officer. He may, for example, chide the officer for doing what he considers "white man's work." If he finds that this approach will not work to gain his release, he may become belligerent or even physically abusive. A variation of this theme was offered by a detective who claims to have made "hundreds" of arrests in ghetto precincts:

He [the offender] takes it for granted that the black officer will go easier with him when an arrest has to be made. He feels that because the officer is a "brother," he can get away with more.

This is an interesting observation when one considers the different expectations that are generally attached to police encounters with blacks. As suggested earlier, white policemen seem to be more sensitive than black officers to the possibility of harm coming to them during confrontations with blacks, and may communicate this feeling in ways that tend to forestall resistance during the arrest situation—for example, the white officer may be quicker to reach for his gun or raise his night stick. Through repeated exposure to reactions such as these or through contact with other blacks who have personally experienced, witnessed or heard about such reactions, the black offender may come to define an arrest situation involving a white policeman as one in which he risks substantial injury should he forcibly resist arrest, or even challenge the officer's authority.

The arrest situation involving a black policeman, on the other hand, may evoke an entirely different set of images and expectations for both the officer and the offender. During most routine arrests, the offender may perceive that the black officer does not feel especially threatened and therefore will be less likely to respond with excessive force to a challenge or defiant gesture. This expectation, especially if it has been supported by other experiences with black policemen in the past, may encourage the offender to put up a little more resistance because he feels he can probably get away with it. For example, one black officer explained that

> I believe that for the most part, black and white cops are given an equal amount of trouble by the black offender. But when more static is given, it is given to the black officer because the guy knows from experience that the white officer is more apt to pull his gun and shoot him.

Most troublesome, we are told, is the individual who defines each and every confrontation between a black policeman and a black citizen in racial terms and who then attempts to embarrass the officer for occupying a role which he considers detrimental to his own race.[13] The officer who introduced this explanation went on to recall an incident in which he was personally singled out during a civil disturbance, was accused of ethnic disloyalty, and was reminded of his "real" identity.

> When I was in TPF during the Brooklyn riots, I had a male black approach me while I was standing in formation with a number of

predominantly white officers. He stated, "You're supposed to be a brother and you're out here coming down on us." I found out later from some of the people in the street that he was an agitator. He hated police and he especially hated black police and he gave them a hard time whenever he could.

The arrest situation, whether it occurs during a racial disturbance or not, seems to present a most opportune moment for some blacks publicly to condemn the black policeman as a traitor to his race and then try to provoke him into retaliating with violence. An officer said,

> I can recall being in situations in which black officers, myself included, were called "Traitors," "Uncle Toms" and names like that by certain people in the community because we were in a situation in which police action had to be taken. We had a real hard time with these people on a number of occasions.

A detective characterized these blacks as "rabble rousers" and offered the following insight into their motives for attaching a special significance to the actions of black policemen in the arrest situation:

> I would say that some people are out there looking to give the police a hard time and it's usually the black officer who they single out. These people have little commitment to the community, most of them. They just want to stir up trouble. They always seem to be around when a cop stops someone in the street. I would describe them as rabble rousers. They see the black officer as taking sides in a racial issue. They see him as doing harm to black people. It's not the "police" against the "criminal" issue, the way they see it. It's "black" against "white" and the black cop is seen as taking the (wrong) side.

The brief analysis presented here suggests that status distinctions take on importance not only within a specified normative context but within cultural ones as well. It also suggests that certain distinctions, e.g., "superordinate versus subordinate" are operative only at certain times and that status holders may attempt to replace distinctions which they feel are irrelevant with ones they feel are important. For example, the black offender may attempt to disengage the operative distinction "superordinate versus subordinate" when the former position is occupied by a black officer and replace it with the new distinction "white against black," in which the black officer is now cast into the "white" category. As we discussed before, real problems can arise when the offender's definition of the situation conflicts with that of the black officer, since it is the black officer (or for that matter, any officer) who invokes the operative distinction and its attendant rules of behavior.

As we have seen, the provocative and sometimes physically aggressive actions of the black offender can under certain circumstances create special management problems for the black policeman. How he reacts to the offender and to black criminality in general thus may differ from the way the white policeman reacts. With this in mind our respondents were asked whether the black officer is generally tougher than the white officer on the black offender and, if so, why. In answering the question most of the policemen responded in ways which strongly suggested that the color of the officer no longer plays a decisive role in the way blacks are treated when taken into custody. In fact, many of these same men went so far as to state that during most "routine" arrests, policemen of both groups tend to respond to the black offender in an emotionally detached, even-handed manner. This, however, was not always the case. In the past, we are reminded, unprovoked assaults committed upon black suspects and prisoners were commonplace in all of the city's police precincts.

> Ten years ago, the white policeman [was tougher]. I saw incidents that turned my stomach; mistreatment of prisoners and the like. Today, basically now, white and black cops approach toward the black offender are pretty lenient. Cops are cool now—although there are some psychos running around in the street—the majority are pretty fair with the offender.

> In the past, the white officer was much more brutal. I haven't witnessed any of this lately. Since the sixties, things have changed. They have gotten better. I don't believe the race of the officer has that much to do with the way the offender is treated anymore. Both black and white cops are pretty fair with the offender now.

Not only are police now seen to exercise greater physical restraint during routine arrests but, in the view of a few respondents, "cooperative" suspects and prisoners are often provided considerations beyond official department requirements. The following series of comments, for example, tend not only to support this view but also provide evidence of police behavior which seems to border on actual benevolence:

> Police are much more humane now. . . . Most cops now go out of their way to make life easier for prisoners. . . . For instance, they ask if prisoners want food or if they want to use the phone. Cops today make notifications [phone calls to the prisoner's family or friends]. Years ago, they didn't do this much. There is a better overall attitude now.

> I wouldn't say it's a racial thing. I think most police now are fairer than they were say ten years ago . . . especially in the station house when a guy brings a prisoner in. I don't see them dragging prisoners upstairs or into the backroom bleeding all over for no reason. If a guy comes in bleeding, chances are he really deserved it. I see cops sending out for coffee or sandwiches for these guys. This type of thing you rarely saw years ago.

> I think the whole department has changed in the way they treat prisoners. Many prisoners are even given money to buy smokes or coffee and even sometimes I've seen them send out for a little taste. . . . Cops don't beat on prisoners anymore, at least I haven't seen any of this.

Although the accounts given above clearly suggest that in most routine arrest situations police treatment of black offenders is more lenient and humane today than in the past, the men we interviewed conceded that force would be used quickly and effectively to overcome resistance to arrest or to reaffirm the officer's official position. The following typical comment gives evidence of this view:

> The majority of black cops can understand what's happening. And most white cops who are over the "shakes," they too understand what's happening. They use a little psychology with the offender in the arrest. However, if a dude gets down and starts calling him, he's going to get his ass kicked by either cop.

Black police do not always insist upon strict compliance with informal interactional codes in the street. Sometimes the black offender will be allowed to manipulate him by drawing in nonrelevant cultural issues such as race. However, as is made clear in the above comment, when the situation involves a personal attack upon or affront to the officer and especially when it leads the black officer to believe that he is losing control of the situation, he is likely to reestablish his authority and redefine the arrest in more formal terms.

Studies of the police have shown that "type of crime" can also influence the policeman's reaction when he is attempting to arrest an offender regardless of the officer's race. Especially despised by police and thus deserving of "special" treatment are cop fighters and sex degenerates who prey on children and the elderly and who, when caught, show no outward concern or remorse for their actions. Our interviews reveal that black police are no different from their white counterparts both in terms of feeling and reaction to those whose behavior violates "commonly accepted" standards of criminal conduct.[14] Consider the following typical comment:

> Well, I think the way an officer reacts to an offender depends on the crime generally. There are a few cops who are tough on all offenders. You see them in the precinct. Most cops, I would say, react according to the situation. I think some cops are probably tougher on sex offenders, particularly those guys who get picked up after committing some forceable crime against a child, or someone who seriously injures the person after attacking them. Also, I think the guy who shows that he doesn't give a fuck about what he did. These guys probably have it a little tougher. On the other hand, you have guys who break into apartments, steal a few articles and then leave, or guys who rip off pocketbooks or stick people up. As long as they don't bash in someone's head to get the money, there's no problem. In fact, in most instances, they're not treated badly at all.

As is evident from the following brief accounts, however, not all black policemen believe that time has significantly modified the attitudes and behavior of white policemen toward the black offender. Indeed, a few of our respondents remain convinced that the white officer, regardless of his time on the job or where he is assigned, still treats black suspects and offenders more harshly than do black cops.

The white policeman is generally tougher. Everyone he locks up is a "shithead" or "scumbag."

The white cop is more brutal. Opportunity to vent his hostility toward blacks. Its rare to find a black officer who is tougher. There is no reason for the black officer to be tougher.

Generally, the white cop is tougher. But there are some black, older cops who are very tough with the black offender. This is a throwback to the old school.

At one time the black cop was tougher. This has changed now. Now the white cop is tougher.

It may well be that under ordinary arrest situations white police are somewhat tougher than black police in their dealings with black criminals. But what about extraordinary situations? Are white police, for example, more apt to use their weapons to terminate a crime in progress or to effect an arrest? In short, are they more inclined to respond with violence to a serious situation involving the black offender? Recent data collected by a reporter for *The New York Times* suggests that if "toughness" is measured in part by involvement in fatal shooting incidents, then the black cop is indeed tougher than the white cop. According to official departmental statistics examined by David Burnham between 1969 and 1973, one out of every 250 white policemen killed someone while one out of every 38 black policemen did so. Specifically, during this period, the 30,000 white policemen in the department killed 64 blacks, 32 whites and 20 Hispanics. The 1987 black policemen killed 44 blacks, five whites, and three Hispanics.[15] If, as these figures suggest, the black cop is more likely to use deadly physical force in serious confrontations with black suspects, then it is also possible, as a number of men in this study claim, that he will respond more aggressively to the black offender in other, less threatening situations.

A number of explanations have been offered by those taking the position that black officers tend to resort to more extreme measures than the white. For one, it has been suggested by police authorities and sociologists as well as by the men in this study that the black policeman is as vulnerable as other members of the service to the pressures and frustrations of police work in ghetto communities.[16] And, in one important sense the black officer may be more susceptible to these strains. He often resides in communities populated largely by lower-class blacks and may have relatives and friends living in these same areas, sometimes in the very same precinct to which he is assigned. For the black officer, who has relatives or close friends, especially living in his work area, is sometimes inclined to take a tough stand with regard to ghetto crime and the black offender. The officer who responds in this manner can then justify his position on the grounds that the offender is presenting a threat to the safety of his friends and loved ones and to the future stability of his community. A black officer agreed as follows:

> I believe that some black cops are tougher on the black offender, not all of them, but some. . . . I would also have to say that many black cops, myself included, have family here and naturally we are concerned about what goes on. These people (criminals) are letting down their own race. They're forcing good people out of the area. They're committing crimes against each other, not robbing impersonal banks. The law-abiding person is paying all his money on a T.V. set and this is the only pleasure he gets when he comes home from work. And someone hits him over the head and steals it from him. Or he may work all week long and one of these bums comes along and takes it [his paycheck] from him or maybe he kills the guy.

This is quite obviously not the case with white policemen who, while they may work in the ghetto, return home to their white communities after their tour of duty.

> Sure black cops are tougher. They have to be. The black cop takes it to heart when honest people in the community are robbed or killed. The white cop works eight hours and then leaves. He has no family here. Many black cops have relations living in the ghetto. They are concerned about their people, what kind of a place it will be in the next few years.

Whether black policemen actually believe that by taking a "hard-line" approach toward the black offender they are in fact making the black community safer for their friends and relatives is questionable. A more likely motive for such reactions is the black policeman's feeling of frustration with the larger criminal justice system or society in general which is simply displaced on to a more available target—the black offender.

A few of the policemen also advanced the notion that some black cops feel they must act tough in the ghetto in order to earn respect and maintain authority in the face of increasing challenges from youthful black hoodlums. For example,

> In my opinion, black cops are sometimes tougher than white cops. However, they are tougher for other reasons and they don't evoke the same hostility and criticism as do white cops. The black cop sometimes feels as though he is not getting the respect due him from the younger blacks he locks up. . . . The ass-kicking they get is deserved; they know it and the people in the street know it and accept it.

Another policeman similarly justified the need to "lean on" the black offender a little harder in order to assert his position in the arrest situation.

> Black policemen are definitely tougher on some occasions. The black officer must lean on the offender a little harder because many blacks take things for granted because the black cop is supposed to be a "brother." If you go easy with them, they will not respect you. Sometimes, you take a lot of shit from these people in the street. . . . As I said, it's mostly a matter of respect. The black cop feels that he has the same authority as the white cop, but sometimes he doesn't get the same respect due his badge.

As we can see from the comments quoted above, the ability of the black policeman to regulate the conduct of other blacks may not always correspond to his own professional expectations. Some blacks in his precinct may view him as a "newcomer" to the police occupation and fail to confer upon him full recognition and acceptance in his official role; otherwise they may simply reject him as being in a position of authority because they consider his role detrimental to the interests of other blacks. Whatever the reason, the resulting disjunction between "official" authority which has been granted by the state and "real" authority which can only be conferred by the community may foster in some black policemen intense feelings of insecurity and frustration—feelings which can only be relieved by striking out first at those individuals who the officer feels are immediately in a position to challenge his authority. As one policeman commented,

> The black officer, being aware of his position as he believes others see it, automatically reacts defensively in an offensive manner to make clear that he is indeed authority and that his authority will be respected the same as the white officer.

Thus far in the discussion a number of observations have been offered concerning the social-psychological dynamics of interaction between police and black offenders. One conclusion reached by many of the men in this study is that police tactics today are geared more toward a humane, professional treatment of lawbreakers whether they are black or white. The claim was made, for example, that police now try to make life easier for criminal suspects who only a few short years ago could be seen being dragged into the station house, subjected to abusive and, at times, brutal treatement, deprived of their right to make telephone calls to members of their family, and denied requests to smoke or send out for food and drink. But what lies behind these apparent changes? One explanation that was offered has to do with the added presence and greater visibility of young black police officers in ghetto precincts. The feeling expressed was that the probability of a black officer arriving on the scene of a crime or showing up at the station house during the processing of a black suspect is now sufficiently great to restrain most overly aggressive (or prejudiced) white policemen from physically abusing prisoners. The assumption conveyed here is that the black officer is no longer going to tolerate abusive treatment of blacks at the hands of white officers. For example, one said,

> I've witnessed some changes and they're for the better. I think the fact that we now have more black officers here has had a lot of influence on the white officer, especially the way he behaves toward the black prisoner. The black officer is now visible. The white officer never knows when he's going to turn around and find a black

cop standing behind him, observing. Most black cops are not going to stand by and watch blacks get hit for no reason and the white cops know this. They are beginning to act more cool now.

Although the addition of greater numbers of black police since the late sixties (and by extension their greater visibility in ghetto precincts) no doubt has acted as a constraint against white police brutality, it is questionable whether this development, by itself, led to such dramatic changes in the behavior of white officers as some of the men claim. A more comprehensive explanation must take into account the possible impact of other recent changes in our legal system and in the general orientation of the police department itself. We are reminded throughout this study, for example, that the growing emphasis on college education for police in the early 1970s has had the effect of creating a small but nevertheless visible corps of policemen who are more professional in their approach toward policing today. Perhaps, as several writers have suggested, exposure to college education does tend to soften hard-line or punitive attitudes toward others by enhancing the officer's own self-image and esteem. The logic put forth here is that those who like themselves are more apt to deal harmoniously with others.[17]

Also contributing to this shift in police behavior towards those arrested was the establishment of the Civilian Complaint Review Board (CCRB) in the mid-sixties. Set up under the Lindsay administration to investigate and evaluate citizen charges of police misconduct (such as excessive or improper use of force), the CCRB presented a very real restriction on those policemen who consistently abused their power and authority when dealing with minority groups. For the first time in the history of the police department, criminal offenders could initiate charges of brutality against individual policemen   charges which if substantiated at an official departmental hearing could result in loss of pay, suspension, or, if serious enough, arrest and dismissal from the force. The threat of these sanctions seems to have had a very definite effect on the behavior of policemen. While the overall number of reported complaints alleging misconduct has risen somewhat since the late 1960s, indicating perhaps a growing public confidence in the Review Board, the number of allegations charging serious misconduct dropped substantially. This is most vividly reflected in the statistics for the past few years which show that the incidence of Class A complaints, which are the most serious, decreased from 642 in 1981 to 191 in 1982.[18]

The recent decline in allegations of serious forms of police abuse of authority may also be a reflection of the growing awareness among policemen themselves that they could be held civilly liable for their actions under Federal law.[19] Although there has always existed the possibility that a citizen, whether a criminal offender or not, could bring a civil suit against an officer for abuse of authority, only recently have the courts invoked Section 1983 of the Civil Rights Act of 1871 and begun to rule in favor of civilian litigants. According to a study conducted by the International Association of Chiefs of Police, the number of civil suits brought against police in this country more than doubled between 1967 and 1971. Although the great majority of these cases were lost in court by the civilian complainants, of those remaining judgements leveled against the police, the average penalty was $3000.[20] In New York City, the police department, under Commissioner Robert J. McGuire, has taken a firm position with regard to the question of liability. If the accused officer can show that he was in compliance with departmental procedures and orders and that he did not *intentionally* violate the complainant's civil rights, the city will assume liability for his actions. If, however, he is found in violation of departmental regulations, then the financial burden falls directly upon the officer.

Finally, substantial salary increases and related fringe benefits won by city cops during the Lindsay administration constitute another powerful factor in gaining an officer's compliance with departmental directives. Police in New York, despite the severe fiscal crisis of the mid-seventies, are still among the highest paid in the country and now may think twice before placing their jobs and economic security in jeopardy by intentionally abusing their authority or by otherwise engaging in unlawful acts against citizens. In short, the combined efforts of city administrators, high police officials, and the courts to curb the incidence of police misconduct has, among other things, sharpened the policeman's awareness to the fact that accountability and responsibility no longer rest solely with upper management but also with the individual officer. Without proper supervision and training, however, it may be years before every police officer becomes aware of this. Until then, and especially while the rate of violent crime continues to escalate in New York City, there will be individual officers who will feel compelled to act out their own personal shortcomings, biases, and frustrations with the larger criminal justice system by taking the law into their own hands.

NOTES

1. The following quote, taken from a woman whose son was murdered in Harlem, recently appeared in *The Daily News:* "There's a code: I guess you'd call it Ghetto Courtesy. No one will testify. No one will help a cop." James Stolz, "Trapped in the Courts," *The Daily News,* July 21, 1980, p. 44.

2. We are referring here specifically to crimes such as loitering, prostitution, gambling, and alcohol-and drug-related offenses.

3. See Allan N. Kornblum, *The Moral Hazards: Police Strategies for Honesty and Ethical Behavior* (Lexington, Mass.: Lexington Books, 1976).

4. On some street corners in Harlem, for example, heavy concentrations of drug addicts can be seen regularly "taking care of business." Yet, uniformed police for the most part seem to wink at these activities. Likewise, prostitutes, winos, and street deviants of all sorts congregate in certain locations in Harlem at all hours of the day, soliciting, harassing, and generally interfering with the normal activities of law-abiding citizens. Here too, these deviant groups seem to remain essentially free from police intervention.

5. It should be added that black migration to Northern urban areas of the country was also a consequence of the mechanization of Southern agriculture which left many, if not most, blacks without substantial means of employment.

6. Paul Chevigny, *Police Power: Police Abuses in New York City* (New York: Pantheon, 1969).

7. See, *The Knapp Commission Report on Police Corruption* (New York: George Braziller, 1972).

8. See, for example, Martin R. Haskell and Lewis Yablonsky, *Crime and Delinquency,* 3rd ed. (Chicago, Ill.: Rand McNally College Publishing, 1978), pp. 361–378.

9. The accomplishments of the PEP Squad from its inception in 1969 are indeed noteworthy. For example, between October of that year and October of 1970, this *20* man unit effected 298 felony narcotic arrests and seized 13,415 decks of heroin and 51 firearms. By comparison, the Tactical Patrol Force, which is comprised of over *1000* officers, effected only 77 felony narcotic arrests in the first 10 months of 1970. It is significant that this unit has been acknowledged in *The New York Times, The New York Daily News,* the black periodical *Amsterdam News,* T.V. news coverage, and by community leaders. These statistics were taken from the Guardians report entitled, *We Have a Responsibility,* dated March 1971, pp. 16–18.

10. See Richard A. Cloward and Lloyd E. Ohlin, *Delinquency and Opportunity: A Theory of Delinquent Gangs* (New York: The Free Press), 1960.

11. See William M. Kephart, *Racial Factors and Urban Law Enforcement* (Philadelphia, Pa.: Univ. of Pennsylvania Press, 1957), p. 116; also, Nicholas Alex, *Black in Blue: A Study of the Negro Policeman* (New York: Appleton-Century-Crofts, 1969), pp. 149–154.

12. See, for example, William H. Hohenstein, "Factors Influencing the Police Disposition of Juvenile Offenders," in Thorsten Sellin and Marvin Wolfgang (eds.), *Delinquency: Selected Studies* (New York: Wiley, 1969), pp. 138–149; Richard J. Lundman, "Routine Arrest Practices: A Commonwealth Perspective," in *Social Problems,* Number 22 (1974), pp. 127–141; William Westley, *Violence and the Police: A Sociological Study of Law, Custom and Morality* (Cambridge, Mass.: MIT Press, 1970).

13. See Nicholas Alex, who makes the same point in *Black in Blue,* op. cit., p. 150.

14. In one sense this finding tends to support Sudnow's interpretation of "normal" crimes. See David Sudnow, "Normal Crimes," in Earl Rubington and Martin S. Weinberg (eds.), *Deviance: The Interactionist Perspective,* (New York: Macmillan, 1968), pp. 158–169.

15. See David Burnham, "3 of 5 Slain by Police are Black," *The New York Times,* August 26, 1973. For a more recent study of police shootings see James J. Fyfe, "Who Shoots? A Look at Officer Race and Police Shootings," *Journal of Police Science and Administration,* Volume 9, Number 4 (December 1981). This study supports the findings of Burnham which disclose that minority officers are *disproportionately* involved in police shootings.

16. See, for example, Arthur Neiderhoffer, *Behind the Shield: The Police in Urban Society* (New York: Anchor Books, 1969), p. 193.

17. See Irving B. Guller, "Higher Education and Policemen: Attitudinal Differences Between Freshman and Senior Police College Students," *The Journal of Criminal Law, Criminology and Police Science,* Volume 63, Number 3 (September 1972), p. 401.

18. Data provided by a captain assigned to the New York City police department's Civilian Complaint Review Board.

19. We are referring here specifically to Section 1983 of the U.S. Federal Code which provides a legal foundation for the civil and criminal prosecution of instances of police abuse of authority. Concern about being sued in Federal court was personally conveyed to me on several occasions by police colleagues in New York City who stated rather grimly that they were aware of instances in which members of the department were sued in Federal civil court for actions taken by the officer in the performance of his duty. It was further reported that in a few of these cases the department absolved itself entirely from liability, leaving the officer(s) with full responsibility for his actions. Whether or not police in New York City have personally suffered severe monetary losses for their actions is perhaps less important than the belief that they have, or might. See also, David H. Bayley and Harold Mendelsohn, *Minorities and the Police: Confrontation in Amer-*

ica (New York: The Free Press, 1968), pp. 103–105, for a further discussion of the feelings of police toward this recent problem.

20. See Gerald D. Robin, *Introduction to the Criminal Justice System* (New York: Harper & Row, 1980), p. 88. Also see, George L. Kirkham and Laurin A. Wollan, Jr., *Introduction to Law Enforcement* (New York: Harper & Row, 1980), p. 356.

CONCLUSIONS

In this book I have attempted to report on the accomplishments and failures of black policemen during a period of massive social change by drawing upon material found in journals, newspapers, books, and department documents. But mostly I have relied upon a long series of interviews with 46 black New York City policemen who, by and large, were quite willing to tell me how they are treated by their superiors, how they get along with white officers, and how they view their role in the black community. This work seems incomplete, however, without offering my own views on the issues discussed by my respondents. As a member of the NYPD since 1966, and one who has served in a variety of investigative, patrol, and supervisory capacities in predominantly black areas of the city, I have become increasingly sensitized to a number of these issues and to the problems facing blacks and other minorities who have had to deal with a "white-dominated" department. While my assessment of these aspects of the black policeman's working world has undoubtedly been influenced by what my respondents have told me, it has also been shaped by what I have read and by what I have observed in the streets and station houses and have generally experienced as a member of the department. It is to these views largely that the remaining pages of this book are devoted.

Discrimination on the Job

In the foreword to a recent book depicting the history of blacks in the NYPD, Robert J. Magnum, a black New York State judge and former member of the police department between 1941 and 1958, summed up the conditions under which black police worked in those days:

Conditions . . . were almost unbearable, and we, in the third generation, were informed that they were even worse before 1931 and during the 1930s. . . . The assignment of Black police officers had been confined almost exclusively to three precincts throughout the city—the 28th and 32nd Precincts in Central Harlem and the 79th Precinct in Bedford-Stuyvesant.

Blacks at the time were almost never assigned to special assignments, such as the Detective Division, Plainclothes, Radio Motor Patrol and were completely excluded from elite special squads, e.g., Missing Persons, Burglary, Forgery, Safe and Loft and Truck, Pickpocket, Emergency Service, and so on. . . . Black superior officers were almost non-existent; Black officers received the most undesirable assignments; disciplinary actions against Blacks and against Whites were uneven at the expense of Blacks and racial slurs by White patrolmen and superior officers against Black officers and Black citizens were commonplace.[1]

Is racial discrimination still rooted in the system-wide operation of the police department as Judge Magnum implied? Are black police still confined to black precincts and districts? Are they still arbitrarily denied access to promotions and to specialized assignments, positions and duties? In short, how far have black cops come in recent years toward achieving full equality and acceptance in the New York City police department? I think it is safe to say that the type of institutional discrimination outlined by Judge Magnum above has been all but eliminated in the department. Today, blacks are not only actively encouraged to join the police service but, once hired, they are assigned the same basic duties as whites, promoted through civil service without regard to race, occupy in many instances command positions over whites (a situation that rarely obtained prior to the 1950s) and have available for the first time avenues of grievance redress both within and outside the organization.[2]

While the data collected for this study generally support the contentions expressed above, they also clearly indicate that black accomplishments did not occur in a vacuum, but were linked to and shaped by an interconnecting series of legal, social, and political events that were taking place in larger society. In a great number of major cities, for example, legislation had been enacted in the seventies to insure that local government agencies were in compliance with earlier Federal rulings aimed at eliminating discrimination in hiring, promotion, and assignment. Yet, as I have attempted to show, neither the enactment of antidiscrimination laws nor the creation of city agencies to oversee departmental practices regarding racial minorities were, by themselves, responsible for the entry of blacks into the police service in substantially greater numbers or for the movement of many of these officers out of routine patrol assignments. Toward the late sixties, there was a growing recognition on the part of local government leaders that blacks could serve the police department in important political ways. New York City, it might be recalled, had recently experienced a series of racial disorders that resulted in injuries to both police and citizens, widespread property damage, and a growing division between its white and minority populations. There was, no doubt, also a concern among high city officials that the predominantly "white-owned" businesses located in the ghetto would continue to suffer economic losses if new and more effective means of preventing disorders were not immediately found. By incorporating greater numbers of blacks into the actual process of policing and by assigning these officers to commands situated in ghetto districts, the city hoped to strengthen the bonds that linked the police with the black community, securing peace in the process.[3] Also, once sworn in, black cops could infiltrate black subversive groups suspected of instigating race riots and could serve in other specialized positions in which white police could not operate unnoticed. These were, of course, not the only compelling factors in the decision to open the doors to eligible black police candidates. The city also faced the very real threat of loss of Federal revenue-sharing funds should it be found in violation of Federal statutes prohibiting discrimination in the hiring of minorities.

Yet, perhaps, the greatest gains in the area of minority hiring were made by minorities themselves. Beginning in the late sixties black police, who felt that black candidates were being short-changed by the city, began to organize themselves into active political groups (such as the Guardians Association) to fight discriminatory hiring practices. Once organized, one of the first steps taken by the Guardians was to file suit in Federal court charging the city with using "culturally biased" entrance standards in an attempt to limit the numbers of minorities in the police department. When this failed to substantially "speed up" the pace at which blacks were being hired, the Guardians then challenged the use of what they claimed were "biased" exams. What eventually emerged from these and other attempts to bring about a more racially balanced department in the seventies was a quota system which insured that of every four officers hired beginning in 1980 one would be of minority extraction.

Largely as a result of the efforts of the Guardians Association to do away with discriminatory hiring practices in New York City, the proportion of blacks on the force is now over 10 percent, nearly twice what it was in the late sixties. This accomplishment may not seem that great in a city where nearly half the population is either black or Hispanic and where the current 24,000 member force is still 83 percent white. But one must also examine these gains within the socioeconomic context in which they occurred as well as the prospects for improvement in the future. Beginning in 1975, for example, as a result of a deteriorating economy, the city laid off 18 percent of all black cops and 22 percent of all Hispanic ones, compared to only 10 percent of its white force.[4] In actual numbers these figures represented a total of 632 minority officers whose service to the department had been "involuntarily" terminated because of civil service policies by which the "last-hired" minority members were released first. While clearly not an act of intentional *racial* discrimination on the part of city government, this loss represented, nevertheless, a tremendous setback for black and Hispanic groups who only a few years earlier had succeeded in adding some 1400 minority police or nearly 19 percent of all new appointments to the force.[5] During the next five years few, if any, recruits entered the Police Academy. However, by 1980, in part because of a recovering economy in the city, minorities once again began to see progress being made toward achieving a more racially balanced department. Under Judge Carter's court-imposed racial quota about 750 blacks joined the police ranks between September of that year and January 1982.

As for the future, if the current racial quota remains in effect during the 1980s—and there is no indication that it will be rescinded unless, of course, minority police candidates pass entrance tests in numbers that Judge Carter finds acceptable—and if attrition in the department continues at its present rate of approximately 2000 officers each year, then by the late 1980s the racial composition of the force should reflect more closely the proportion of minorities in the city.[6] This estimate is based upon the following facts and related assumptions. The overwhelming majority of police officers who will be retiring from the department during the 1980s will be white. This follows from the fact that most officers who joined the force in the 1960s (some 20 years ago) were white. Nearly half of all the nonranking black and Hispanic officers on the job today joined the department in the early 1980s and *will not* be eligible for pension retirement until the late 1990s. This new corps will provide a pool of minority officers who will, in all probability, attain ranking positions themselves under a different but also recently enacted racial quota system in promotions and who may well decide as some whites have in more favorable economic times to remain on the job past their eligible retirement date. Now, as blacks (and Hispanics) enter the department in increasingly greater numbers and advance in rank, a more favorable image of police work as a career should emerge in the eyes of members of the larger minority community. This new image should, in turn, attract even larger numbers of minority police candidates in the future as the community itself will have less reason to suspect black and Hispanic officers of being tools of the white society. This does not necessarily mean that the *actual* number of minority cops in the department will greatly increase in the near future. That will depend upon both population and economic stability in the city. Should the city's economy, for example, once again take a turn for the worse, then we may very well see fewer police positions available in the future, fewer promotions to ranking positions, and perhaps most important of all, fewer retirements of whites due to a decrease in outside job opportunities. But even if the city were to experience a declining economy the overall proportion of minority officers in the department should increase as a result of the racial quota system in hiring. Thus, while blacks (and Hispanics) may not gain much in terms of absolute numbers under a deteriorating economy, they should still gain proportionately to whites.

Besides being able to count upon increased opportunities for police employment in New York City, blacks, once hired, can expect to be assigned to precincts in the future on a more-or-less random basis. Unlike their brother officers in the past, the black cop will not find himself excluded from assignments in more affluent, white areas of the city because of his skin color. As we know, this was generally the case in the sixties. For "political" reasons, largely, black cops were routinely assigned to lower-class ghetto districts. Today, the virtual absence of unrest in the city's black communities coupled with recent pressure from the Guardians Association to do away with "restrictive" assignment practices, has resulted in a more balanced distribution of newly hired black officers. This pattern is evident in most, if not all, of the city's "mixed" communities where the current proportion of black police ranges anywhere from 10 to 35 percent, and even in such affluent areas as Manhattan's "silk-stocking" district, where in the past year or so close to half of all newly assigned cops are of minority extraction. The recent trend toward nonrestrictive assignments can also be inferred from the racial distribution of civilian members of the service. Like the black and Hispanic officer, the minority civilian can expect to be assigned to commands located outside as well as within the ghetto.

Black police not only fought and succeeded in modifying geographical assignment practices to accommodate their own special interests, but they made equal, if not greater, gains in the areas of task assignment and advancement. Restricting black cops to foot patrol duties, for example, is clearly a thing of the past. Today, and for some time now, assignments to motor-patrol duty depend largely, although not entirely, upon seniority and performance. Officers who have only a few years in rank and who show a willingness to meet even average performance standards can expect to be assigned to motor-patrol duty sooner than junior members of the precinct regardless of their color. Advancement to the detective bureau is another area in which blacks (and Hispanics) have made significant strides since the 1960s. Data collected by the department's Office of Equal Employment Opportunity consistently show that during the seventies nonwhite officers have been assigned to detective commands in *greater* proportion than their numbers in the patrol force and, once there, advanced in grade at an equal rate as whites. This suggests that the department has for some years now at least supported a policy of proportional representation for its minority police in the detective bureau if not a policy of merit advancement.

Although the data in this study show that the black officer is clearly better off today than he was some years ago, he may find nevertheless that his chances for upward mobility on the job are still restricted in some cases by factors beyond his control; that is, they are not affected by court action, increased political activism, or by above-average performance ratings. For example, the black officer may discover that even though he is fairly represented in the department's 70 or so specialty units, he is likely to be more fairly represented in some than in others. Emergency Service, Harbor, Highway Patrol, Auto Crime, Arson/Explosion, and Inspections are but a few examples of "preferred" specialty units in which black participation is not only below but in some instances well below the average of 10 percent.[7] Even at the precinct level in some commands, the black officer may find opportunities somewhat limited for movement out of routine patrol. As I mentioned earlier this situation may be due in part to a "self-elimination" process activated by the black officer who deliberately chooses not to volunteer for certain specialty assignments because of the belief that occupational values held by members of these units often run counter to his own. But mostly, I believe, it is tied directly to his "newcomer" status in the organization; that is, to the fact that he is not yet considered a member of the established group. Because the black officer is a "partial outsider," he may find in some precincts that he is not entitled to all the benefits full membership brings. His ties to most white cops in the precinct are, for the most part, limited largely to matters of official police business. Rarely is the black uniformed officer in a position to cultivate the type of relationships with white officers that can lead to privileges or preferential treatment on the job.

The black officer's connections and relations with whites outside the work setting is, generally speaking, even more limited. Because he is not a member of the dominant ethnic group, he does not belong to their social fraternal clubs. Because of continuing social pressures exerted by both sides, he does not, as a rule, fraternize with white cops after work. And, finally, because white society still has the means to exclude most blacks from white surburan communities, he doesn't live near white cops and consequently doesn't travel to and from work with them. Together, these restrictions, which are linked largely but not entirely to his position within both the department and the larger society, hinder the development of the kind of informal intergroup ties needed by the black officer to compete on equal terms with his white colleagues in the precinct. The black officer similarly finds that he cannot turn to his white superiors for preferential treatment. For all of the above reasons, his relations with most white bosses are also limited to matters of an official nature. Nor, can the average black officer always count on his brother officers of higher rank to help him move ahead on the job. For, like himself, blacks in supervisory and command positions also occupy a "newcomer" status with many of the attendant disadvantages.

How then is the black patrol officer to overcome the disadvantages arising from partial membership in the organization? It has been my feeling for some time now that the answer does not lie *solely* in further court action or in greater political activism on the part of black police groups, since these avenues only redress problems which are tangible and therefore amenable to such tactics. Blacks, if they are to compete on truly equal terms with whites, must establish, at least for the time being, independent sources of power and influence within the structure of the organization. This means, for one thing, that more of them must attain supervisory and command positions. Yet evidence presented earlier shows that even as late as 1981 black bosses accounted for no more than 4 percent of the entire command structure of the police department, hardly an encouraging picture.

Some would argue that this condition is due in large part to the persistence of discrimination in the police department; but this seems barely an accurate assessment of the problem. What has historically accounted for the small number of black bosses is a seniority system which has, as far back as I can determine, allotted credit on promotional exams (up to 50 percent on some) in proportion to longevity on the force. Since blacks, as a group, were relative newcomers to the department in the 1960s and early 1970s, this arrangement, although clearly not aimed at keeping minority candidates down, did operate to their greater disadvantage. As well, a promotional testing system which emphasized education and reading skills as requisites to successful exam-taking adversely affected blacks who have suffered disproportionately in the past from educational deficiencies. It was unlikely that they would have scored as well as whites on exams which stressed the acquisition of these skills. Also, it is clear from speaking with the men in this study that some blacks lack motivation to prepare for competitive civil service examinations.[8] This, however, may have been due in some part to the fact that in past years, and especially during the late 1960s, blacks who did attain ranking positions in the department were often "hidden away" in nonuniformed, specialty units such as Narcotics and the Bureau of Special Services. Because these bosses were not accessible to lower-level blacks, they did not serve as a reference group to which black officers could aspire to belong or even relate themselves psychologically. In this sense, then, the placement of black bosses in "low visibility" specialty units in the late 1960s, early 1970s, had the unanticipated and somewhat dysfunctional consequence of lowering the motivation of lower-level blacks to aspire to ranking positions in the department. Finally, and perhaps most importantly, there was a sharp reduction beginning in the late 1960s in the frequency with which promotional exams were being given—a condition owing largely to the city's growing fiscal problems during this period. In the past 12 years, for example, only two civil service tests have been offered for promotion to the rank of sergeant, one in 1973, the other in 1978. And it is only from the more recent exam and only in the past year or so that minorities have been promoted to the rank of sergeant under a court-imposed quota system. Similarly, the last promotional exam for the rank of lieutenant—a position in which blacks make up a scarce 2 percent of the command structure—was last given in 1973, nearly a decade ago.[9] This meant that only those blacks who had been appointed prior to the late 1960s would have been eligible to take this test and of this group only those few who had passed a prior sergeant's exam. Clearly, while it was neither the city's fault nor its intention that so few promotional tests have been offered since the early 1970s, it is impossible nevertheless to integrate blacks and other minorities into upper management positions where they can begin to effect policy change, if they have not first been afforded the opportunity to take lower-level sergeant and lieutenant promotional exams.

While there is a clear trend in New York City today toward reducing the importance of seniority in promotions to supervisory and lower-management positions,[10] there still remains the dual question of black educational deficiency in exam taking and along with that the problems generated by the infrequency with which promotional tests have been given in recent years. In attempting to deal with these specific problems the city has recently moved in two directions. First, there are indications that the Department of Personnel will be scheduling promotional tests on a more frequent basis in the future due to the growing number of vacancies in lower and middle-management positions which have, in turn, been created by greater-than-average numbers of retirements and a newly expanding work force.[11] There also is evidence that future promotional exams will test job-related issues and attempt to measure the candidates' knowledge of police procedures, policies, and law rather than acquired reading skills or mathematical ability as they have in the past.[12] In conjunction with this, evidence has also come to my attention which suggests that as a group, black police may be considerably better educated today than whites.[13] If this is true, then black candidates for promotion should be able to compete on more equal terms with whites whether future tests are "job-related" or not. Of course, as has been mentioned, the more important question is whether blacks will be sufficiently motivated in the future to study for competitive promotional tests. If reference group theory does explain, in part, the lack of motivation among members of this group in the past (and I suspect it does) then the steadily growing number and visibility of black uniformed sergeants ought to provide the incentive needed for lower-level blacks to adequately prepare for these exams in the coming years. But even if this is not the case, or if for any number of other reasons blacks continue to fare less well than whites on competitive promotional exams, the recent enactment of a racial quota in lower-level promotions should serve to insure greater representation of black supervisors in the near future. And as blacks move into supervisory and command positions in increasingly larger numbers, their sphere of influence should begin to expand, altering in the process existing patterns of informal power relations.

The other factor which, in past years, has effectively blocked the building of an independent and interlevel black power base in the New York City police department has been the near-total concentration of senior white officers in key clerical positions. Data from the department's OEEO show, however, that this pattern is changing. Beginning in the early seventies, the police department has slowly but systematically replaced police officers occupying these positions at all operational levels with (predominantly) black and Hispanic civilians. In 1975, for example, there were some 5400 civilians employed by the department in various clerical, technical, and professional positions, of which nearly 1500 or 28 percent were black. By the early 1980s the total civilian force had climbed to over 7000, while the proportion of black civilians jumped to 47 percent.[14] What accounted for this sharp increase in civilian representation in the department was the belief (shared by many city officials) that well-trained and supervised civilians could perform most routine adminstrative tasks as well as police and for substantially lower salaries and fewer fringe benefits.

Besides reducing expenditures during a critical period in the city's history and freeing thousands of uniformed officers for more important field assignments, "civilianization" systematically stripped away one of the key bases of "informal" power for whites in the organization. Once removed from the "office setting" and assigned to patrol duties, these officers soon lost the "connections" that were the source of their power and influence. Gradually, the informal power that was once in their hands exclusively was being transferred to minority civilians who clearly were not going to continue to favor whites over other emerging groups.

Changing economic and social patterns in the city during the past decade or so have not only begun to alter traditional power arrangements among lower-level police, as evidenced above, but they have triggered changes in relations among officers of unequal rank as well. It might be recalled once again that, as a result of the mass exodus of white police to the suburbs beginning in the late 1960s, new friendships based upon residential proximity and the need to travel together in car pools were beginning to emerge between white patrol supervisors and white subordinates—friendships that would later carry over on to the job and affect the informal distribution of rewards and privileges.[15] Because blacks lived predominantly in the city, they did not become involved in car-pooling and therefore missed out on the opportunity to become part of these newly emerging networks. But evidence suggests that this pattern, too, is reversing itself. Rising divorce rates among city police have forced many of these white officers to return to the city rather than rent an apartment in the suburbs.[16] Not only are these officers moving back into the city in greater numbers but the rapidly escalating interest rates on new home mortgages is effectively limiting the pool of newly hired officers who can afford to live outside the city. Now as the older whites retire from the job and as they are replaced by minorities—who in all probability will be forced to remain within or close to the city—and as members of these groups advance in rank themselves, patterns of informal power relations linked to hierarchical ties in the department should begin to shift in favor of the newly emerging groups. In short, preferential treatment based upon group membership and informal ties will never completely disappear in the police department even under the most egalitarian conditions as long as the power to provide services to others is built into the structure of positions themselves. My own personal experiences, along with data provided by this study, do suggest, however, that the *bases* from which informal arrangements develop and grow will continue to shift in the future, reflecting in the process changing social, economic, and political trends both within and outside the department.

Although I argued earlier that favoritism in its various forms operates on all levels of the department, its impact on blacks in recent years seems least acute in the detective bureau. This is not because blacks have been able to establish an independent base of power at this level, but because the changing structure and needs of the bureau in the 1970s provided for the application of more egalitarian standards in distributing rewards and privileges. As the detective bureau shifted to specialization, for example, the role of detectives underwent considerable transformation. Case clearance, teamwork, and the acquisition of "social" skills replaced long-standing "quantitative" indicators of performance, prompting detective supervisors themselves to adopt a more rational, race-free basis for rewarding members of their units. Whether these new criteria continue to govern the way rewards and privileges are distributed in the future will depend in part, I suspect, upon further structural changes in the organization. Should the department perceive a need for the detective bureau to revert to its earlier form (with an emphasis on "quantity" rather than "quality" arrests and case clearance), it is conceivable that rewards (advancements in grade) and privileges will once again be distributed largely among

members of the dominant group who, in the past, were more willing than blacks to undertake activities which futhered this goal.

There is yet a final problem facing black police in New York City
and elsewhere. This is the deliberate attempt by *individual* whites
in the department to deny blacks all the opportunities and advantages attached to membership in the dominant group *solely* because
they are black. Individual racism, regardless of the work level in
which it is found, differs in several important ways from favoritism. For one, whites who engage in the practice of favoritism make
distinctions based largely upon friendship ties, past allegiances, or
group affiliation. They do not, as a rule, single out other whites
for preferential treatment because of their dislike or distrust of blacks.
Indeed, the racial factor is seldom ever consciously considered. The
racist, in contrast, makes his judgements affecting positions and
duties based upon group membership and disdain for nonmem-
bers and unlike the white who practices favoritism, places race over
all other personal values and individual characteristics. Second, even
though both favoritism and racism may result in the unequal distribution of rewards and privileges along racial lines, the two practices are often quite different in terms of personal impact. It might
be recalled that favoritism in its earlier form (political patronage)
was defended as a means of adjustment or way of circumventing
the political systems of this country which failed to satisfy the dis-
tinctive needs of immigrant American groups. In this sense, it served
a positive function for those who had few alternative means at their
disposal to pull themselves up out of poverty. While its form has
changed somewhat over the years in New York City, favoritism or
patronage is still regarded by many cops as an accepted or customary "way of life" in the organizational arena. This feeling is evident
even among many blacks in the department who, ironically, benefit less from the practice than do members of the established group.
To my knowledge no black cops have defended racism or even attempted to justify its existence.

Personal experience over the years suggests that racist cops, while
admittedly few in number, are more often than not senior members of the service set in their ways and beliefs about black people.
Their view of blacks as being primitive, inferior, and quite often
"different" regardless of the individual's background, occupation,

or position in the community, undoubtably was formed prior to their entry into the police department and reinforced by racist folklore and selected contacts with members of the black community. But it is not this view that sets the racist apart from the great majority of his white colleagues: There are many whites on the job who think of blacks in these terms. Rather, it is an attitude toward and treatment of *black* police as indistinguishable from all other blacks that identifies this type of individual. The uniform the black cop wears, the authority he represents, and the accomplishments he has achieved over the years have in no way altered this perception. In the eyes of the racist white cop, the black officer is viewed not as a colleague but as an unwanted "outsider" who has systematically infiltrated the ranks of the "established group" and devalued the prestige of the job.

What is especially harmful about the racist cop's view of blacks is not that he simply has them but that he often translates them into racially-discriminatory behavior. Because of intense negative feelings about blacks, the racist white officer, for example, finds that he cannot or will not act in an objective way toward them. His predispositions often prevent him from backing blacks in troublesome situations, from being receptive to advice they may have to offer, or from recognizing their superior performance. The black cop may also find that the racist white is never satisfied with the quality of work no matter how hard he tries to please. He knows, moreover, that he cannot be outspoken, especially on racially-sensitive issues and can never take a position contrary to that held by the white police. But what disturbs him most is the feeling he gets that these very same standards are hardly ever applied to whites in the same command—that he is being singled out for special treatment only because of his color.

Most detrimental to the acceptance and position of blacks in the department is that the racists' views are often contagious, especially when communicated by someone in a position of authority and leadership. The casual use, for example, of the demeaning term "nigger," when referring to blacks on the job, not only affects the subordinate's attitude toward members of this group, but at the same time conveys the feeling that the department itself condones notions of black inferiority and subordination. Yet, it is because the racist's true feelings are generally hidden from blacks in his command that this individual represents a most serious challenge to their position. One simply, after all, cannot fight that which one cannot document and prove. Therein lies perhaps one of the most difficult problems facing progressive police agencies today—that of identifying and separating from sensitive command assignments those individual bosses who still harbor racist attitudes *and* treat blacks in ways that reflect these views. In the past there has been a tendency among some police commanders to ignore (or even deny) behavior on the part of a subordinate officer that was *racially* discriminatory in both intent and impact. Through such tactics the commander avoided a direct confrontation with an unpleasant problem. Unfortunately, by doing so he was also conferring approval upon existing practices in his unit. It should be recognized, in conclusion, that police agencies are hierarchically structured and that changes in behavior and attitude usually come about when those in charge take a firm position against discrimination.

Interpersonal and Intergroup Relations

Perhaps, as some of the men in this study claim, the single most important determinant of racial change in the NYPD has been the early civil rights movement. Operating as it did on a number of levels this movement was directly responsible for eliminating legal barriers to equality by providing avenues through which blacks and other minority groups could effectively challenge racially-biased policies and practices in the work setting. But the early black movement influenced racial patterns in the NYPD in other ways as well. For example, because of the accomplishments they achieved in the area of job opportunities, black police were beginning to feel better about the department, feelings that would eventually carry over into their relationships with white cops. Of course, white police who had actively demonstrated in the sixties for higher pay and improved working conditions were also beginning to change their view of civil protest and of black police as they themselves gradually began to identify in this regard with oppressed groups.

While the early black movement was setting the stage for positive changes in interracial patterns on the job, it was, ironically, the more militant phase that would eventually have the greatest impact on relations between the two groups. Yet, as some have asked me, how could a movement that clearly opposed established and cherished values and that occasionally called for violence as a solution to America's racial problems, draw black and white cops closer together? It did so in several ways: First, the latter movement with its emphasis on racial pride provided the stimulus for a new self-conception and sense of identity among many black officers in the city. Rather than being dysfunctional to racial integration in the department, as might be expected, this new identification resulted, in the long run, in greater acceptance of blacks as equals on the job.[17] Second, and perhaps more critically, the militant movement provoked in some instances violent, guerilla-type attacks upon black and white patrol teams in the city. By altering the policeman's perception of the "enemy" and by directing attention away from internal racial issues and problems, these assaults succeeded in reducing the importance of race and in fostering a closeness and sense of common identity between the groups. In fact, it was shortly after a series of fatal attacks on black and white teams in Harlem and in the East Village by members of the Black Liberation Army that I became aware of a new sense of comraderie developing between black and white policemen assigned to central Harlem precincts. Mutual hostilities and division which had for some time characterized interpersonal relations in this area seemed to diminish even among the more overtly prejudiced and militant officers.

At about this time other developments were taking place in the city that would reduce further the division between the groups. For one, the police department itself was in the process of hiring additional black officers and assigning them to neighborhoods populated largely by blacks. Of course, not all white police reacted with enthusiasm to the influx of blacks, but in time many did come to recognize and appreciate the advantages of having black cops assigned to work in the ghetto. Gradual acceptance rather than outright rejection became the norm in most of the city's police precincts.

The problem of racial polarization in some police commands at the time also came under direct attack by Commissioner Patrick Murphy. In a number of experimental precincts, human-relations training programs were set up. Their primary purpose was to strengthen cooperation and team work between white and black cops at the command level and to promote a sense of mutual respect and acceptance for their views. According to several official reports issued by the department, this program was an overwhelming success. Most officers who participated found it, as did some of the men in this study, to be a rewarding experience and expressed a desire to extend the program into the future.[18] In addition to this, the Commissioner embarked upon an all-out effort to encourage police officers to pursue a college education. Murphy remained convinced (in spite of the controversy surrounding the issue of police education) that college-trained officers were more likely than those that were not to develop a sensitivity to the problems facing urban police and minority groups. This effort too was deemed a success. By the mid-seventies well over 6000 police officers, or roughly a third of the force, were attending college on their own time; over 1800 of them had already attained degrees.[19]

Another development that appeared to weaken the *racial* basis of group solidarity in some police commands was, ironically, the Knapp Commission's investigation into organized police corruption during the early 1970s. In its attempt to root out corrupt influences in the department and prevent patterns of misconduct from reemerging in the future, the Commission intentionally created an atmosphere of suspicion among police officers that any one of their colleagues could be working for the Commission or the department's Internal Affairs Division. In response to this tactic, police officers throughout the city and especially those assigned to commands in corruption-prone districts such as Harlem, soon developed strategies of their own to screen out fellow officers who, regardless of color, were either suspected of or known to be sympathetic to the Commission. It was during this period and for some time after that I began to see new relationships emerging along lines of mutual trust, rather than race. Both black and white officers suspected of having breeched the police "code of silence" were systematically separated from those who were not suspect. Of course, once suspicion was dispelled after the Commission hearings, old friendships were reestablished in many of these commands, but the new ones which had developed prior to and during the hearings (many of which were interracial) also remained intact.

As with any attempt to alter long-standing practices and feelings in a particular social setting, however, there is bound to be both resistance and differences of opinion as to its success. So it is with a number of policemen in this study who remain essentially unconvinced that relations between blacks and whites on the uniformed patrol level have substantially improved over the past few years. These men point to factors which, because they are thought to be so deeply imbedded in the belief systems and work routines of white police, constitute a persistent source of intergroup conflict. Racial exclusivism, whether it results from genuine feelings of aversion toward members of another group or from a natural tendency on the part of black and white cops to keep to themselves, is thought to be one potential source of strain between the groups. Racial incidents, and especially the kind that result in an assault upon or shooting of a black, nonuniformed policeman by a white officer are another. However, as we know, since 1974, when the department first instituted formal procedures standardizing the manner uniformed cops would use to verify the identity of a member in civilian clothes, there have been no instances of mistaken-identity shootings by either group against the other. The one problem remaining in this regard are the incidents which result from the use of unnecessary force or inflammatory language during the verification process and even these, I am told, are practically unheard of today.[20]

Another potential source of intergroup conflict at the patrol level (and the only one I am inclined to believe constitutes a threat even to established relationships today) is the abusive treatment some black citizens receive at the hand of white cops. Although I have argued earlier that the black officer's understanding of the white cop's reasons or motives for behaving in this particular way may be distorted by the "racial" factor operating in the ghetto, the fact remains that white uniformed police are, on the whole, apt to treat blacks as a group differently than whites because it is blacks, not whites who are numerically overrepresented in lower-class ghetto communities where the actual conflict lies. In other words, actions taken by white police, while seemingly influenced solely by visible racial factors are in fact influenced, both consciously and unconsciously, by factors linked to social class. What color a person is, is, in my view, of less importance as a predictor of police decisions regarding the treatment of a citizen. If the person is presumably or actually of middle- (or upper-) class standing in the black community, the police, while they may not always think of him as such, will nevertheless treat him the same as they would a white person from a similar background.

Yet while white uniformed police and people living in the ghetto continue to experience conflict, evidence collected from this study suggests that the more blatant and unchecked abuses of police power that gave rise to interracial dissension on the job in the past are on the decline. This is a consequence, in part, of the introduction in the seventies of new police procedures and policies aimed at improving relations between the races. But mostly, I sense, it is the result of the greater presence and visibility of minority officers in the streets and of the increasing use of civil litigation against the police for abuse of authority. Indeed, "lawsuits against officers for everything from failure to act and excessive force to false imprisonment . . . reached near-epidemic proportions" during the 1970s.[21] And given the increasing frequency with which Federal courts have been ruling in favor of civilian complainants, along with the publicity these decisions have generated over the past few years, it is not at all surprising to find that even the most unstable, brutal, and irresponsible officers are being effectively deterred from intentionally violating the rights of minority citizens.[22]

In analyzing the changing character of police race relations, it would appear that while there has indeed been some improvement over the years in the way black and white patrol officers get along on the job, structural factors operating on this work level continue to produce the potential for conflict and division between the groups. One factor identified in this study is the nature of patrol work itself, that is, its routine, demanding, socially restricting and potentially dangerous character. Stated another way, patrol work in those areas of the city where black and white officers experience the greatest exposure to each other is of such a nature as to limit rather than increase the type of intergroup contact needed to form attachments and friendships across racial boundaries. Yet, it is in this particular area that the department is perhaps least able to effect change. It cannot, for example, regulate the kind or frequency of jobs police routinely handle while on patrol. Nor has the department much control over the physical environment in which most patrol officers work. Another factor mentioned earlier concerns the actual assignment of patrol officers itself. It has been argued along these lines that if black and white cops could only experience more contact with each other, racial difficulties would be resolved. However, we also know from observations of the behavior of whites and blacks in the Republic of South Africa and in parts of the American South that increased interracial contact can, under certain conditions, intensify rather than lessen hostility and conflict between the groups.

What then can be done to reduce the potential for conflict between white and black uniformed cops in the coming years? For one thing the department could structure the work environment for its newly hired officers so that they would experience greater interracial contact under conditions that are more conducive to the growth of mutual respect and acceptance. In fact, while the department is probably unaware of it, the Neighborhood Stabilization Unit (NSU), originally formed in 1978 to project a "high visibility" police image throughout the city, was one step in this direction. Comprised of rookie police officers fresh from the academy, the NSU operates out of designated precincts in the city's five boroughs. Members assigned to this unit ordinarily work in teams of two on foot or in patrol cars under the supervision of hand-picked sergeants and field training specialists. Except under the most unusual of circumstances NSU officers are expected to respond only to certain types of jobs while on patrol. They are not required to handle most routine jobs assigned to members of the regular patrol force.

While assigned as a precinct sergeant first in the Bronx and then in Manhattan, I had the opportunity personally to observe NSU officers both in the street and during more relaxed moments in the station house. What impressed me most was the ease with which this mixture of young black, Hispanic, and white officers worked together—the virtual absence of any display of friction and the seemingly total disregard of their racial differences. None of the NSU officers I observed or came into contact with between 1980 and 1981 seemed to experience even the slightest difficulty adjusting to their visible and sometimes sociocultural differences and accepting each other as equals on the job. What was crucial in terms of bringing about these desirable results was, first of all, the fact that these officers from the day they left the Police Academy worked apart from members of the regular patrol force and were consequently shielded from the negative influences of the older, more cynical and prejudiced cops in the precincts. Secondly, even though it is true that members of both the NSU and regular patrol force are experiencing greater interracial contact in their respective commands nowadays, the types of contact situations experienced by white and black cops assigned to the NSU differ greatly from those experienced by members of the regular patrol force. And, as I suggested above, it is not simply *increased* contact between the groups that leads to mutual respect and acceptance on the job but, as Gordon Allport and others pointed out some years ago, contact under *controlled* conditions under which the races interact with the positive support of law or authority, possess equal status, are cooperatively dependent upon each other, and seek common goals.[23]

The critical issue here is to what extent do the NSU and regular patrol force meet the criteria for furthering cooperation and respect. In the police department today clearly the first condition obtains for both. All cops, regardless of rank or assignment, work together under the support of law and local authorities. But beyond this differences between the two units begin to emerge. And it is these differences that I believe account in large part for the virtual absence of racial difficulties in the NSU on the one hand and for the lingering potential for interracial problems among cops assigned to precinct patrol. For example, all bottom-level police officers have the same official status within the organization. Yet for some whites assigned to the regular patrol force even recent Federal and local rulings have failed to alter their erroneous perception of blacks as possessing a subordinate or inferior status. This comes across most clearly in their disparaging remarks directed not only at members of the black community but at black cops themselves. These men simply do not view blacks as "equals" regardless of whether they are merchants in the community, political leaders or co-workers on the job. Some white patrol officers also do not see themselves in a position of cooperative dependence upon their black colleagues. For them, the average black cop is not viewed as a member of the police fraternity but rather as an "outsider" who is invading the white policeman's territory, monitoring his behavior in the streets and station houses, and siding with other outsiders in decisions affecting his authority and autonomy in the black community. In addition, the nature of patrol assignments, most of which are handled effectively with little or no assistance from other police units, serves to dull the officer's sense of dependence upon others in his precinct except, of course, under the most demanding or dangerous of situations.

Perceptions of status equality, dependence, and cooperation are, as far as I can see, manifestly different among members of the NSU. Largely because officers assigned to this unit are required to spend the first six months of their field training in virtual isolation from members of the regular patrol force they have, like members of other specialty units in the department (e.g., detectives), come to depend almost exclusively upon one another for support, direction, companionship, and, perhaps most importantly, protection in the street. This mutual dependence leads, in turn, to a sense of status equality among the officers which is evidenced not only by the respect they show each other at work, but by their occasional willingness to establish and maintain relationships after working hours.

Perhaps the greatest single difference separating the NSU from the regular patrol force involves the area of common or mutually agreed-upon goals. There is rather strong evidence in both this and other studies which shows that even though white and black patrol officers often share a common definition of their role in the black community, there remains some difference between them as how best to achieve certain departmental goals.[24] The issue of aggressive patrol in the ghetto, for instance, has come under sharp attack from some of the younger blacks on the job today, who see it not as a way of *preventing* street crime but as a means of *harassing* black people. Most white cops, in contrast, support the policy of aggressive street patrol despite the potentially harmful effect it has on the attitudes of some black groups toward the police. There is, in addition, disagreement between some white and black patrol officers as to the priority that should be attached to certain traditional police goals. Many blacks who joined the department in the late 1960s adopted "peace keeping" and "order maintenance" as predominant organizational goals while most white cops on patrol clung to the belief that the policeman's primary job should be fighting crime. In the NSU, by contrast, conceptions of occupational roles and job priorities are determined largely, although not entirely, by the officers themselves during the first six months of their careers and have an important and relatively permanent effect on their later identity. While there is an obvious concern among these officers with protecting the public from criminal victimization and engaging in other traditionally defined law enforcement pursuits, extreme positions and work styles tend to be effectively tempered by the process of interaction and informal negotiation which takes place in the field between the officers. Here the "racial" factor, that is, the constant interaction between white and black NSU cops under equal status conditions, combines with the more "relaxed" setting in which these officers work to produce a more "balanced" view of the police role—one which is then carried with the officer to his permanent precinct command. Moreover, working on foot (or in a radio car) by themselves and not having to deal with the seemingly uninterrupted flow of "tension-producing" jobs routinely handled by members of the regular patrol force provides an optimal setting for police of different racial backgrounds to discover that they share similar beliefs, interests, and values which are totally unrelated to their job. And it is this discovery or in some instances the actual growth of similar personal characteristics that supplies many officers with a basis for mutual attraction and lasting friendships. Indeed, many of the white NSU cops that I have worked with and come to know on a more personal basis since their reassignment to precinct commands, have not only brought with them a set of attitudes toward their work and their black colleagues that is more in keeping with current notions of equality and fair play, but have maintained these positive attitudes in the face of unpleasant, adverse citizen contacts and occasionally countervailing pressures from older white precinct officers.

It would thus finally appear to me that there is considerably more accord between the NSU and the detective bureau in terms of meeting Allport's four conditions for reducing interracial conflict than between the NSU and the regular patrol force. But this should not be surprising. Both (NSU officers and detectives) work in the type of environment that invariably leads to a reduction of prejudice through increased interracial contact under equal status conditions. Both share within their own respective work settings a common definition of their role which is predicated, among other things, upon a mutually dependent effort that involves little or no competition along racial lines. And both can boast of experiencing few, if any, internal racial difficulties. Based upon these observations alone it would seem that the department would do well to preserve the concept of NSU in the future and to establish a policy that would provide, where possible, for the random pairing of newly assigned officers. This arrangement would avoid the necessity of applying a strict racial formula in assigning members to teams, thereby eliminating the problem of "race accenting" inherent in such a formula. Of course, this approach would not, in all instances, cure the problem of individual dislikes and hostilities, but it might help discourage the growth of group distinctions that, in the past, were made along strictly racial lines. Furthermore, considering the growing numbers of blacks, Hispanics, and women who are joining the police department each year, as a practical matter, this arrangement would present few hardships on the officers involved. In fact, it would be far easier to achieve integration at this early stage in the officers' career than at a later point when role conceptions, work habits, and attitudes have been set. The department might also consider extending the period of assignment in NSU, thereby providing newly hired officers with even greater opportunities for cross-racial contact under conditions that are conducive to the growth of mutual respect, acceptance, and lasting friendships. Finally, and in conjunction with this, the department might consider efforts to modify the precinct patrol officer's *perception* of his working environment and role in the black community so that both are more compatible with current policing requirements. But, this will take, among other things, a renewed emphasis on both higher education and in-house training of the kind that will break down, in a way acceptable to most police, traditional definitions and belief systems.

The Black Community

As the data in this study show, the black struggle to achieve equality and acceptance has over the years taken a variety of forms. First, there were court battles and formal government intervention initiated mostly by prominent civil rights leaders. These actions were followed by more direct challenges to America's dominant value system—challenges which culminated at times in violent confrontations with those in established positions of power and authority. Finally, there was a collective effort on the part of black groups and government leaders in some cities to incorporate minorities not only into the ranks but into the policy-making structure of its social, political, and legal institutions.

While efforts in the 1960s often occurred simultaneously, it was not until the early 1970s that government agencies such as the police began to experience real changes in their policies and practices. In New York City the decision, for example, to increase black police representation was based, among other things, upon a number of political considerations; most important, perhaps, was the belief that, once hired, blacks would behave in ways that were more acceptable to racial minorities, in the process transforming community hostility toward the department into trust and support, as has been discussed a number of times. It was also felt, as a practical matter, that since black cops would be welcome in ghetto communities, they would be more effective in these areas. But, as the interviews in this book tend to show, these assumptions did not always translate into reality. Many blacks who joined the department in the 1970s soon found themselves facing conflicting demands for loyalty. As members of the black community they were expected to bring into their neighborhoods definitions of the police role that were more compatible with black culture and interests. As police officers, they also were expected to conform to a set of occupational values and beliefs that were often at odds with those held by some sectors of the black population.[25]

For a number of younger black officers entering the department during this period, being part of the larger black experience heightened their sense of identity with the community and led to a rejection of many traditional police values. These younger men openly expressed interest in the affairs and problems of the black community, an attachment foreign to all but a handful of white officers. Because they grew up in the ghetto themselves, they had a better understanding of its culture. Consequently, when assigned to patrol, they were less apprehensive than white cops in their dealings with black people and more likely to attempt to mediate problems without resorting to provocative behavior, unnecessary force, or arrest. Also, because these younger officers felt less threatened in contact situations with other blacks, they tended to integrate themselves into, rather than isolate themselves from, the community. In short, for many blacks living in the ghetto, the added presence of the young black cop in the street represented a significant break with traditional methods of patrolling these areas and a move toward fulfilling the real meaning of the "service" model of policing.

The belief that the black cop could serve as a buffer between an outwardly prejudiced and insensitive white department and the black community prompted a number of men in this study to recommend that precincts with a large black population be staffed with mostly black cops or, if that was not feasible, mixed with whites and assigned to patrol in integrated teams. While on the face of it this seems like a practical response to conflicts between police and blacks, there are in fact a number of problems that arise. Considering first the question of integrated patrol teams, aside from the problems that might develop due to the reluctance of precinct commanders to insure proper compliance with such a directive, it seems unwise for the department, especially at a time when white and black cops are working together with little or no *outward* display of friction, suddenly to "accent" the racial issue. By *forcing* white and black cops to work together under a "racial" formula, the department is, in effect, publically admitting that a problem exists. Second, the *forced* integration of patrol teams would probably come under sharp attack from police union officials as well as individual officers of both colors on the grounds that it would be disruptive to internal morale. It is important to remember that patrol officers have traditionally chosen partners on the basis of similar work styles and job values and more recently with regard to the need to work together or at least be assigned to the same team if they travel together long distances to and from work in car pools. To the extent, then, that car-pooling serves, among other things, a vital energy-saving function, it could reasonably be defended by police line organizations as both a legitimate and practical reason to maintain traditional assignment practices. In short, any deliberate disruption of long-standing arrangements that results in undue hardships, economic or otherwise, would not only meet, I suspect, with political resistance from the officers, but would lead to increased racial polarization, lowered morale, and reduced productivity.

As for the staffing of precincts located in predominantly black areas of the city with black officers, a different set of problems emerge. For one, the drastic cutback in police personnel during the mid-seventies resulted, as I noted earlier, in the disproportionate layoffs of minority police. Although this condition eased somewhat with the recall of a number of these officers and with the institution of a racial hiring quota in the early eighties, it is still uncertain whether the department will be able to attract in the very near future sufficient numbers of eligible blacks to insure a predominance of black cops in all or even in most of the city's black districts. Second, even if the racial composition of the department were to undergo substantial change in the 1980s and minority representation began to approximate the city's larger population, it is still not at all clear whether the department would greatly benefit by assigning its black cops exclusively to black precincts. There is, for example, the question as to whether black cops themselves prefer working in ghetto precincts, and if some do not if these same officers will perform up to par. Moreover, even if some black cops might prefer ghetto assignments, the demand on the part of other black officers to serve in patrol areas outside the ghetto has been so great that the Guardians Association has recently sought to do away with racially based assignment practices altogether. Besides the other disadvantages attached to working in high-crime, physically demanding ghetto precincts, such assignments may symbolize for some black policemen their subordinate status in the department and suggest to the larger public that they are not capable or worthy of policing white areas of the city. Finally, and perhaps most importantly, there remains the question of whether black police are as warmly received by people in the black community as some claim. If, in fact, they are not held in such high regard by significant sectors of the black population and if for individual reasons some black officers prefer, even demand, assignments elsewhere, then it would seem less justified or even counterproductive to saturate black areas with black police or even to consider forcibly integrating patrol teams to begin with.

Actually, there is evidence in this and earlier studies of the police which strongly suggest that among certain sectors of the black community, the black officer is viewed and treated in much the same way as his white counterpart.[26] Distrust of the legal system as a whole and of the police in particular is apparently so great among these groups that the black officer is suspect simply by virtue of the uniform he wears and the interests he is presumed to represent. Yet the perception of the black officer as a "white cop in black skin" is linked obviously to more concrete circumstances. For example, by joining the police department during a favorable economic period (such as the late sixties), black cops were provided not only with needed jobs but with a means to escape from the ghetto to more advantaged surroundings. This led in some instances to a disassociation from the values and lifestyles that once were the basis of their identification with the very same people they were hired to serve. Indeed, it is not all that uncommon today to find among black cops who fled the ghetto soon after joining the department, an attitude devoid of any special attachment to the community, its people or its internal problems.

But some black policemen did more than just disassociate themselves from the problems of the inner city. A few contributed directly to these problems by systematically engaging, along with some white cops, in serious forms of misconduct including the accepting of illicit payoffs from narcotics' dealers, gamblers, numbers' operators, and local businessmen.[27] In fact, it was the exposure of these unlawful activities among members of the "elite," and largely black, Preventative and Enforcement Patrol Squad during the early 1970s that, according to a number of men in this study, greatly undermined the positive image other blacks in the department were attempting to project in Harlem. There is, in addition, the charge that some black cops are overly harsh in their dealings with certain groups in the black community, especially criminal offenders. Whatever the motivation for this type of behavior, whether it derives from legitimate concerns for law-abiding people or from cultural values internalized during the socialization process, it can only be interpreted by sections of the black community as further proof that underneath their black skin lies a "white" mentality.

Rejection of the black policeman by segments of the black community has, over the years, taken a variety of forms ranging from subtle innuendos to more direct attacks upon his identify and physical well-being. There is, for example, a feeling shared by some black cops today that authority is not automatically built into their official position as it is with the white officer. This comes across most strongly in routine encounters with senior black citizens (especially crime victims and complainants) who often seem to prefer dealing with white officers, with a substantial portion of the younger black population who view the black officer's position in the department and community as marginal, and with the black offender who occasionally reveals his contempt for the black officer by challenging his right to make an arrest of another black or even to take police action to begin with.

Besides experiencing rejection from hostile and suspicious segments of the black community for the reasons given above, the black officer has also had to come to grips with the feeling that he is actually no more effective in combatting crime and reducing victimization in the ghetto than his white counterpart. And, like the great majority of his white brother officers who work in these areas, he has turned outward in assigning the blame. He contends, for example, that in the black community there is a growing disrespect for law and order, that he is not receiving cooperation and support from the public, that because they do not understand or refuse to accept the legal constraints under which he must operate in today's changing society, they have become increasingly bitter toward the police and indifferent to *their* problems. But the black officer is equally critical of both the administration, which he claims has substantially weakened his power over the criminal element by instituting changes in police procedures, and the Supreme Court, which he now sees, as do most white cops, as favoring and protecting through its recent decisions the criminally guilty. It is perhaps an irony to the black officer that many of the same rulings and departmental directives that were enacted during the 1960s and early 1970s to curb formerly unchecked abuses of police power in minority communities have also effectively limited his ability to deter crime in these areas, to make arrests that stick and to collect evidence for successful prosecution. Understandably, such experiences have tended to alienate many black (and white) cops not only from the department and larger legal system, but from the community they are sworn to protect. Not only have these experiences led to frustration, cynicism, and resigned apathy, but they have undermined the officers' own self-image, pride in his work, and commitment to the higher ideals of police service.

Some blacks in the department have attempted to meet the frustration generated by changing laws and procedures, contradictory roles, greater citizen demands for protection, and growing community indifference to their problems by applying for transfers to less demanding assignments where they could pass the time studying for promotional exams or waiting for retirement. But even here they experienced rejection and added frustration because, until very recently, the ghetto was precisely where the department felt it needed its black officers the most. It was at this point that the job ceased to be viewed within a professional context for many of these men and became instead simply a means to a paycheck. Unfortunately, this definition of police work reinforced in the eyes of some black citizens the negative images and expectations they had of the black officer to begin with.

Perhaps, then, the basis for improving police effectiveness in the ghetto does not lie exclusively or even predominantly in saturating these areas with black cops. Rather it would seem to lie, as I have indicated earlier, in efforts to inculcate in *all* police coming on the job an understanding of, and receptivity toward, their changing role in today's society. And I remain firmly convinced that, in spite of the various arguments to the contrary, one way this can be accomplished is through higher education. Again, I am not speaking of education in the natural sciences or even the police sciences, but education in the social and behavioral sciences. It has been my experience that police college students trained even minimally in these areas are better able than most who are not college educated to recognize, accept and deal with changing situations both within the department and the larger society. Serious students are, on the whole, more sensitive to ghetto problems, less abrasive in their dealings with minority citizens, and more apt to apply the "spirit" rather than the "letter" of the law. In short, they are more effective police officers.

However, a great deal more focused research is needed not only into the kind of social science curriculum that police ought to be exposed to, but research dealing with the length of time police students must attend institutions of higher learning before they begin to experience measurable change in attitude and behavior.

That is, it seems to me that any evaluation of the substantive benefits of college training would of necessity have to take into consideration both the content of academic curricula as well as the length of time spent gaining a higher education. In the meantime the police department must renew its support for the concept of higher education for police and possibly even consider requiring that future promotions to higher rank be predicated upon completion of a college degree.

In concluding, one final point ought to be made. I have tried to show throughout this book that while the situation of black police in New York City has indeed improved over the past decade or so, this change was inspired mostly by events occurring outside the organizational setting. For example, as the political system in New York City underwent reform in the mid-sixties and as local government began to experience a need for greater accommodation of its minority groups, these groups began to experience a parallel move toward greater acceptance and equality. However, as we know, the political climate on both the Federal and local levels has once again shifted direction, bringing with it new governmental priorities. Whether the NYPD will maintain its position as a progressive institution in the area of race relations during the next decade will depend not only on the direction these priorities take, but upon a renewed commitment by local government, its minority leaders, and constituents (both within and outside the department) to resist, through political, and if necessary legal, expression, any attempts to turn the calendar back. If it is to maintain this position the department must also take steps on its own to eliminate the remaining vestiges of racism and inequality in the work setting by increasing the number of police whose views are more consistent with the democratic ideals of this nation.

NOTES

1. James I. Alexander, *Blue Coats-Black Skin: The Black Experience in the New York City Police Department Since 1891* (New York: Exposition Press, 1978), pp. ix, x.

2. Part of this statement is not entirely correct; the recently established racial quota in promotions now allows blacks with lower exam scores on civil service tests to advance in rank over whites with higher scores. So, in effect, these officers are being promoted *with* regard to race.

3. See Nicholas Alex, *Black in Blue: A Study of the Negro Policeman* (New York: Appleton-Century-Crofts, 1969), p. 27.

4. See Janice Prindle, "New York's Whitest—Keeping the Melting Pot on the Back Burner," *The Village Voice,* October 15–21, 1980, p. 21.

5. Ibid, p. 20.

6. Information on police retirements was provided in November 1982 by Police Officer Lou Matarazzo of the Patrolmen's Benevolent Association.

7. Data provided by the New York City police department's OEEO.

8. A number of men interviewed for this study claim that although they put some effort into studying for promotional exams, they did not put in enough to pass the tests. Others told me that they weren't really interested in being promoted to supervisory positions and therefore did not study at all. And still others stated that their only goal was to achieve the rank of detective (a nonsupervisory position). Having accomplished this, they had no interest in moving beyond this position.

9. Data provided by the New York City police department's OEEO.

10. Since this writing a civil service promotional exam to the rank of lieutenant has been given in which full seniority (i.e., ten years in rank as a sergeant) added *only* five points to the candidate's final mark.

11. Beside the recently held exam for promotion to lieutenant, the department has tentatively scheduled exams for promotion to captain in 1984 and to sergeant in 1983.

12. Unlike all past civil service promotional tests, the written portion of the recent lieutenant's exam contained no questions which were directly aimed at measuring the candidate's ability to read and understand lengthy paragraphs. The questions themselves consisted of a few short sentences and focused on work-related duties of precinct lieutenants and on information members holding this rank ought to have in order to effectively carry out their assigned duties.

13. In the 5th and 6th Homicide Zones in Harlem, for instance, black detectives attending colleges and universities during the late 1970s outnumbered white detectives by at least three to one. I have also found similar proportional representation in colleges in some of the patrol precincts from which I collected data. These are, of course, only rough estimates which do not speak for black and white police in other parts of the city. Yet, I strongly suspect that these commands (located mostly in Manhattan and the Bronx) are fully representative of other commands in the city. See also, Bernard Cohen and Jan M. Chaiken, "Police Background Characteristics and Performance," (The New York City-Rand Institute, August 1972), p. xi. In this study the authors noted that black officers in New York City were considerably better educated than white officers. Nearly 40 percent of the black appointees sampled had attended college for at least one year as compared to slightly over 20 percent of the whites. For further evidence of the higher educational level of black New York City police officers, see James Sordi, "Do the New York City Police Department Efforts to Recruit Black and Hispanic Officers Clash with its New Appointment and Promotion Proposals," John Jay College of Criminal Justice, unpublished M.A. thesis, 1973, p. 44.

14. Data provided by the New York City police department's OEEO.

15. Car pooling is not an issue among detective sergeants and their subordinates since detective bosses, unlike their uniformed counterparts, work a different chart (schedule) than their subordinates. Uniformed sergeants, for example, are normally scheduled to work the same tours as members of their squads thus allowing them to travel to and from work together. Precinct detective bosses, on the other hand, work an overlapping chart so that they are able to supervise members of all teams over a designated period of time. The irregularity with which a detective sergeant supervises any particular team of detectives serves, in effect, to preclude car-pooling as a feasible arrangement.

16. Many researchers have commented on the high divorce rate among police in this country. Anthony Pate of the Police Foundation, for example, has compiled data from the National Institute of Occupational Safety and Health which show that the current divorce rate among police is twice that of the general population. See W. Clinton Terry, 111, "Police Stress; The Empirical Evidence," *Journal of Police Science and Administration,* Volume 9, Number 1 (March 1981), footnote number 9, p. 67. In addition, personal knowledge of the marital status of a great many of my friends, acquaintances and their friends on the job today strongly suggests that once separated, police officers living in suburban communities are moving back into the city.

17. For further support of this position see, Marcel L. Goldschmid (ed.), *Black Americans and White Racism: Theory and Research* (New York: Holt, Rinehart and Winston, 1970), p. 341.

18. A departmental memo dated April 23, 1971 from a sergeant assigned to the 16th Division to the Chief of Personnel, comments on the effectiveness of one such dialogue program involving black and white patrolmen in the 105th precinct. This memo and other information pertaining to the department's Human Relations Workshop programs was supplied by the Community Affairs Division of the NYPD.

19. Police Department City of New York, Press Release, Public Information Division, dated February 20, 1970, Number 17.

20. According to this officer, who wishes to remain anonymous, the Guardians Association tries to maintain a careful record of such incidents in case of court litigation. The feeling conveyed to me by this officer was that, in the past, it was common practice to challenge blacks who claimed to be cops because there were so few blacks on the job at the time.

21. See George L. Kirkham and Laurin A. Wollan, Jr., *Introduction to Law Enforcement* (New York: Harper & Row, 1980), p. 356.

22. I am of the firm belief that recent civil suits brought by aggrieved citizens under Section 1983 of the Civil Rights Act of 1871, have effectively reduced instances of deliberate abuse of police authority in New York City. A recent conversation with a sergeant assigned to the department's Advocates Office supports this belief. He stated that he was personally aware of only *two* cases in the past few years in which members of the department were found liable for improper action taken against civilians. This, he added, constituted a substantial decrease in the number of adverse judgements leveled against police officers in the city. See also, Gerald D. Robin, *Introduction to the Criminal Justice System* (New York:

Harper & Row, 1980), pp. 86–88, for a discussion of recent civilian law suits against police agencies in this country.

23. For an excellent discussion of contact and racial change see, Thomas F. Pettigrew, *Racially Separate or Together?* (New York: McGraw-Hill, 1971), especially pp. 274–280.

24. See Nicholas Alex, op. cit. See also, Alex's, *New York Cops Talk Back: A Study of a Beleaguered Minority* (New York: Wiley, 1976).

25. See James B. Jacobs and Jay Cohen, "The Impact of Racial Integration on the Police," *Journal of Police Science and Administration,* Volume 6, Number 2 (June 1978).

26. In a number of "riot" situations in this country it has been dramatically shown that black police alone have been as ineffective as white police in restoring order. For example, on July 24th, 1968, Cleveland's Mayor, Carl Stokes, decided to remove all white law enforcement officers and National Guardsmen from the riot-torn areas of Cleveland. These officers were replaced by approximately 100 black officers and deputy sheriffs who were assisted by 500 black civilians wearing "Mayor's Committee" armbands. This experiment failed to restore order and Mayor Stokes, the next day, returned the National Guardsmen and white police to the area. See, David N. Lawyer, Jr., "The Dilemma of the Black Badge," *The Police Chief,* November 1968, p. 22; see also, Nicholas Alex, *Black in Blue,* op. cit., especially pp. 135–160.

27. The Knapp Commission's report on police corruption in New York City offers evidence of organized corruption among groups of black cops assigned to Harlem precincts. This note is not meant to malign black cops as a group or to devalue their accomplishments to date, but to make the point that, once hired, they were as susceptible as white officers to payoffs, bribes and other forms of misconduct. In addition, since most black cops were assigned to ghetto precincts prior to the Knapp investigation in 1972, there was more opportunity for them as a group to become involved in corrupt activities.

INDEX